Higher Education Rulemaking

Higher Education Rulemaking

The Politics of Creating Regulatory Policy

REBECCA S. NATOW

JOHNS HOPKINS UNIVERSITY PRESS | *Baltimore*

© 2017 Johns Hopkins University Press
All rights reserved. Published 2017
Printed in the United States of America on acid-free paper

2   4   6   8   9   7   5   3   1

Johns Hopkins University Press
2715 North Charles Street
Baltimore, Maryland 21218-4363
www.press.jhu.edu

Library of Congress Cataloging-in-Publication Data

Names: Natow, Rebecca S., author.
Title: Higher education rulemaking : the politics of creating regulatory policy /
   Rebecca S. Natow.
Description: Baltimore : Johns Hopkins University Press, [2016] | Based on
   author's thesis (doctoral - Teachers College, Columbia University, 2013)
   issued under title: Making Policy in the United States Department of
   Education : The Political Process of Federal Rulemaking for Higher
   Education. | Includes bibliographical references and index.
Identifiers: LCCN 2016010237 | ISBN 9781421421469 (hardcover : alk. paper) |
   ISBN 9781421421476 (electronic) | ISBN 1421421461 (hardcover : alk. paper) |
   ISBN 142142147X (electronic)
Subjects: LCSH: Education, Higher—Law and legislation—United States. |
   Administrative regulation drafting—United States. | Higher education and
   state—United States. | United States. Office of Postsecondary Education. |
   United States. Higher Education Act of 1965
Classification: LCC KF4225.N38 2016 | DDC 344.73/074—dc23
LC record available at https://lccn.loc.gov/2016010237

A catalog record for this book is available from the British Library.

*Special discounts are available for bulk purchases of this book. For more information,
please contact Special Sales at 410-516-6936 or specialsales@press.jhu.edu.*

Johns Hopkins University Press uses environmentally friendly book materials,
including recycled text paper that is composed of at least 30 percent
post-consumer waste, whenever possible.

CONTENTS

ACKNOWLEDGMENTS

I am very grateful to all of the individuals and groups who, either directly or indirectly, contributed to the completion of this book. I wish to acknowledge them here.

I thank the scholars who reviewed and critically commented on various aspects of this work. I am deeply grateful to Kevin Dougherty for helping me to conceptualize this study from the very beginning, for providing constructive criticism throughout each step of the research and writing process, and for serving as a fantastic mentor for many years. I am also indebted to Jeffrey Henig for encouraging me to pursue the higher education rulemaking process as a research topic and for providing guidance and criticism from the early days of the study. Aaron Pallas and Judith Scott-Clayton also provided valuable feedback that helped to shape and to improve this work. William Zumeta provided insightful thoughts and comments on papers that later became the bases of chapters 4 and 5. I also thank Anna Neumann and the other faculty of the Higher and Postsecondary Education Program at Teachers College, Columbia University, for teaching me and challenging me to think critically about higher education in the United States. I thank Kenny Nienhusser for his assistance, insights, and thoughtful critiques of this research from the earliest days of the project. I also thank Monica Reid Kerrigan for early feedback on theoretical and methodological conceptualizations of the research. Milagros Castillo-Montoya and Sosanya Jones also served as valuable sources of moral support as we completed our dissertations and doctoral studies together at Teachers College, Columbia University.

I thank my colleagues (current and former) at the Community College Research Center—particularly Thomas Bailey, Melinda Karp, Shanna Smith Jaggars, Nicole Edgecombe, Davis Jenkins, Michael Armijo, Vikash Reddy, Markeisha Grant, Hana Lahr, Lara Pheatt, Lisa Rothman, Doug Slater, Sarah

Prescott Phillips, Tam Do, and Tatev Papikyan—for being wonderful and incredibly supportive colleagues.

I owe tremendous thanks to my study participants for taking the time to speak with me about the higher education rulemaking process. I am humbled, honored, and very grateful that so many respected higher education and policy leaders set aside time from their busy schedules to answer my questions and to take a real interest in my work. Needless to say, this book would not have been possible without their contributions.

I thank the editors and anonymous reviewers of Johns Hopkins University Press and *The Journal of Higher Education* for their critiques and commentary on earlier versions of this work. I particularly thank Greg Britton of Johns Hopkins University Press for all of his efforts that helped to move the book forward.

I thank my extended family for their many years of love and support, particularly my mother and fellow education scholar Rosemary Carolan. I thank the wonderful individuals who babysit and teach my children and who assist me with my housework, without whose tireless efforts I would never be able to complete my own work.

This research was funded in part by the Teachers College Dean's Grant for Student Research, the Teachers College Policy Research Fellowship, and the Teachers College Higher & Postsecondary Education Program Endowed Fellowship. My doctoral dissertation, on which this book is based, received the Outstanding Dissertation Award from the Politics of Education Association and was a finalist for the Outstanding Dissertation Award from Division J (Postsecondary Education) of the American Educational Research Association. I am very grateful to these organizations for the tremendous honors.

Lastly and most importantly, to my husband Steven Natow, and my children Adam and Charlotte Natow: Thank you for all of the love, joy, inspiration, support, and encouragement you provide every day. There is nothing more important to me than you.

Earlier versions of portions of chapters 1, 2, 3, 4, and 9 and the appendix were previously published in Rebecca S. Natow, "From Capitol Hill to Dupont Circle and Beyond: The Influence of Policy Actors in the Federal Higher Education Rulemaking Process," *The Journal of Higher Education*, 86(3): 360–386. © 2015 The Ohio State University. Reused with permission.

Higher Education Rulemaking

CHAPTER ONE

Introduction

In November 2014 the Association of Private Sector Colleges and Universities (APSCU) sued President Barack Obama's secretary of education and the Department of Education itself[1] over the most recent iteration of the Gainful Employment Rule (Devaney, 2014; Field, 2014a). The rule, which had been issued a few days earlier, sought to impose heavier regulations on for-profit higher education institutions. The new regulations could jeopardize these institutions' eligibility to participate in federal student financial aid programs if they failed to meet certain standards, primarily relating to their graduates' debt-to-income levels and ability to repay student loans (Dundon, 2015; Field, 2014a; Program Integrity: Gainful Employment, 2014). The regulations were based on a section of the Higher Education Act that requires career-focused higher education programs (such as those offered by many for-profit colleges) "to prepare students for gainful employment in a recognized occupation" in order to qualify to receive federal student aid dollars (Higher Education Act, 2012, §§ 1001[b][1], 1002[b][1][A][i], [c][1][A]; Program Integrity: Gainful Employment, 2014, p. 64890; see also Dundon, 2015, p. 382; Mettler, 2014, p. 93; Zemsky, 2013, p. 69). But the institutions that were to be subject to these requirements strongly opposed the rule. The chief executive of APSCU, an association representing the for-profit higher education sector, argued that the anticipated "impact" of the Gainful Employment Rule "on student access and opportunity, [would be] so unacceptable and in violation of federal law, that [the group was] left with no choice but to file suit" (Devaney, 2014).

This litigation was not the first lawsuit the for-profit higher education sector had brought against the Obama administration over rulemaking that targeted the industry. In 2012 a federal court ruled in favor of APSCU in a lawsuit against the secretary of education over a previous version of the Gainful Employment Rule. In that case the court invalidated a key portion of the rule because the

Department of Education had "failed to provide a reasoned explanation for a core element of its central regulation" (*APSCU v. Duncan*, 2012, p. 38). Because the decision substantially weakened the earlier version of the rule, the Department of Education began the process of recreating the Gainful Employment Rule, and this process resulted in the regulation issued in October 2014 that became the subject of APSCU's 2014 lawsuit (Dundon, 2015; Field, 2014a).

In addition to the lawsuits, the for-profit sector fought the Gainful Employment Rule in a variety of other ways. APSCU created a website and issued Internet advertisements critical of the regulation (Stratford & Fain, 2014). Representatives of the sector served on the negotiated rulemaking committees that were charged with drafting both proposed rules (Gainful Employment Negotiated Rulemaking Committee, 2013; Team I—Program Integrity Issues, 2010). All told, the for-profit higher education sector spent in excess of $10 million trying to defeat both Gainful Employment Rules (Stratford & Fain, 2014). These rules have attracted the attention of numerous other interested actors as well: members of Congress, consumer advocates, think tanks, higher education students, and others have all spoken out on one side or the other of the Gainful Employment debate (see, e.g., Marcus, 2012; Stratford & Fain, 2014). During the public comment periods, each proposed Gainful Employment Rule received more than 90,000 comments (Program Integrity: Gainful Employment, 2011, 2014).

The criticism of the Gainful Employment Rule centered not only on the substance of the rule—tighter regulation of the for-profit sector—but also on the process for creating the rule. In the lawsuits challenging the rules, APSCU claimed that the Department of Education had "exceeded its authority" in creating the Gainful Employment Rules (Field, 2014a). Some interested actors sent written comments to the Department of Education arguing that the second proposed Gainful Employment Rule constituted "federal overreach into higher education" (Program Integrity: Gainful Employment, 2014, p. 64902). In nullifying a key provision of the earlier version of the rule, a federal court found that the development of the "debt repayment standard" in the rule had not been "based upon any facts at all" and, as such, was "arbitrary and capricious" (*APSCU v. Duncan*, 2012, pp. 1, 31). Indeed, the very process of developing the two Gainful Employment Rules sparked a significant amount of opposition, controversy, and debate.

The sometimes contentious process by which regulatory agencies develop and promulgate legally binding rules and regulations is known as rulemaking (Kerwin & Furlong, 2011; Lubbers, 1998). Rules and regulations that implement and support the federal Higher Education Act are typically created in the US

Department of Education's Office of Postsecondary Education. This book presents a research-based description of this process—the higher education rulemaking process—and also provides a thorough analysis of the political influences that help to shape the process and contribute to the substance of regulations affecting postsecondary education in the United States. The volume examines the following important aspects of the federal rulemaking process for higher education: why higher education rulemaking is an important policymaking process; how the higher education rulemaking procedure unfolds, from start to finish; who influences the higher education rulemaking process, both within and outside of government; what strategies and other powers actors employ in attempts to influence higher education rulemaking; how surrounding political, social, and economic contexts relate to higher education rulemaking; how policy and higher education actors view the rulemaking process, including their perspectives on how expansive the Department of Education's rulemaking authority should be and their perspectives on how effective their own participation in rulemaking is; how technology has influenced the rulemaking process; and future prospects for higher education rulemaking. This chapter introduces the higher education rulemaking process, describes the types of policies that have been created through this process, and introduces the research on which this work is based.

Higher Education Rulemaking: Its Significance and Its Stakeholders

As stated above, rulemaking refers to the process of creating legally binding regulations, or "rules" (Anderson, 2006; Furlong & Kerwin, 2005; Golden, 1998; Kerwin & Furlong, 2011; Lubbers, 1998; O'Connell, 2008). After a piece of legislation such as a Higher Education Act reauthorization is signed into law, the implementing agency is charged with crafting the details of programs and regulations designed to bring the statute's policy goals into being. This policy implementation occurs within the Department of Education through the creation of higher education rules, as well as through the provision of guidance and interpretation of the law and regulations (Hillman, Tandberg, & Sponsler, 2015; Pelesh, 1994).

Based on the definition of "rule" in the Administrative Procedure Act (2012, § 551[4]), Kerwin and Furlong (2011) identify three general categories of agency rules.[2] First, there are rules that simply *implement* provisions of laws issued by other bodies of government, such as the legislature; these rules do not create new policies in their own right, but merely elucidate and transmit into the regulatory code the "procedures" and "instructions" for implementation that have already been enacted (p. 5). A second category of rules, those that *interpret* policy, are often required when existing laws or regulations must be reevaluated in light of new or unexpected conditions, or when nonbinding guidance is provided. Finally, there are rules that *prescribe* new policies in their own right. These types of rules are typically promulgated when an authorizing statute sets broad policy standards "but provides few details as to how they are to be put into operation or how they are actually to be achieved" (p. 6). Such rules allow a substantial amount of discretion for agencies to develop substantive and broad-reaching policy (Kerwin & Furlong, 2011).

Though rulemaking generally receives less attention than legislative policymaking, it is nonetheless an important and powerful policymaking process. Numerous regulations are created annually through rulemaking procedures taking place across the federal government, and the final rules resulting from the process can affect a wide variety of industries and have huge economic impacts (West & Raso, 2013). Bryner (1987) has characterized rulemaking as "the most controversial exercise of government power by regulatory agencies" (p. 203), no doubt because rulemaking involves the creation of policy by government entities composed of unelected individuals (Bryner, 1987; Golden, 1998; Kerwin & Furlong, 2011; Lubbers, 1998; Mantel, 2009). In other words, rulemaking amounts to policymaking by a government agency that is "accountable to the American people only through indirect means" (Kerwin & Furlong, 2011, p. 167). The process, therefore, should be observed to ensure that the people's interests are sufficiently respected (Golden, 1998). If there is a lack of public influence—either directly or via elected public officials—then the participatory features incorporated in rulemaking practices may not be fully reflective of democratic principles. Identifying democratic involvement in rulemaking is important to confirm "the legitimacy of resulting regulations" (p. 256).

It is also important to understand the rulemaking process because, as Kerwin and Furlong (2011) note, "the way rules are written profoundly affects what they contain, and the content of rules determines, to a very large extent, the quality of our lives" (p. 43). That is, what happens during rulemaking influences the substance of final regulations, which in turn can have important implications for constituents. In fact, regulations created through the higher education rulemaking process affect numerous stakeholders. The willingness of the for-profit higher education sector to spend millions of dollars to oppose the Gainful Employment Rule demonstrates just how significant the impact a rule—or even a potential rule—can have for proprietary institutions. But the for-profit sector is not the only type of higher education institution affected by rulemaking: community and technical colleges, public universities, minority-serving institutions, religiously affiliated colleges, and private nonprofit institutions also have a stake in the outcome of many higher education rules, and all these have actively participated in higher education rulemaking. Students are stakeholders of the process as well: when rules restrict institutions' eligibility to participate in federal student financial aid programs, financially needy students may be priced out of attending certain institutions (Stratford & Fain, 2014). On the other hand, students may take on an enormous amount of debt to finance their higher education, and regulations created through the rulemaking process may seek to ensure student-outcomes accountability on the part of institutions, so that students can have confidence that their degree will help them to find work after graduation and repay their student debts (see, e.g., Program Integrity: Gainful Employment, 2011, 2014). Sometimes, higher education rules directly regulate issues relating to student and college-graduate eligibility for certain financial aid programs, such as debt forgiveness programs (see, e.g., Federal Perkins Loan Program, 2008) and certain federal scholarships (see, e.g., Academic Competitiveness Grant Program, 2007; Teacher Quality Enhancement Grants Program, 1999a).

In addition to students and institutions, organizations in the student lending industry (such as banks and guaranty agencies), accreditors of higher education institutions (national, regional, and program accreditors), organizations that do business with higher education institutions, state government agencies, and members of the business community also have a stake in higher education regulations and have taken part in the higher education rulemaking process (see, e.g., Gainful Employment Negotiated Rulemaking Committee, 2013). Consumer advocates and legal aid attorneys have participated on behalf of students and their families (see, e.g., Gainful Employment Negotiated Rulemaking Committee, 2013; researcher's data set).[3] Given the number and diversity of individuals and groups who are affected by higher education regulations, the process of creating those regulations is likely to be fraught with politics and power struggles. Scrutinizing the process not only helps interested parties understand how the content of final regulations develops, but may also provide insight for policy actors regarding how to influence higher education rulemaking. In any event, a policymaking process that affects so many stakeholders is an important matter. Observing the process can help to ensure that stakeholders are well represented in the creation of the policies.

Policies Created through Higher Education Rulemaking

Higher education rulemaking takes place in the US Department of Education's Office of Postsecondary Education and primarily involves the creation of regulations that implement provisions of the Higher Education Act and its various amendments and reauthorizations. As Parsons (1997) points out, "the Higher Education Act of 1965 is an authorizing statute," which "means that it defines the purpose of the programs under the act and sets the life span at the end of which programs must either be reauthorized or come to an end" (pp. 38–39). Since 1965 the Higher Education Act has been reauthorized numerous times (Parsons, 1997), most recently in 2008 (National Conference of State Legislatures, 2014). The Higher Education Act is also an authorizing statute in the sense that it is the starting point for higher education rulemaking (Kerwin & Furlong, 2011). This section describes the policies and programs authorized under the current iteration of the Higher Education Act and identifies some of the specific regulations created through the Office of Postsecondary Education's rulemaking process.

The Higher Education Act

First enacted in 1965, the Higher Education Act provides federal funding for numerous higher-education-related programs (see also Parsons, 1997). Currently, the act contains nine main sections, known as "Titles." Title I, called "General Provisions," explains some key terms; contains an antidiscrimination clause; creates the National Advisory Committee on Institutional Quality and Integrity; establishes programs to prevent alcohol and drug abuse on college campuses; and requires institutions to report large gifts from international sources (Higher Education Act, 2012, §§ 1001–1019d). Also included in this title are provisions relating to higher education costs, including requirements for tuition "transparency" (§ 1015a) and in-state tuition charges for members of the US military and their families in states in which the service members are stationed (§ 1015d). The title also contains administrative provisions for student financial aid delivery (§§ 1018–1018b).

Title II of the Higher Education Act governs federal programs designed to enhance the quality of teaching, including grant programs for organizations that provide teacher preparation training, incentives for placing teachers in "high-need" fields (i.e., science, technology, engineering, and mathematics [the STEM subjects] and special education [§ 1036]), accountability metrics to evaluate such programs, and teacher professional development with regard to such matters as using new technologies and educating students with disabilities (§§ 1021–1041). The thinking behind Title II programs is that they will promote student success and learning by encouraging high-quality teaching (Clewell et al., 2000).

Title III, currently entitled "Institutional Aid," provides federal funding directly to minority-serving institutions and colleges that serve large numbers of low-income students (Higher Education Act, 2012, §§ 1051–1068h; see also Harper, Patton, & Wooden, 2009). Funds awarded through Title III can be used for various purposes, from purchasing lab equipment, to building new classrooms, to enhancing tutoring programs, to—in some cases—building the institution's endowment (see, e.g., §§ 1057, 1059c, 1059e, 1062, 1065). This title contains some specific provisions relating to institutions designated as Historically Black Colleges and Universities (HBCUs), including grant funding and record-keeping requirements related to the funding, capital financing (§§ 1060–1066g), and special provisions designed to increase minority involvement in the STEM subjects (§§ 1067–1067k). When the Higher Education Act was first enacted, Title III "sought to support HBCUs during the period in which increased numbers of African American students were beginning to seek educational opportunities elsewhere" (Harper et al., 2009, p. 397).

Title IV of the Higher Education Act governs the provision of federal student financial aid, to assist eligible students with paying for college by providing need-based grants, loans, and work-study positions (Higher Education Act, 2012). Much of the rulemaking that takes place in the Office of Postsecondary Education is based on this title of the Higher Education Act. Among other things, Title IV governs need-based Pell and supplemental grants, merit-based scholarships,[4] need-and- merit-based grants, a variety of types of student loans, and financial aid programs for special populations of students, among other federal student aid programs (§§ 1070a–1087ii). It also contains provisions for determining the amount of financial need students have (§§ 1087kk–1087vv). Federal need-based student grant aid is dispersed to institutions for each eligible student who is enrolled in that institution (see, e.g., § 1070a). Both a student and the student's institution must be eligible to receive Title IV funds. Student eligibility mostly has to do with financial need and US citizenship status. But as the Gainful Employment Rule discussed above demonstrates, policymakers have conditioned institutional eligibility on the completion of certain institutional activities or standards (Program Integrity: Gainful Employment, 2011, 2014). Thus, through Title IV, Congress and the Department of Education are able to incentivize particular institutional behavior, and noncompliant institutions risk losing their federal student aid funds. Disruptions to Title IV funding eligibility could constitute a significant financial detriment to an institution and may even lead one to cease operations, as has happened in the past (see, e.g., Borrego, 2001a, 2001b).

Title IV also funds federal TRIO programs (Higher Education Act, 2012, §§ 1070a-11–1070a-28; Pitre & Pitre, 2009). The name "TRIO" recalls that there were three programs established by this title in 1965 (Pitre & Pitre, 2009), but as of this writing there are eight federal TRIO programs (US Department of Education, 2015b). TRIO programs are designed to aid in postsecondary access and success for students who are underrepresented in higher education, such as low-income students, first-generation college students, and underrepresented minority students (Pitre & Pitre, 2009; Swail, 2000). These programs allow eligible students to participate in programmatic activities and to receive information, advice, tutoring, and other services, with the goal of helping participants to attend and to complete college (Swail, 2000).

Title V, called "Developing Institutions," provides federal funding to Hispanic-Serving Institutions (Higher Education Act, 2012, §§ 1101–1103g). Permitted expenditures for these programs are similar to those granted to Title III institutions, as discussed above (see, e.g., § 1101b). Title VI pertains to federal funding for postsecondary education programs in international studies (§§ 1121–1132-7). These include programs in foreign languages (§§ 1121–1128b) and international business (§§ 1130–1130b). Funds provided through Title VI may go toward library collections, centers and institutes, outreach programs, research, technology, and student travel, among other things (see, e.g., §§ 1122–1126, 1130-1).

Title VII finances "Graduate and Postsecondary Improvement Programs" (Higher Education Act, 2012, §§ 1133–1140r). This title provides postgraduate financial and informational support for students in the areas of art, social science, law, the humanities (§§ 1134, 1136), and "areas of national need" as determined by the secretary of education after consulting with other federal agencies (§ 1135a). This title also provides funding for master's-level study in the STEM subjects at certain minority-serving institutions (§§ 1136a–1136c). The Fund for the Improvement of Postsecondary Education is also authorized under Title VII (§§ 1138–1138d), as are certain programs designed to assist postsecondary students with disabilities (§§ 1140–1140r). Title VIII contains some miscellaneous provisions, such as the establishment of an educational program on the historic Underground Railroad (§§ 1151–1155). Finally, Title IX of the Higher Education Act (2012) provides federal funding for additional specialized programs (§§ 1161a–1161aa-1).[5] These include Teach for America (§ 1161f), programs designed to enhance nursing education (§ 1161d), grants for rural institutions of higher education (§ 1161q), programs designed to assist students who are military veterans (§ 1161t), and several others.

Policies and programs authorized under the Higher Education Act are funded through a separate appropriations process (Parsons, 1997). Thus, not all provisions of the act will necessarily be fully (or even partially) funded at any given time. For example, recent federal budget cuts have left several Title VI programs at least temporarily unfunded (Feal, 2016). So the fact that the Higher Education Act authorizes a program does not necessarily mean that the program will be active at all times. Moreover, Congress may legislatively repeal a Higher Education Act program and has done so in the past (for example, an urban community service program established under Title VII was repealed in 2008 [Higher Education Act, 2012, §§ 1139–1139h]).

Because the Office of Postsecondary Education's authority to create rules derives from the Higher Education Act, higher education rulemaking is intended to implement provisions of the act. Therefore, the subjects covered in higher education rulemaking resemble the policies and programs established under the Higher Education Act.

Substantive Policy Areas of Higher Education Rulemaking

While all rulemaking under the Higher Education Act is considered "higher education rulemaking" for purposes of this analysis, some sections of the act prompt more rulemaking than others. Provisions of the act that are lengthy, highly technical in nature, and require much federal funding tend to have more regulations than other provisions. A review of the substance of higher education rules has revealed five distinct substantive policy areas that are most frequently regulated. The first is the regulation of higher education students. Rules setting student eligibility to participate in federal student aid and other federal scholarship programs fall under this category. The second category is student debt management. Rules in this category regulate matters such as qualifications for loan forgiveness or deferred loan repayments, among other matters relating to student debt. These rules are distinct from the regulation of students because they regulate anyone holding federal student loans, including parents and college graduates as well as current students. However, there may be some overlap between rules falling into this category and rules that regulate students.

The third category of substantive policy areas governed by higher education rules is the regulation of higher education institutions, which often involves rules setting institutional eligibility to participate in federal financial aid programs.

Fourth is the regulation of banks, guaranty agencies, and other lending organizations. Requirements for such organizations to participate in Title IV financial aid programs fall under this category. The final category, the regulation of federal grants not related to student financial aid, involves grants related to minority-serving institutions under Titles III and V, grants pertaining to teacher education programs under Title II, federal-funded TRIO programs under Title IV, and other grants under titles VI, VII, VIII, and IX. Some regulations fall under more than one of these five broad areas of higher education policy regulated through higher education rulemaking.

Examples of Higher Education Rules

The study on which this book is based closely examined 32 regulations created through the higher education rulemaking process. The methodological appendix contains details about the identity and substance of all 32 of these rules; however, some of the more noteworthy and typical of these regulations are described in the next few pages. Three of these "focal" rules—the two Gainful Employment Rules and the Accreditation and Student Outcomes Rule—are chronicled throughout the book as illustrative examples of the various topics analyzed.[6] However, all of the focal rules described in the remainder of this chapter have provided valuable data on how the higher education rulemaking process operates, as well as who and what influences it, and will occasionally also serve to illustrate factors affecting higher education rulemaking.

GAINFUL EMPLOYMENT RULES

The two Gainful Employment Rules have been among the most closely watched and controversial higher education regulations. Targeting mostly for-profits but also some programs at nonprofit institutions, the goal of these rules is to ensure that most students in career-focused postsecondary programs who receive federal student loans will be in a financial position to repay those loans after completing their programs (Mettler, 2014; Zemsky, 2013). Emerging from a broader rulemaking procedure concerned with improving the "program integrity" of Title IV student financial aid, the original Gainful Employment Rule took on a life of its own during the rulemaking process and was eventually published as a proposed rule separate from the other program integrity regulations (Program Integrity: Gainful Employment, 2010; Program Integrity Issues, 2010b; see also Zemsky, 2013). As mentioned above, a key section of the original Gainful Employment Rule was nullified by a federal court in 2012 (*APSCU v. Duncan*, 2012).

A new Gainful Employment Rule was issued in 2014 (Program Integrity: Gainful Employment, 2014).

Both versions of the rule contain the requirements that career-focused programs provide public disclosure of certain information about the programs, that program alumni's debt-to-earnings ratio remain within certain limits, and that new career-focused programs be subject to a special approval process. Failure to comply with the provisions of the Gainful Employment Rule could mean the revocation of an institution's permission to participate in Title IV financial aid programs, at least temporarily (Program Integrity: Gainful Employment, 2011, 2014; see also American Council on Education, 2011, 2014; Fain, 2014; National Association of Student Financial Aid Administrators, 2014). Shortly before the 2014 rule was issued, Secretary of Education Arne Duncan "estimated [that] 1,400 academic programs that enroll 840,000 students would fail to meet the standards with their current performance" and that "99 percent of those programs [were] at for-profits" (Fain, 2014).

ACCREDITATION AND STUDENT OUTCOMES RULE: AN INCOMPLETE RULEMAKING PROCEDURE

One important higher education rulemaking procedure that did not actually result in a final rule will, together with the Gainful Employment Rules, serve to illustrate many of the phenomena regarding higher education rulemaking that are described throughout this book. This rulemaking can best be described as the Accreditation and Student Outcomes rulemaking. In 2005 Margaret Spellings, then secretary of education, created the Commission on the Future of Higher Education, which became known as the Spellings Commission (Lowry, 2009). The purpose of the commission was to analyze issues relating to higher education quality and access and to make recommendations for reform (Secretary of Education's Commission, 2006; Zemsky, 2007). One recommendation of the commission, reported by the US Department of Education in 2006, was that "student achievement . . . be measured by institutions on a 'value-added' basis that takes into account students' academic baseline when assessing their results" and that "this information . . . be made available to students, and reported publicly in aggregate form" (quoted in Lowry, 2009, p. 510).

Not long after the Spellings Commission's report was released, the Department of Education commenced a rulemaking procedure to create a regulation that would have connected higher education student outcomes to institutional accreditation and would have implemented new data-gathering requirements

(Lederman, 2007a; Lowry, 2009). These regulations could have hindered institutions' ability to participate in Title IV financial aid programs if their students' achievement levels did not meet certain standards. The rulemaking drew immediate criticism, including criticism from congressional officials of both major political parties. Members of Congress sent letters to the secretary of education and gave speeches opposing the attempt of the Department of Education to regulate in this regard (Lederman, 2007b; Lowry, 2009). Senator Lamar Alexander (Republican from Tennessee), speaking on the Senate floor, warned that he might "offer an amendment to the Higher Education Act to prohibit the department from issuing any final regulations on these issues until Congress acts" (Lederman, 2007b; Office of Senator Lamar Alexander, 2007). And an appropriations subcommittee in the House of Representatives sought to forbid the Department of Education to use agency funding for the purpose of regulating higher education accreditation (Lowry, 2009). Ultimately, the Department of Education did not move forward with this rule (Lowry, 2009; US Department of Education, 2007d). Nonetheless, this experience demonstrates how politics—and politicians—can influence higher education rulemaking and how perspectives on what matters are appropriate to regulate can ignite passionate debate and change the entire course of a rulemaking procedure.

OTHER ILLUSTRATIVE FOCAL RULES

Several additional focal rules are particularly illustrative of some of the aspects of higher education rulemaking described throughout this book, such as the policy actors who are influential in the process, the various strategies that actors employ to influence rulemaking outcomes, and the manner in which political, economic, and other contexts influence higher education rulemaking.

Incentive Compensation Rules. Also created as part of the large 2010–2011 "program integrity" rulemaking were changes to incentive compensation regulations for admissions personnel at higher education institutions. This rule change was the latest in a series of changes that occurred over several presidential administrations. In the 1992 reauthorization of the Higher Education Act, Congress forbade the practice of compensating college admissions and financial aid staff by incentive (Kantrowitz, 2010). This meant that institutions of higher education could not financially reward staff members for bringing new students into their organizations. This provision was enacted amid concern that some higher education institutions were using questionable recruiting practices that had prompted "unqualified students" to attend college, where they were struggling (p. 3). Shortly after the 1992 reauthorization became law, the Department of Education issued a series of regulations aimed at implementing the statute's provisions. One regulation, issued in April 1994, banned colleges and universities that received federal student aid from paying "any commission, bonus, or other incentive payment" to a person who admitted or provided financial aid to new students, with limited exceptions (Student Assistance General Provisions . . . Interim final regulations, 1994, p. 22427; see also Kantrowitz, 2010).

During the George W. Bush presidential administration, the Department of Education issued a regulation elucidating exceptions—or "safe harbors"—to the incentive compensation ban (Federal Student Aid Programs, 2002). Under this new rule, institutions could make some incentive-based payments without fear of violating the Higher Education Act. Such "safe harbors" included providing compensation based on students' completion of all or part of their programs and compensation for certain types of recruiting via the Internet, among other practices (Federal Student Aid Programs, 2002; see also Kantrowitz, 2010). This rule change was seen as helpful to the for-profit sector (Burd, 2014; Mettler, 2014) and was implemented by a famously business-friendly presidential administration (Jacobe, 2004).

Then in 2010, President Obama's Department of Education eliminated those safe harbors through its comprehensive "program integrity" rule (Program Integrity Issues, 2010a; see also Mettler, 2014). The leading association representing for-profit higher education, APSCU, claimed that the elimination of the safe harbors "dramatically affects private sector schools and their students, yet [the regulations] are unsupported by factual evidence or logical reasoning" (Burd, 2014). APSCU once again sued the Obama administration, this time over the elimination of the safe harbors (Burd, 2014; Stratford, 2014). In October 2014 a federal judge in the District of Columbia agreed with one of APSCU's legal arguments and ordered the department to provide a sufficient evidence-based explanation for certain aspects of its incentive compensation prohibitions. The judge stopped short of vacating the prohibitions, and the Obama administration's incentive compensation rules remain in effect (*APSCU v. Duncan*, 2014; Stratford, 2014). More recently, however, the Department of Education has stated that it will loosen the restriction on incentive payments based on students' completion of their programs, citing a lack of strong evidence that such payments were being made "as a proxy for enrollment-based compensation" (Stratford, 2015).

Academic Competitiveness and National SMART Grants Rules. In 2005 Congress created two federal scholarships for undergraduate students—the Academic Competitiveness Grant (ACG) and the National Science and Mathematics Access to Retain Talent (National SMART) Grant—based on both financial need and academic merit for students going into particular fields, such as the STEM subjects (US Department of Education, 2014a). In 2006 the Department of Education began creating rules to implement these new scholarship programs and immediately drew criticism. Among other things, critics claimed that the department would overstep its authority if it made final a proposed provision requiring that, to remain eligible to receive Pell Grants (a separate, much larger, and entirely need-based grant program), institutions with relevant academic programming "must also participate in the ACG or SMART Grant program" (Lederman, 2006). This provision did, in fact, become part of the final rule (Student Assistance General Provisions . . . Final regulations, 2006).

In 2007 the Department of Education conducted another rulemaking regarding the ACG and National SMART Grants. The final regulation that resulted from that rulemaking did not eliminate the institutional-participation–Pell Grant eligibility requirement, but it did prohibit students enrolled in college certificate programs from receiving ACG and National SMART Grants (Academic Competitiveness Grant Program, 2007; see also Field, 2007). Certificate programs have historically enrolled a relatively high percentage of women and minority students, and more often than not the programs have been offered at community colleges (Henderson, 1995; Horn & Li, 2009). Thus, this rule had negative implications for community colleges and for the demographics of students who tend to enroll in certificate programs. Less than a year after this rule was issued, Congress passed the Ensuring Continued Access to Student Loans Act (2008), which specifically allowed students in postsecondary certificate programs to receive Academic Competitiveness Grants (see also US Government Accountability Office, 2009).

Distance Education and Teach-Out Plans Rule. An example of a lower-profile rule is a higher education regulation issued in 2009 that addressed the issue of accrediting distance learning programs (Institutional eligibility, 2009). Among the changes this rule made was to define "distance education" as distinct from "correspondence education" and to require that accrediting organizations be well informed about distance education (p. 55414). Another aspect of this rule required colleges and universities to create policies that would assist the institution's students in the event that the institution closed a program before all enrolled students were able to complete it. These policies are known as teach-out plans (Council for Higher Education Accreditation, 2009; Institutional eligibility, 2009).

As this rule dealt specifically with accreditation, the negotiated rulemaking committee included several different types of accreditors as both primary and secondary negotiators. Because the rule was more technical and less controversial than the Gainful Employment, Incentive Compensation, and even the ACG and National SMART Grants rules, the rule and its rulemaking process received considerably less attention than those other rules received.

Rules Reflecting High-Profile Events. Every so often, a high-profile event influences the content of higher education regulations. Some major events in recent decades that have led to new higher education rules include hurricanes Katrina and Rita, Operation Desert Shield and Operation Desert Storm, and the terrorist attacks of September 11, 2001. The higher education rule that followed the two hurricanes provided student aid reform for students who withdrew from college as a result of the hurricanes (Federal Student Aid Programs, 2006). Specifically, it allowed the secretary of education to "waive a student's Title IV grant repayment if the student withdrew from an institution because of a major disaster" (p. 45671). Similarly, a 1992 regulation extended certain Pell Grant protections to military service members who served in Operation Desert Shield and Operation Desert Storm (Pell Grant Program, 1992). More recently, a 2007 rule provided for the forgiveness of some federal student loans for certain 9/11 victims' families (Federal Perkins Loan Program, 2007a).

Typically, rule content reflects a major event because rulemakings are spurred by new legislation prompted by the event. For example, the regulation reforming student financial aid for certain victims of hurricanes followed the passage of such legislation as the Pell Grant Hurricane and Disaster Relief Act; the Student Grant Hurricane and Disaster Relief Act; and the Emergency Supplemental Appropriations Act for Defense, the Global War on Terror, and Hurricane Recovery (Federal Student Aid Programs, 2006). The rules changing financial aid provisions for veterans of Operation Desert Shield and Operation Desert Storm and for certain 9/11 victims were similarly reflective of statutory changes.

Rules Affecting TRIO Programs. As explained above, TRIO programs—the federally sponsored programs designed to increase access and student success in postsecondary education—were established and continue to be authorized by the Higher Education Act. Thus, regulations administering these programs are created through the higher education rulemaking process. These regulations sometimes take the form of "priorities" rather than rules. Priorities are funding preferences for certain federal grant programs, which serve to alert potential grantees to "the areas in which the Secretary [of Education] is particularly interested in receiving applications" (US Department of Education, 1998). Just like rules, priorities are published in the *Federal Register* in proposed form ahead of a notice-and-comment period before being finalized by the Office of Postsecondary Education.[7]

Although TRIO program priorities are often straightforward and low-profile, they may occasionally engender controversy, as occurred when an Upward Bound priority led some institutional officials in 2006 to question whether the Department of Education was "attempt[ing] to circumvent congressional authority" (*Public Regional Hearing for Negotiated Rulemaking*, 2006a, p. 121) or "effectively chang[ing] a congressional priority for an administrative one" (*Public Regional Hearing for Negotiated Rulemaking*, 2006b, p. 34). Other regulations of TRIO programs involve regulating program costs, setting selection standards for participants, and other mandates (see, e.g., Talent Search Program, 1993).

Overview of Research Methods

The description and analysis provided in this book are based largely on an extensive empirical study of the higher education rulemaking process. The findings presented derive from embedded case study research (Scholz & Tietje, 2002) that involved examining the higher education rulemaking process as a case of rulemaking in a US federal agency and, within that overall case, a comparative case study of 32 individual instances of higher education rulemaking.[8] The case-study rules cover a period of more than 20 years and span several different substantive areas within higher education policy. Subject matters of the rules include eligibility for students and institutions to participate in federal student aid programs, regulation of federal scholarships and TRIO programs, changes to accreditation requirements, and federal student loan forgiveness, among other issues. Some of the rules involve controversial, high-profile matters, while some involve issues that are more technical in nature and not as highly visible. These sampling criteria were employed to maximize diversity among the rules studied, making it possible to identify both consistent patterns over time and factors related to differences in rulemaking proceedings and results.

Data sources include in-depth interviews with 55 policy and higher education actors, during which those individuals commented regarding their experiences with and perspectives on the higher education rulemaking process. Interviewees included US Department of Education staff (both political appointees and career personnel), congressional staff, representatives of various kinds of higher education institutions, student and consumer representatives, mediation experts, state government agents, and representatives of the lending industry, among others. Additionally, rulemaking documents (including the texts of final and proposed rules as well as available negotiated rulemaking records and a sample of public comments) relating to the case-study rules were analyzed. Other data sources for this study include a sample of news articles covering higher education rulemaking and the websites of certain governmental and nongovernmental organizations with a stake in higher education rulemaking. A detailed methodological appendix appears after the final chapter of the book.

Overview of the Book

The remainder of this volume describes the procedures and politics of the higher education rulemaking process and other influences over the process. Connections are made, throughout, between the study's findings and relevant theoretical literature, including theories of bureaucratic politics (see, e.g., Hill, 1991; McCubbins, Noll, & Weingast, 1987, 1989; Niles, 2002; Niskanen, 1971; Stigler, 1971), theories of power (Gaventa, 1980; Lukes, 2005), and theories of policymaking processes (Kingdon, 2003; Sabatier & Jenkins-Smith, 1999; Sabatier & Weible, 2007). Chapter 2 describes the role of the federal bureaucracy in higher education policy and practice, which includes the rulemaking process but also numerous other powers and responsibilities. The conceptual framework of the empirical study is also explained in chapter 2. Chapter 3 provides a detailed description of how the higher education rulemaking process operates procedurally—that is, the legal procedures through which a rule must proceed to go from conceptual to proposed to final. Chapter 4 identifies the various policy and higher education actors who influence the process and describes the types of influence that these actors have. Chapter 5 explains the strategies and powers that actors employ in their attempts to influence higher education rulemaking. Chapter 6 discusses the beliefs of policy actors regarding higher education rulemaking, regulation, and the subject matters of higher education rules; it also explores how such beliefs influence higher education rulemaking participation and the content of final rules. Chapter 7 describes the ways that surrounding political, economic, and social contexts have influenced higher education rulemaking. Chapter 8 describes how advances in technology have influenced the higher education rulemaking process and, in some cases, have made participation in the process easier. Chapter 9 summarizes the study's findings, discusses its implications, and provides a perspective on future prospects for higher education rulemaking. As a whole, this book is a definitive guide to, and analysis of, the higher education rulemaking process and the politics that surround it.

CHAPTER TWO

The Federal Bureaucratic Role

To understand the important role that higher education rulemaking plays in the policymaking process, it is important to understand the broader role of the federal bureaucracy in higher education policy and practice and to situate the rulemaking process within that bureaucratic role. The "bureaucratic role" in this context refers to the influence of federal agencies that are managed by unelected officials and administer and implement federal programs and policies (see, e.g., Anderson, 2006; Howlett, Ramesh, & Perl, 2009). As explained in chapter 1, the US Department of Education attempts to control certain aspects of higher education, such as accreditation and academic standards, through creating rules such as the Gainful Employment Rules and the attempted Accreditation and Student Outcomes Rule. But other tools of bureaucratic power can influence these matters as well, such as officially recognizing accrediting agencies, issuing nonbinding guidance and interpretations of laws and regulations, and commissioning studies and reports about particular matters affecting higher education. Indeed, agencies such as the Department of Education and others hold a wide range of powers and responsibilities, and they can influence higher education policy and practice in various ways and through many mechanisms, rulemaking being but one of them. But other actors, such as the president, members of Congress, and powerful interest groups influence bureaucratic policy and regulatory outcomes in many ways as well.

This chapter describes the bureaucratic role as it relates to higher education policy and practice. First, it explores various theories of bureaucratic policymaking and describes how the creation of regulatory policy—including higher education regulations—reflects aspects of those theories. The chapter then identifies federal agencies that have influenced postsecondary education policy and practice and describes the mechanisms through which the federal bureaucracy creates and implements higher education policy.

Theories of Regulatory Policymaking

Scholars of political science, policy processes, and public administration have long theorized about bureaucratic policymaking and the policy actors who influence it. As Lowi (1972) observed long ago, "policies determine politics" (p. 299), meaning that the character of the policy outcome predicts the types and magnitude of political activity that will take place during the policy's creation (see also Lowi, 1970; Smith & Larimer, 2013). The policies that result from the higher education rulemaking process fall into the category of "regulative policy," according to Lowi's typology (1972, p. 300).[1] Regulations seek to compel certain types of conduct on the part of particular actors or groups of actors through a system of incentives (for following the rules) or punishments (for not following the rules) (Anderson, 2006; Lowi, 1972; Smith & Larimer, 2013). According to Lowi, the creation of such policies can draw political processes that are active and highly conflictual, with much negotiating and coalition building on the part of policy actors (Anderson, 2006; Lowi, 1970, 1972; Smith & Larimer, 2013). But who are the actors who are involved in these conflicts and build these coalitions? And how, if at all, do external factors influence the contentious political process of regulatory policymaking?

When considering which actors have the most influence over regulatory outcomes, historically the literature has focused on three categories of actors: bureaucratic actors, their political principals, and powerful regulated entities (Moe, 2012; Yackee, 2003). These categories are reminiscent of the so-called iron triangles, consisting of bureaucratic agencies, interest groups, and committees and subcommittees in Congress, which together exercise a great deal of influence over policymaking and other government activities (see, e.g., Freeman & Stevens, 1987; Hayden, 2002; Howlett et al., 2009). But different theories view each of these actors as holding varying levels of control over bureaucratic policymaking.

The Discretion of the Bureaucracy

According to one perspective, which emphasizes the power of the bureaucracy (see, e.g., Hill, 1991; Niskanen, 1971; Rourke, 1969; see also Anderson, 2006), bureaucracies and the individual bureaucrats who work within them possess discretion in how they fulfill their official tasks, and thus they are able to exert considerable authority in bureaucratic policy and operations. While recognizing that elected officials, interest groups, and other factors all have some influence over bureaucratic decision making, this theory contends that bureaucrats often make decisions that advance their own preferences and interests as well as those of their organizations (Anderson, 2006; Hill, 1991; Niskanen, 1971; Rourke, 1969). Additionally, this theory recognizes that bureaucrats are often in possession of more and better information than their political-branch principals (Meier, 2008). And in fact, bureaucracies often do exercise discretion with regard to many of their policymaking tasks, including decisions to commence rulemaking and decisions about at least some of the content of the regulations issued (O'Connell, 2011).

There are various reasons for the existence of bureaucratic discretion. Bureaucracies have been delegated a great deal of influence from the executive and legislative units of government (Kerwin & Furlong, 2011; Rourke, 1969). After delegation, the political branches—which can be short of resources and preoccupied with a myriad of other matters—tend not to micromanage the bureaucracy (Kerwin & Furlong, 2011; Wilson, 1989; see also a similar argument in McCubbins & Schwartz, 1984). Additionally, the fact that authorizing legislation often provides only "broad and ambiguous statutory mandates" allows bureaucrats a fair amount of discretion to decide the details of a particular program (Anderson, 2006, p. 206; see also Stone, 2002).

The fact that bureaucracies may possess much discretion in policymaking raises some complicated issues regarding democratic processes. First, bureaucrats are not elected and therefore cannot be voted out of office for creating policy that large portions the voting public might not support (Bryner, 1987; Mantel, 2009). Second, many bureaucratic decisions are made with less public inspection and publicity than typical congressional and presidential decisions receive (Rourke, 1969, 1972). Thus, considerable bureaucratic power may cause apprehension among those who believe that public policy should be made by democratically elected individuals with substantial public oversight (Bryner, 1987; Mantel, 2009; Rourke, 1969, 1972). But theories emphasizing bureaucratic discretion have been criticized for downplaying the role that elected political actors play in influencing regulatory policy and activity (Moe, 2012).

The literature on rulemaking and bureaucratic policymaking indicates that agency bureaucrats do have substantial involvement in the rulemaking process and are typically faced with many opportunities to exercise discretion. Although administrative agencies and their employees may feel the influence of other branches of government as well as private interests, there are instances when the agencies operate relatively independently of outside forces (Kerwin & Furlong, 2011; Wilson, 1989). Moreover, as Golden (1998) observes, agency bureaucrats determine the ultimate language and substance of regulations. Although inter-

yikes!

ested persons outside an agency may comment on proposed rules, agencies may decide not to take those comments into account when rendering a final rule (Golden, 1998; Yackee, 2006).

In addition to finalizing the text of regulations, agency representatives construct and publish rulemaking notices, organize and oversee public hearings, and consider comments on proposed rules (Golden, 1998; Kerwin & Furlong, 2011). Additionally, Kerwin and Furlong (2011) explain that an agency influences the "types and sequencing of the rules that it produces" through "setting priorities" within its own organization as to which regulations and policy areas deserve the most attention (p. 131). Kerwin and Furlong also note that agencies often decide the internal procedures for planning, commencing, and scheduling a rulemaking and for determining the amount of agency moneys to apportion to rulemaking activity.

Pelesh's (1994) experience with one higher education rulemaking procedure illustrates several ways in which the Department of Education has exercised discretion in this process. Pelesh found that the department determined which individuals would be part of negotiated rulemaking committees, wrote early drafts and revisions of rule proposals, created negotiated rulemaking "protocols," and served on the negotiated rulemaking committee (pp. 158–159). He describes a situation in which the department exercised a fair amount of discretion in the rulemaking process, ultimately taking "a dominant position"; it "was not just one of the negotiating parties" (p. 164).

Political Control

According to a different theory, government bureaucracies are agents of the legislative and executive branches, and as such, bureaucracies make policies that align with the objectives of and the policies created by the political branches (see, e.g., McCubbins et al., 1987, 1989; Wood & Waterman, 1991; see also Moe, 2012). Through various mechanisms such as the creation of required administrative procedures, the political branches can control—often in advance of agency rulemaking activity—the manner in which bureaucracies carry out their policymaking tasks. They can also set limitations on what an agency may do (McCubbins et al., 1987, 1989). Although some theories of "political control" tend to argue that "congressional dominance" of bureaucratic activities is accurate, others recognize the unique and important powers of the president as well (Moe, 2012).

The political units' supervisory powers over the bureaucracy may take different forms (see McCubbins et al., 1987, 1989; McCubbins & Schwartz, 1984;

O'Connell, 2011; Waterman & Meier, 1998; Yackee, 2003). McCubbins et al. (1987) distinguish between "oversight" mechanisms (such as congressional hearings and the imposition of penalties) and less direct, "procedural" mechanisms of control (p. 244). The former mechanisms have sometimes been dubbed "police patrols" in the literature because they involve a "surveillance" of bureaucratic behavior and a meting out of punishments for agency misbehavior (McCubbins & Schwartz, 1984, p. 166). Political actors may also rely on what have been called "fire alarms" to notify them of potential problematic matters occurring in government agencies (McCubbins & Schwartz, 1984; see also McCubbins et al., 1987, 1989; Yackee, 2003, p. 9). "Fire alarms" occur when citizens, interest groups, or other policy actors alert elected officials that an agency has taken some action believed to be outside the agency's appropriate range of discretion (McCubbins & Schwartz, 1984; see also McCubbins et al., 1987, 1989; Yackee, 2003). Upon receiving this information, political actors can look into the matter, determine whether there has been a breach of the principal-agent relationship, and—if they desire—take action to correct the agency's missteps (McCubbins et al., 1987).

In addition to "police patrols" and "fire alarms," McCubbins et al. (1987, 1989) point out that elected officials also create the legally binding procedures that require agencies to fulfill certain obligations before they may create and implement bureaucratic policy, such as through rulemaking. For example, the Administrative Procedure Act requires that departments publicize their plans to create a new rule and seek input from external sources about the content of a potential rule (Administrative Procedure Act, 2012; McCubbins et al., 1987). Through procedures such as these, the political units can control—in advance of any agency rulemaking activity—the manner in which bureaucracies carry out their policymaking tasks and can establish limitations on what an agency may do (McCubbins et al., 1987, 1989). The political branches can also include language in authorizing statutes that limits the amount of rulemaking that is permitted to take place in implementing the statute, thereby reining in some bureaucratic discretion (O'Connell, 2011).

Presidents, of course, play a role in the passage of legislation such as the kinds described above, by signing or vetoing legislation passed by Congress (Moe, 2012; O'Connell, 2011). But presidents can control the bureaucracy independently of Congress by signing executive orders that mandate particular procedures to be followed in the rulemaking process (see, e.g., Executive Order No. 12866, 1993). Also, the president appoints (subject to Senate approval) agency leadership, such as the secretary of education and other high-level managers of the

leadership

Department of Education, which may likewise influence rulemaking or bureaucratic decision making (Anderson, 2006; Bernstein, 1955; Furlong, 1998; McCubbins et al., 1989; Moe, 2012; O'Connell, 2008, 2011). Moreover, previous research indicates that pressure from presidents can weigh heavily on bureaus: in a survey of agency officials' beliefs about political influences on regulatory activities, agency officials identified the presidency as highly influential over agency behavior (Furlong, 1998).

Theories that emphasize political control have been criticized for assuming, perhaps unrealistically, that the political branches have the opportunity to obtain full and accurate knowledge about the details of bureaucratic work and also have "numerous opportunities to signal their preferences" (Meier, 2008, p. 4). Moreover, such theories take a view of the bureaucracy as "respon[sive] to politicians in a stimulus-response pattern," a similarly unwarranted supposition, and do not recognize that in many cases, bureaus "force political institutions to respond to them" (p. 4). Just as bureaucratic discretion theory has been criticized for underestimating the power of political actors in regulatory policymaking, political control theory has faced the critique of giving insufficient credence to the authority and expertise of the bureaucracy (Carpenter & Krause, 2014; Moe, 2012).

There is much evidence of the political units' influence over the bureaucracy. Through the authorizing legislation it enacts, Congress has the power to define the extent, substance, and procedure of many rulemakings (Kerwin & Furlong, 2011; Lubbers, 1998; McCubbins et al., 1987). The more specific authorizing legislation is in defining the terms of government programs or the extent of permissible bureaucratic activity, the more control Congress exerts over bureaucratic policymaking (Anderson, 2006). Congress may also define the terms of rulemaking itself (McCubbins et al., 1987, 1989), for example, by mandating regional meetings or negotiated rulemaking as part of regulation development (1998 Amendments, 1998; Higher Education Opportunity Act, 2008; Lubbers, 1998) or by specifying time frames for concluding the construction of new rules (Kerwin & Furlong, 2011; Lubbers, 1998). Through statutes such as the Higher Education Act, Congress (in conjunction with the president who signed the legislation) has exerted these very kinds of influence over higher education rulemaking.

The Accreditation and Student Outcomes Rule provides an example of congressional influence over a higher education rulemaking procedure. As explained more fully in chapter 1, this rulemaking controversially sought to link higher education accreditation to student outcomes. Some members of Congress disagreed with what the Department of Education was trying to do via this rule and communicated to the department (both directly and indirectly) that it should cease regulating in this area, at least until the next reauthorization of the Higher Education Act (Lowry, 2009). Some members of Congress sent a letter to the secretary of education asking her to delay the prospective rule and took steps through the legislative process to prohibit the department from regulating in this area; one member of Congress even made a floor speech expressing displeasure with the rule (Lederman, 2007b; Lowry, 2009; Office of Senator Lamar Alexander, 2007). That particular rulemaking procedure was discontinued and never completed (Lowry, 2009, p. 510). As this case demonstrates, congressional wishes with respect to rulemaking can be quite influential over the Department of Education's regulation of higher education. Presidents also exert influence over the rulemaking process in a variety of ways, for example by signing legislation and issuing executive orders, which have affected both the substance and the process of higher education rulemaking. A president may also issue signing statements or guidelines to explain the administration's policy positions that bureaucracies are expected to accommodate (Anderson, 2006; Halstead, 2008; Kerwin & Furlong, 2011).

Another important way the president influences the process is through the Office of Management and Budget (Kerwin & Furlong, 2011), which is involved in various aspects of the higher education rulemaking process, for example through the OMB's required review and approval of certain proposed and final rules (see also Executive Order No. 12866, 1993; Kerwin & Furlong, 2011; Lubbers, 1998). West and Raso (2013) state that the OMB's review power may render the White House's influence over rulemaking even greater than that of Congress, once rulemaking has commenced. The OMB also has the ability to make "recommendations on agencies' budgets"—a power that might persuade agencies to make rules as pleasing as possible to the OMB (Kerwin & Furlong, 2011, pp. 241–242). OMB powers are linked with presidential powers because the OMB is a White House office and is closely aligned with the president (Anderson, 2006; Bryner, 1987; Yackee, 2003). Indeed, Bryner (1987) identifies "OMB review" as a presidential power (p. 14).

The Power of Regulated Entities

Other theories recognize the power of interest groups over regulatory policymaking. One such theory, known as regulatory or agency "capture" theory, argues that certain regulated entities possess a substantial amount of influence over the government agencies that profess to regulate them, persuading the agencies to promote policies that benefit powerful interest groups (Bernstein, 1955; Laffont & Tirole, 1991; Makkai & Braithwaite, 1992; Niles, 2002; Stigler, 1971; see also Kerwin & Furlong, 2011). Such beneficial policies may include relaxed regulations, the provision of grants or contracts to certain regulated parties, the restriction of competition within the industry, the allowance of profitable collaboration among powerful regulated actors (for example, "price-fixing" [Stigler, 1971, p. 6]), and the advancement of related industries that benefit the regulated party (Niles, 2002; Stigler, 1971).

The marked influence that interest groups and regulated parties can have over government agencies may derive from several sources. The influence may result from the often close relationship between regulated entities and their governing agencies (Kerwin & Furlong, 2011; Laffont & Tirole, 1991; Makkai & Braithwaite, 1992; Wagner, Barnes, & Peters, 2011). Indeed, the "iron triangles" mentioned above have also been dubbed "cozy triangles" by some observers (Durant, 2015, p. 210; Freeman & Stevens, 1987, p. 9). Moreover, bureaucrats sometimes desire future employment within the industry being regulated, and this may influence them to treat the industry—composed of prospective employers—favorably (Johnson, 1983; Laffont & Tirole, 1991; Makkai & Braithwaite, 1992). Conversely, former industry leaders may go to work for a regulatory bureau but remain biased toward the industry's positions and interests (Johnson, 1983; Makkai & Braithwaite, 1992).[2] Also, regulated entities hold expertise in their own fields and can provide a unique data source for regulators (Wagner et al., 2011). The influence of interest groups over government agencies may also be the consequence of vocal demands and effective lobbying efforts— whether before the agencies themselves or before the political units to which the agencies must answer—that interest groups undertake in attempts to secure particular bureaucratic outcomes (Laffont & Tirole, 1991; Niles, 2002). Business organizations in particular may be able to influence government agencies because such organizations often have considerable resources (Wagner et al., 2011).[3]

It is problematic for regulated entities to have a substantial level of influence over government agencies because such "capture" may interfere with agencies' ability to regulate the industry effectively and consistently and to perform bureaucratic policymaking responsibilities in a manner that promotes the best interests of the general public. In other words, a captured agency's top priority will be to aid the powerful organizations that have captured it, and these organizations' interests may not align with the general interests of the larger society (Fernández, 1994; Niles, 2002).

The literature on rulemaking and bureaucratic policymaking demonstrates that some well-resourced regulated parties do exercise a fair amount of power over the creation of agency regulations. However, interest group influence is often uneven. Some interest groups possess greater assets and more information relating to rulemaking than others, and consequently the more advantaged interest groups are better positioned to influence rulemaking than less advantaged ones (Coglianese, 2006; Golden, 1998; Kerwin & Furlong, 2011). Research has shown, for example, that business and regulated industries may play a greater role in the notice-and-comment phase than other interested individuals or groups (Coglianese, 2006; Golden, 1998). In an analysis of formal comments on 11 proposed rules promulgated by three federal agencies, Golden found a disproportionate number of comments authored by business and industry among two of the three agencies' proposed rules. Moreover, according to Golden, some types of policy actors are "more sophisticated" than others in the "monitoring techniques" they use to keep themselves informed about rulemaking (p. 257). Businesses, groups representing their interests, and well-resourced public interest groups tend to engage in highly effective screening strategies, such as learning about new rulemakings from other organizations and receiving electronic notifications of agency activities (Golden, 1998).

In addition to commenting and monitoring, there are various other ways that interest groups may influence the rulemaking process. Policy actors sometimes communicate with rulemaking entities outside the notice-and-comment or rulemaking-hearing contexts (Furlong, 1998; Furlong & Kerwin, 2005; Kerwin & Furlong, 2011). Another way that a nongovernmental actor may influence rulemaking is by petitioning an agency to commence rulemaking when the actor sees the need for a new rule (Administrative Procedure Act, 2012; Furlong, 1998; Furlong & Kerwin, 2005; Kerwin & Furlong, 2011; Lubbers, 1998). Departments need not commence a rulemaking upon receiving a petition; however, they are obligated "to acknowledge the petition and consider the request" (Kerwin & Furlong, 2011, p. 79). Interest groups may also influence rulemaking by joining forces with other policy actors—whether part of the same organization or not—to advocate in favor of desired rule provisions (Furlong, 1998; Furlong & Kerwin, 2005; Kerwin & Furlong, 2011). Furlong and Kerwin's survey found that a large percentage of interest groups and other organizations identified "forming coalitions with other organizations/firms" as a tactic they used either "sometimes," "often," or "always" when attempting to influence rulemaking (p. 363). And of course, interest groups may influence rulemaking by taking part in public rulemaking hearings or negotiated rulemaking (Furlong, 1998; Furlong & Kerwin, 2005; Kerwin & Furlong, 2011).

Combination and More Comprehensive Theories

As Bertelli (2012) observes, "no single view of public sector governance is sufficient" (p. 171). Indeed, a number of scholars have more recently recognized the advantages of combining certain aspects of different bureaucratic policy theories (Bertelli, 2012; Bertelli & Lynn, 2006; Carpenter & Krause, 2014; Yackee, 2003; see also Moe, 2012). Bertelli and Lynn, for example, combine theories of political economy with concepts prevalent in "the classical tradition of public administration" to analyze US bureaucracy (p. 8). Moreover, Carpenter & Krause delineate "transactional authority" theory, which views bureaucratic power as a shared agreement between the political units and government agencies. This viewpoint recognizes that both types of actors hold power and that "a cooperative hierarchical relationship reflect[s] mutual agreement, albeit at times the nature of the politician-agent relationship is contested with each party winning some conflicts while losing others" (p. 9).

Other theories take a much broader view of policymaking, not focusing mainly on policy actor power but taking into consideration the broader context in which public policy is created (see, e.g., Kingdon, 2003; Sabatier & Jenkins-Smith, 1999; Sabatier & Weible, 2007). The Advocacy Coalition Framework (ACF), for example, does not focus on the power of one category of actor versus other categories. Rather, the ACF sees policy development as a prolonged process in which coalitions of individuals and groups possessing comparable beliefs promote the adoption of certain policies (Sabatier, 1986, 1993; Sabatier & Jenkins-Smith, 1993, 1999; Sabatier & Weible, 2007; Weible, 2007). Actors with similar beliefs form advocacy coalitions, which work to promote their own favored policies within "a policy subsystem" (Sabatier & Jenkins-Smith, 1999, p. 119). Coalitions involve all kinds of policy actors, and powerful coalitions are often successful at influencing policy (Sabatier & Jenkins-Smith, 1999; Sabatier & Weible, 2007). The ACF notes that policy actors' beliefs influence their public advocacy behavior, including the determination of coalition membership and the specific details of the programs and policies they desire. The ACF also views certain contextual phenomena—such as economic conditions and shifting political power—as crucial determinants in the policymaking process, because such phenomena influence coalitions' actions and can lead to the creation or alteration of public policy (Sabatier, 1986; Sabatier & Jenkins-Smith, 1999; Sabatier & Weible, 2007).

Kingdon (2003) similarly argues that shifts in context may precipitate the consideration of certain types of policies (see also Zahariadis, 2007). "Policy windows," according to Kingdon, are brought on by "politically propitious events" that do not occur often, may serve to move prospective policies onto the government's "decision agenda," and have preceded "major changes in public policy" (p. 166). Though often attention-grabbing events, these are sometimes more subtle but still mark important shifts in the policy environment. Examples of these contextual changes include reauthorizations of statutes, critical events, and the election of different public officials (Kingdon, 2003). Likewise, West and Raso (2013) note that certain "contextual factors" and changes in the surrounding "policy-making environments" have influenced rulemaking (pp. 505–506). This includes changes in economic conditions, advances in technology, and changes in extant policies (West & Raso, 2013).

But regardless of how various theories view the power of the bureaucracy, they all recognize bureaucratic agencies as important actors in the policymaking process. In the realm of higher education, several federal agencies routinely play a role in the shaping of policy affecting postsecondary education in the United States. The next section describes the federal agencies that are most typically involved in higher-education-related matters.

Federal Agencies That Influence Higher Education Policy and Practice

From conducting the research that forms the bases for technological advances and medical breakthroughs to educating the populace in preparation for workforce and civic participation, higher education plays an increasingly crucial role in our society. The significant and ubiquitous presence of higher education means that it is affected by policy changes in a vast number of areas, from collective bargaining to environmental protection to (more directly) education policy, and beyond. As such, the actions of a wide variety of federal agencies have at least some impact on higher education policy implementation and the day-to-day activities of colleges and universities.

The federal agency that most directly and frequently affects higher education is the US Department of Education (Cook, 1998). Indeed, this department's role in creating regulatory policy relating to federal financial aid programs renders the agency "a major actor in the postsecondary policy issue space" (Hillman et al., 2015, pp. 38–39). Through its Office of Postsecondary Education, the Department of Education is responsible for implementing federal financial aid programs as well as federal programs related to minority-serving institutions (Cook, 1998; Higher Education Act, 2012; Hillman et al., 2015; Office of Postsec-

a lot of diff. areas affected!

ondary Education, 2015b). This office is also responsible for administering federal grants to states and higher education institutions. One such program is the Fund for the Improvement of Postsecondary Education, which provides grants for diverse programs with the goal of improving the higher education experience (Cook, 1998; Office of Postsecondary Education, 2015a). The Office of Postsecondary Education also "administers programs to strengthen foreign language learning, international and area studies teaching, and research and curriculum development on global issues at the undergraduate, graduate, postgraduate, and K-12 levels" (Office of Postsecondary Education, 2015b). Other segments of the Department of Education that handle matters affecting higher education include the Office of Career, Technical, and Adult Education; the Institute of Education Sciences; the Office for Civil Rights; and the Office of Innovation and Improvement, among others.[4]

Other federal agencies that administer programs or implement policies affecting some aspect of postsecondary education are also relevant to a discussion about the power of bureaucracy in the higher education policy arena. The National Oceanic and Atmospheric Administration offers postsecondary student scholarships (National Oceanic and Atmospheric Administration Office of Education, n.d.) and a "Sea Grant" research program in partnership with more than two dozen universities (National Oceanic and Atmospheric Administration, n.d.). Agencies such as the Department of Labor, the National Labor Relations Board, and the Department of Health and Human Services regulate issues regarding employees and labor unions, including student employees and the part-time faculty workforce (Hillman et al., 2015; Jaschik, 2015). The Department of Labor has also provided grants to higher education institutions for the development and implementation of workforce training programs (US Department of Labor, 2011). The Department of Veterans Affairs offers postsecondary scholarships to veterans (Hillman et al., 2015). The Department of Justice carries out civil rights policy in educational settings, including the Civil Rights Act, the Americans with Disabilities Act, and the Equal Educational Opportunities Act (US Department of Justice, n.d.). And numerous federal agencies—including but not limited to the Department of Defense, the National Science Foundation, and the National Institutes of Health—provide funding for university-based research and development to expand scientific knowledge and further governmental goals (Hillman et al., 2015; National Science Foundation, n.d.; Rosenzweig, 2001; see also Cook, 1998).

But what are the specific mechanisms through which the bureaucracy acts to influence higher education policy and practice? Although some of these

So many departments!

mechanisms have been alluded to previously, the next section describes in more detail the various actions that may be taken by bureaucracies to enact their influence.

Methods of Bureaucratic Influence on Higher Education Policy and Practice

The federal bureaucracy can influence higher education policy and practice through numerous mechanisms. Some of the main ones are funding decisions, inspections, adjudication, nonbinding rules and guidance, and rulemaking (Anderson, 2006; O'Connell, 2008).

Funding Decisions

One way that federal bureaucracies influence higher education policy and practice is through funding decisions. Federal agencies are responsible for administering funding for a variety of purposes to colleges and universities. By setting the eligibility criteria, terms, and conditions of receiving such funding, bureaucracies can influence the behavior of higher education institutions. Agencies that provide university research funding determine funding requirements, issue requests for proposals, and review periodic reports about the research (see, e.g., Association of American Universities, 2011; National Science Foundation, 2013). Moreover, federal agencies have provided funding to colleges and universities for such things as the development and improvement of particular types of academic programs (see, e.g., Office of Postsecondary Education, 2015a; US Department of Labor, 2011). The federal government has also provided funding to build institutional capacity to, for example, better meet the needs of underserved student populations, such as through the Department of Education's "Strengthening Institutions Program" (US Department of Education, 2013a). Additional important types of funding for higher education include funding for minority-serving institutions, funding for TRIO programs (which, as explained in chapter 1, aim to improve higher education access and success for traditionally underrepresented students [Pitre & Pitre, 2009; Swail, 2000]), and the provision of need-based student aid for higher education (Higher Education Act, 2012). Higher education institutions that want to receive funding from federal agencies will ensure that their behavior and activities comply with the requirements to be eligible for funding.

Two things are important to note when considering the influence of the federal bureaucracy on higher education via funding decisions. First, the legislature has control over bureaucracies' budgets and sometimes provides details about how funding should be used (see, e.g., Bertelli, 2012). For example, the Trade Adjustment Assistance Community College and Career Training Grant program, which provided funding for community colleges to develop training programs in "in-demand" skills (Field, 2014b), was authorized under the legislative enactment known as the American Recovery and Reinvestment Act (Phelan, 2014; US Department of Labor, 2011). That statute provided specific information about the types of educational programs that were to receive funding: those that would assist professionally displaced individuals to obtain training in fields with potential for growth, such as in computing and health occupations (Phelan, 2014). In light of Congress's ultimate control over agency budgets—and the fact that Congress sometimes dictates precisely how parts of the bureaucratic budget should be spent—bureaucracies' funding decisions as an influence over higher education should be considered a joint power held by both the bureaucracy and the political branches.

Second, in addition to requiring recipients of funds to meet eligibility criteria and agree to various terms and conditions, many federal funding programs are subject to regulations created by the bureaucracy through the rulemaking process. For example, institutions and their students must meet eligibility standards in order to receive Title IV student aid funds. But to maintain eligibility, institutions must comply with new regulations, such as changing standards about what types of incentive payments are permissible for an institution's admission staff (see, e.g., Kantrowitz, 2010, regarding these changing standards). Thus, although funding decisions are treated in this section as a method of bureaucratic influence separate from rulemaking, the two are actually quite closely related.

Inspections and Investigations

Bureaucracies undertake inspections or investigations with some frequency to determine whether regulated activity is compliant with law and other requirements (Anderson, 2006). Many federal agencies have an Office of the Inspector General or similar department, whose job it is to review and examine the agency's activities and to make recommendations aimed at "promoting economy, efficiency, and effectiveness and preventing and detecting fraud and abuse in those programs and operations," while providing complete and timely information to both Congress and the agency's leader regarding problematic or concerning issues that may arise (Council of the Inspectors General, 2014, p. 1). The Department of Education's inspector general investigates such matters as "fraud, waste, or abuse of Department of Education funds" and conducts other types of inspections as well (Office of Inspector General, 2015). Additionally, the Department of Education's Office of the Inspector General has been granted law enforcement powers, meaning that criminal investigators within the office have the authority to make arrests and execute warrants (Council of the Inspectors General, 2014). Anderson (2006) notes that law enforcement powers often provide an agency with considerable discretion and are an effective way for the agency to "mold policy" by, for example, enforcing some laws more "vigorously" than others (p. 226).

Offices within the Department of Education other than that of the inspector general conduct investigations as well. For example, the Office for Civil Rights announced in 2014 that some higher education institutions were under investigation to determine whether any violations of Title IX of the Education Amendments of 1972 (prohibiting sex discrimination) took place in the institutions' handling of matters relating to sexual harassment and assault (US Department of Education, 2014b). In addition, the department developed the "Student Aid Enforcement Unit" within the Office of Federal Student Aid in 2016, with one of its responsibilities being "to identify potential misconduct or high-risk activity among higher education institutions" (US Department of Education, 2016).

Commissions, Task Forces, and Similar Groups

Agencies may also appoint commissions or task forces for the purpose of analyzing particular issues or problems, writing reports about them, and making recommendations for policy or practice change. One such group, created by Secretary of Education Margaret Spellings, was called the Commission on the Future of Higher Education and came to be known as the Spellings Commission. Its tasks were to analyze higher education in the United States and the problems it faced with regard to "access, affordability, quality, and accountability" and to make recommendations for addressing those problems (Secretary of Education's Commission, 2006, p. xiii; see also Zemsky, 2007). After the Spellings Commission released its report, the Department of Education held "a forum on accreditation" to consider how the commission's suggestions could be put into practice (Office of Postsecondary Education: Notice, 2007, p. 4221). Later, the never-completed Accreditation and Student Outcomes Rule became one of the consequences of the Spellings Commission's recommendations.

Although that particular rulemaking was halted early in the process and never resulted in final regulations (Lowry, 2009), the Spellings Commission and other similar agency-appointed groups have had influence—both directly and indirectly—on education policy and practice over the years (see, e.g., Basken, 2007; Guthrie & Springer, 2004). For example, the National Commission on Excellence in Education, appointed by the secretary of education in the early 1980s, resulted in the well-known "Nation at Risk" report, which came to heavily influence education policy in the United States (Guthrie & Springer, 2004). Task forces may also influence agency rulemaking, such as when a Department of Education "Task Force on Student Loans" composed entirely of department personnel provided suggestions for proposed regulatory language regarding federal student loan programs in 2007 (Federal Perkins Loan Program, 2007c, p. 32411).

Adjudication 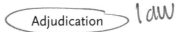 law

Another way that the federal bureaucracy may influence higher education policy and practice is through adjudication, the process through which a bureaucratic agency hears evidence, interprets the law, and makes a legally binding decision about a particular situation, in a similar fashion to a court of law (Administrative Procedure Act, 2012, §§ 554, 556, 557; Anderson, 2006). In the Department of Education, adjudications relating to the student financial aid programs under the Higher Education Act are handled though the Office of Higher Education Appeals and involve such matters as removal of an institution's eligibility to receive federal student aid and the recovery of department funding that was allegedly spent inappropriately. Other matters that may involve higher education (but also often involve other areas of education) are handled by the Office of Administrative Law Judges and the Civil Rights Reviewing Authority, both of which (along with the Office of Higher Education Appeals) are part of the Department of Education's Office of Hearings and Appeals (Office of Hearings & Appeals, n.d.). The decisions that arise from these adjudications create binding policy or precedent, just as judicial decisions do when rendered by courts (Anderson, 2006; O'Connell, 2008). Decisions may be reviewed by the secretary of education or a judicial court (Solomon, 2011).

Nonbinding Rules and Guidance

Nonbinding rules and guidance refer to such documents as "guidance documents, policy statements, and interpretative rules" as well as rules developed through "nonlegislative rulemaking" (O'Connell, 2008, p. 901). An example of nonbinding guidance affecting higher education is a document issued in 2007 that offered directions to schools, other federal grantees, and contractors about the "collection and reporting of racial and ethnic data" ("Final Guidance," 2007).

Various offices within the Department of Education have also issued "Dear Colleague" letters, which provide clarification on how certain rules or laws should be interpreted. An example of a "Dear Colleague" letter issued by the Department of Education is a 2011 document confirming that Title IX gender discrimination and sexual harassment prohibitions cover sexual assault and delineating how institutions should respond to such acts to be in compliance with Title IX (Ali, 2011). Other "Dear Colleague" letters provide information and guidance regarding federal student financial aid programs (see iLibrary, n.d.). Complex regulations may become the subject of more nonbinding guidance than regulations that are less complex and perhaps easier to understand. For example, the Gainful Employment Rules (which are complex as well as controversial) have given rise to dozens of Department of Education guidance documents (Office of Federal Student Aid, n.d.a.).

Although guidance documents and "Dear Colleague" letters such as these are technically not binding (O'Connell, 2008), they are interpretations of and supplements to binding laws, and as such, these documents can influence institutional practices and behavior by providing information from a knowledgeable authority about how to interpret laws that are binding.[5]

Recognition, Program Administration, and Data Collection

In addition to rulemaking (discussed next) and all of the methods for influencing higher education policy and practice explained above, the federal bureaucracy has other responsibilities that can have serious consequences for higher education institutions. For example, the Department of Education makes determinations about institutional eligibility to receive federal student aid, including the recognition of accrediting organizations that can decide whether an institution is sufficiently meeting standards to be eligible for Title IV program participation (Cook, 1998; US Department of Education, 2015a). Federal agencies also directly manage government programs (Anderson, 2006), including the Department of Education's direct student lending program (Cook, 1998; Office of Federal Student Aid, n.d.b.). Some federal agencies also collect data about various matters, including demographic and survey information regarding college students and higher education institutions (see, e.g., National Center for Education Statistics, n.d.). Data collection processes create both responsibilities and opportunities for higher education institutions—responsibilities to submit data to the agency and opportunities to use the data to conduct research. Through

[handwritten margin note, left side top: "do it this way"]

[handwritten margin note, left side bottom: Collect data to complete research.]

administrative responsibilities such as those described in this subsection, the everyday work of federal bureaucrats can have considerable influence on colleges' and universities' behavior, as well as on important policy matters such as higher education access for students, even if indirectly.

Rulemaking

Finally, the federal bureaucracy influences higher education policy and practice through rulemaking. As explained in chapter 1, rulemaking is an administrative procedure that, when carried out to completion, results in the adoption of rules (also known as regulations), which are as binding as laws passed by the legislature (Anderson, 2006; Furlong & Kerwin, 2005; Golden, 1998; Kerwin & Furlong, 2011; Lubbers, 1998; O'Connell, 2008). There are two types of rulemaking: formal and informal. Formal rulemaking involves an adjudicatory process that resembles a trial, much like the adjudications described above (Lubbers, 1998; O'Connell, 2008). In fact, although there are some key differences between adjudication and formal rulemaking (Lubbers, 1998),[6] the same hearing procedures required for adjudications under the Administrative Procedure Act apply to formal rulemaking hearings (see Administrative Procedure Act, 2012, §§ 553–554, 556–557). Formal rulemaking is employed relatively infrequently and is required only when the authorizing statute requires that rules "be made on the record after opportunity for an agency hearing" (§ 553[c]; see also Lubbers, 1998; O'Connell, 2008).

Agencies also create regulations and make policy through informal rulemaking. Also known as "notice-and-comment rulemaking" (O'Connell, 2008, p. 901; see also Lubbers, 1998, p. 5), this procedure generally involves publishing a Notice of Proposed Rulemaking, allowing time for interested persons to comment on the rule proposal (unless the notice-and-comment period is waived), and then publishing a final, binding version of the rule in the *Federal Register* (Kerwin & Furlong, 2011; Lubbers, 1998; O'Connell, 2008). Additional legal requirements must be followed as well for a final rule to be binding. Informal rulemaking is the typical means of creating regulatory policy implementing Higher Education Act provisions within the Department of Education. It is also the form of rulemaking that is under scrutiny in the remainder of this book. The next chapter describes the detailed procedure prescribed by law for informal rulemaking in the Department of Education's Office of Postsecondary Education to implement provisions of the Higher Education Act.

CHAPTER THREE

The Procedural Process

As a policymaking process, higher education rulemaking must follow a legally prescribed procedure. Although the main elements of rulemaking are largely consistent across agencies, the precise process varies not only by agency but also by authorizing statute, and even by the nature of the anticipated rule itself (Kerwin & Furlong, 2011; Lubbers, 1998). For example, occasionally "formal rulemaking," in which hearings and testimony are used to craft rules, is employed when required by an authorizing statute (Kerwin & Furlong, 2011; Lubbers, 1998; O'Connell, 2008). Because this book is concerned with the creation of regulations administering and implementing provisions of the Higher Education Act, this chapter describes the procedural process of "informal rulemaking" (Lubbers, 1998, p. 5); it is the process used in the US Department of Education to make regulations authorized under that act. The process of higher education rulemaking is based on several different statutes and executive orders, which together require particular steps to be taken by the Department of Education to create a binding rule. The statutes include the "Rule Making" section of the Administrative Procedure Act, as well as the Congressional Review Act, the Paperwork Reduction Act, the Negotiated Rulemaking Act, and even the Higher Education Act itself (see Administrative Procedure Act, 2012; Higher Education Act, 2012; Hillman et al., 2015; Kerwin & Furlong, 2011; Lubbers, 1998).

The procedures described in this chapter have been created by the political branches, whether through statute or executive order. This fact is consistent with McCubbins et al.'s (1987, 1989) contention, discussed more fully in chapter 2, that the political branches exercise control over bureaucratic policymaking by determining procedural rules. Within the parameters set by statutes and executive orders, the Department of Education makes some procedural decisions as well, such as scheduling rulemaking, determining when and where

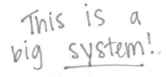

certain meetings will take place, and developing initial drafts of negotiated rule-making protocols (see, e.g., Pelesh, 1994).

Generally speaking, the different phases of the higher education rulemaking process are: pre-rulemaking and initiating rulemaking; drafting a proposed rule (which often involves holding regional meetings around the country and embark-ing on a process known as negotiated rulemaking); the notice-and-comment phase; finalization of a rule; and postfinalization. However, the rulemaking procedure is not as rigid as it might appear. Not every rule goes through every step, and sometimes the steps might occur outside the typical order (Kerwin & Furlong, 2011). In some cases, such as the Accreditation and Student Outcomes rulemaking, the process is discontinued at some point before completion and no final rule results from it. In other cases, such as the Gainful Employment Rule, aspects of the final regulations are challenged and nullified in court, and a new rulemaking process regarding the same subject matter is conducted. The concern of this chapter, though, is the general procedural process of notice-and-comment federal rulemaking as it occurs within the US Department of Educa-tion for the purpose of regulating higher education. This chapter concludes by considering the ways in which the procedural rules allow for diverse participa-tion and viewpoints in the process and the degree to which these rules may favor involvement on the part of powerful policy actors.

Phase 1: Pre-rulemaking and Initiating Rulemaking

The first step in the rulemaking process is generally viewed as the decision to initiate rulemaking. However, it is arguable that the rulemaking process begins even further back in time, when the authorizing statute is enacted (Kerwin & Furlong, 2011). Although the Higher Education Act was first enacted in 1965, it has been periodically reauthorized and amended. Such legislation has been the springboard for higher education rulemaking. *part of system!*

After authorizing legislation is in place, personnel within the Department of Education must decide to initiate rulemaking, and as part of that decision-making process, department officials must decide what and when to regulate. As West and Raso (2013) note, "agencies typically lack the resources to pursue more than a fraction of the initiatives that are warranted by their legal mandates" (p. 495). Determining what to regulate is a crucial agency function because the subject matter of prospective regulations can shape policy discussions, priori-tize funding for certain programs, and draw attention to particular issues (West & Raso, 2013). The decision of when to regulate has also been an important

sneaky !

consideration for agencies. For example, some observers have noticed a surge of rulemaking toward the end of a presidential administration or before a change in party control of Congress, presumably to cement policy relatively quickly, before new leadership and possibly a new ideology come to power. Of course, new administrations have been known to halt and review such "midnight" rulemakings upon taking office (O'Connell, 2008, 2011). Although agencies often have some leeway in deciding when to initiate rulemaking, sometimes the timetable for creating new rules is dictated by statute (Kerwin & Furlong, 2011).

Another important consideration during the initiation stage is the question of why to start rulemaking. Sometimes, an agency has no choice but to create regulations because Congress has placed language in the authorizing statute mandating that rulemaking must occur (Kerwin & Furlong, 2011). Other times, agencies have more discretion. Agency personnel or internal committees within the agency may come up with ideas for new regulations that will implement or administer programs or policies authorized by statute, or for revising existing rules (Kerwin & Furlong, 2011; West & Raso, 2013). Agencies may also be prompted to start rulemaking because a formal petition or request has been received from an outside entity: other agencies, congressional committees, or even members of the public (Kerwin & Furlong, 2011; Lubbers, 1998; Office of the Federal Register, 2011). Moreover, changing environments, new facts coming to light, or the occurrence of a high-profile event may prompt an agency to start rulemaking (Office of the Federal Register, 2011). As a representative of for-profit higher education interviewed for this study explained, the Department of Education may become aware of "complaints" or "program review" results indicating that a particular policy or program is experiencing difficulty with implementation and needs an adjustment to existing rules. Whatever the catalyst, once a decision to commence rulemaking is made, the next step is to determine what language to include in the rule.

Phase 2: Drafting a Proposed Rule, Regional Meetings, and Negotiated Rulemaking

The next step in the rulemaking process is to draft a proposed rule, which will appear in the *Federal Register* as a Notice of Proposed Rulemaking. While personnel within an agency are often tasked with writing the language of an NPRM (Golden, 1998; Kerwin & Furlong, 2011), many higher education regulations are written with the help of negotiated rulemaking committees (Pelesh, 1994). Negotiated rulemaking refers to including in the drafting of the NPRM

allowing affected to have a voice!

individuals and groups who will potentially be affected by the proposed rule (Harter, 1982; Kerwin & Furlong, 2011; Lubbers, 1998; Pelesh, 1994; Pritzker & Dalton, 1995). The Higher Education Act (2012) requires that negotiated rule-making be used when regulating Title IV financial aid programs. In theory, negotiated rulemaking is supposed to result in regulations that are more agreeable to the individuals and groups affected by them, because it makes these parties part of the NPRM drafting process (Coglianese, 1997; Harter, 1982; Kerwin & Furlong, 2011; Pelesh, 1994; Pritzker & Dalton, 1995).

Negotiated rulemaking for higher education tends to follow the following procedure, as prescribed by law.[1] First, the Department of Education holds regional meetings (Higher Education Act, 2012, § 1098a[a][2]), attended by potentially affected parties, at various locations across the country, to discuss the goals and rules of forthcoming negotiated rulemaking sessions and receives recommendations as to which parties should serve on negotiated rulemaking panels. The Higher Education Act states that at the regional meetings, the department should obtain information and suggestions from a wide range of individuals and groups, including higher education institutions, organizations in the student loan industry, students, and legal representatives of student interests (Higher Education Act, 2012). At a 2008 regional meeting at Texas Christian University, a Department of Education official explained in some detail how regional meetings fit into the negotiated rulemaking agenda-setting process:

> Basically, we start off with public hearings like this. We seek public comment about issues—from the public, and concerns the public has. We do it through the hearings here and through written comments you can submit that are—you can submit it to the address in the *Federal Register* notice. We'll take those public comments in a review of what we see in the Act and go back and develop the idea of what areas we need to negotiate on, the subject areas for committees, and we'll be publishing a notice about that, and we'll announce what subject areas we're going to negotiate, what the proposed committees are, and request nominees for those committees to come and participate in the negotiation process. (*Public Regional Hearing on Negotiated Rulemaking*, 2008a, p. 2)

After the regional meetings, the Department of Education meets with selected representatives of stakeholder constituencies for the process of negotiated rulemaking, to discuss the content that should be included in a proposed rule (Higher Education Act, 2012; Higher Education Opportunity Act, 2008; Kerwin & Furlong, 2011; Lubbers, 1998; 1998 Amendments, 1998; Pelesh, 1994; Pritzker & Dalton, 1995). Negotiators are selected by the Department of Education based on nominations received in response to a request for the same; the nominations are to be collected publicly, from across a broad array of stakeholders in the higher education arena (Hillman et al., 2015; Pelesh, 1994). The Higher Education Act requires the department to select negotiators from "industry" in addition to Washington insiders and to include "both large and small participants, as well as individuals serving local areas and national markets" (Higher Education Act, 2012, § 1098a[b][1]).

Negotiated rulemaking meetings are moderated by "a neutral, competent convener, preferably skilled in the techniques of mediation" (Kerwin & Furlong, 2011, p. 207). Negotiated rulemaking sessions often take several days, sometimes separated by weeks at a time. For example, the negotiated rulemaking committee that met to develop what later became the first Gainful Employment Rule met on multiple occasions between the months of November 2009 and January 2010 (Program Integrity: Gainful Employment, 2010).

Ideally, the negotiated rulemaking team reaches "consensus" on the language to be included in the NPRM (Pelesh, 1994, p. 156; Pritzker & Dalton, 1995, p. 1; see also Kerwin & Furlong, 2011, p. 207). Such consensus occurs when "each interest represented concurs in the result, unless all members of the committee agree at the outset to a different meaning" (Pritzker & Dalton, 1995, p. 8).[2] Respondents of this study who have participated in negotiated rulemaking explained that typically, the Department of Education provides some potential language for a proposed rule at the beginning of a negotiated rulemaking session, and then together the negotiators analyze the language and debate recommendations for change. In the course of a few sessions of negotiating, ideally the language of the NPRM becomes increasingly more agreeable to participants and consensus is reached. If consensus on a proposed rule is achieved, then the agreed-upon language is used in the NPRM, and participants in the negotiation are not permitted to comment in a negative manner on it during the notice-and-comment phase. But if all negotiators—including the department's negotiator who is a member of the committee—do not agree on the NPRM language, then the department's personnel draft the NPRM, and all participants are free to comment as they please (see also Kerwin & Furlong, 2011; Lubbers, 1998; Pelesh, 1994; Pritzker & Dalton, 1995).

Negotiated rulemaking is fairly typical when federal higher education policy is being regulated. However, there are several circumstances under which the Department of Education is not required to conduct negotiated rulemaking. The Higher Education Act states that the Department of Education need not conduct negotiated rulemaking if "the Secretary [of Education] determines that applying such a requirement with respect to given regulations is impracticable, unnecessary, or contrary to the public interest . . . and publishes the basis for such determination in the *Federal Register* at the same time as the proposed regulations in question are first published" (Higher Education Act, 2012, § 1098a[b][2]). Also, although the Higher Education Act requires negotiated rulemaking for most regulations of federal student aid programs, the implementation of other aspects of the Higher Education Act do not typically require negotiated rulemaking. In those instances, Department of Education personnel write the proposed rules (Golden, 1998; Kerwin & Furlong, 2011). But even when negotiated rulemaking is not conducted, the agency may nonetheless reach out to experts in the regulated areas and other stakeholders when developing proposed rule language (Kerwin & Furlong, 2011; Office of the Federal Register, 2011). Other considerations that go into drafting an NPRM include the impact the rule would have on stakeholders and how the rule would be implemented once it is finalized (Kerwin & Furlong, 2011). *impact / implemented?*

Sometimes proposed regulations are the subject of the same negotiated rulemaking sessions but are issued as separate NPRMs. This was the case with regard to the first Gainful Employment Rule. The meaning of "gainful employment in a recognized occupation" was negotiated together with several other topics relating to maintaining the "integrity" of Title IV financial aid programs; however, when the NPRM for most of the "program integrity" rule was released, the only aspects of "gainful employment" that joined it were ones that covered "technical, reporting, and disclosure issues" (Program Integrity Issues, 2010b, p. 34808; see also Epstein, 2010). The bulk of the first Gainful Employment Rule's proposal was released separately a short time later, and both went on to become separate final rules (Program Integrity: Gainful Employment, 2011).

The Office of Management and Budget reviews certain draft NPRMs to ensure that they meet particular standards of the law and objectives of the prevailing presidential administration (Kerwin & Furlong, 2011; US General Accounting Office, 2003). Under Executive Order 12866 (1993), the OMB's Office of Information and Regulatory Affairs must review and approve "significant" rules, with "significant" referring to a rule that could

(1) Have an annual effect on the economy of $100 million or more or adversely affect in a material way the economy, a sector of the economy, productivity, competition, jobs, the environment, public health or safety, or State, local, or tribal governments or communities;

(2) Create a serious inconsistency or otherwise interfere with an action taken or planned by another agency;

(3) Materially alter the budgetary impact of entitlements, grants, user fees, or loan programs or the rights and obligations of recipients thereof; or

(4) Raise novel legal or policy issues arising out of legal mandates, the president's priorities, or the principles set forth in this Executive Order. (Executive Order No. 12866, 1993, p. 51738; see also US General Accounting Office, 2003, p. 23).

Occasionally, an agency will issue an "Advance Notice of Proposed Rulemaking," which contains draft language for a proposed NPRM and asks for public input into how a forthcoming NPRM should be written and what content it should include (Lubbers, 1998; Office of the Federal Register, 2011). This process is similar to negotiated rulemaking in that it asks interested parties to participate in the development of an NPRM, but different from negotiated rulemaking in that it relies on written comments rather than face-to-face, mediated negotiations with selected participants to create the proposed rule (Office of the Federal Register, 2011). Although Advance NPRMs are not often used in higher education rulemaking, they are issued at times. One example occurred in 2001, when the Department of Education asked for comments on how to develop an NPRM that would address issues relating to "the accuracy, integrity, and accessibility of electronic records in the administration of the federal student aid programs" following the enactment of the "E-Sign Act," which validated the use of electronic forms and signatures in, among other things, federal student lending transactions (Performance Standards, 2001, p. 13034).

Once an NPRM regulating higher education is written, the typical practice is for the Department of Education to publish it in the *Federal Register* and thus trigger the next phase of the rulemaking process, known as the notice-and-comment period.

Phase 3: The Notice-and-Comment Period

When an NPRM is published in the *Federal Register*, stakeholders and other members of the public may submit comments to the issuing agency regarding the proposed rule (Administrative Procedure Act, 2012; Kerwin & Furlong, 2011; Lubbers, 1998; Wagner et al., 2011). Typically the notice-and-comment phase lasts between 30 and 60 days, although more complicated or controversial proposed rules may establish a longer notice-and-comment period (Lubbers, 1998; Office of the Federal Register, 2011).

In higher education rulemaking, the categories of actors who submit comments during this phase run the gamut from college students and private taxpayers, to congressional members and committees, to lending organizations and higher education associations.[3] But as mentioned above, a specific exclusion from the notice-and-comment phase is that participants in negotiated rulemaking sessions that reach consensus on proposed rule language are not permitted to comment negatively on a proposed rule. According to one of this study's respondents who has participated in negotiated rulemaking, the rationale for this exclusion is that through negotiated rulemaking, the Department of Education has "supposedly gotten all of the key players to the table, they have reached agreement on it, and so the comment period is just kind of perfunctory. Nobody is really going to dissent from what's been agreed to, in fact, that's part of the protocol. If you have given consent, you're not supposed to comment negatively."

Once comments on a proposed rule are provided, the agency reviews the comments, considers their arguments, and determines whether to alter the rule based on them (Golden, 1998; Kerwin & Furlong, 2011). However, it is the Department of Education's prerogative to either adhere to the wishes of commenters or disregard them (Golden, 1998; Yackee, 2006). As one respondent put it, "The department doesn't have to take [the comments]. They have absolute control." An agency's rationale for changing or not changing a proposed rule's content is discussed as part of the final rule (Kerwin & Furlong, 2011).

A rule may go through more than one notice-and-comment period if, for example, comments raise issues that require additional attention or if substantial changes are going to be made to the text that was originally proposed (Kerwin & Furlong, 2011; Office of the Federal Register, 2011). Occasionally, rulemaking may be scrapped at a late stage in the process, if it is deemed unnecessary or highly problematic (Kerwin & Furlong, 2011). Moreover, the notice-and-comment procedure does not need to occur in every instance of rulemaking (Administrative Procedure Act, 2012; Kerwin & Furlong, 2011; Lubbers, 1998). Under the Administrative Procedure Act, agencies are not obligated to publish rulemaking notices and receive public feedback in the following circumstances:

(A) . . . [for] interpretative rules, general statements of policy, or rules of agency organization, procedure, or practice, or

(B) when the agency for good cause finds (and incorporates the finding and a brief statement of reasons therefore in the rules issued) that notice and public procedure thereon are impracticable, unnecessary, or contrary to the public interest (Administrative Procedure Act, 2012, § 553[b][3]).[4]

Phase 4: Finalization of a Rule

During this stage, the Department of Education's personnel write the final rule, taking into account what has been learned from interested parties during previous stages of the process. The OMB once again reviews significant rules before they become final (Kerwin & Furlong, 2011; US General Accounting Office, 2003). A former Department of Education official explained that OMB review is one of the reasons for the sometimes lengthy process of rulemaking: "OMB often doesn't like a rule or will have multiple questions, sometimes dozens of questions, and sometimes it kicks back and forth between the agency and OMB. And that could go on for months."

A rule becomes effective at least 30 days after it appears in final form in the *Federal Register*, with the exception of rules that are deemed "major," which do not become effective for a minimum of 60 days after final rule publication (Administrative Procedure Act, 2012; Anderson, 2006; Congressional Review Act, 2012, § 801[a][3]; Kerwin & Furlong, 2011; Lubbers, 1998). The Congressional Review Act requires the extra time between a "major" rule's announcement and its effective date so that Congress can examine the rule and determine whether to override it (Kerwin & Furlong, 2011, p. 84; Lubbers, 1998, pp. 17, 136–137). If the rule is not overridden, it becomes effective after expiration of the review period.

Phase 5: Postfinalization

The completion of any OMB or congressional reviews, publication of a final rule in the *Federal Register*, and passage of sufficient time for the rule to become effective do not necessarily signify the end of the higher education rulemaking process. Although not technically part of "rulemaking," several potential occurrences after a rule becomes final can shape regulatory policy and perhaps lead to alteration of the rule.

One important postfinalization activity is litigation. An interested party who is unhappy with a final rule may file a lawsuit against the agency, asserting, for example, that the rule was improperly developed or that rules of procedure were not appropriately followed during its creation (Kerwin & Furlong, 2011; Lubbers, 1998).[5] The Gainful Employment Rules, for example, have been challenged in court by representatives of for-profit higher education, and in the case of the first Gainful Employment Rule, the lawsuit succeeded in getting part of the original version of the rule struck down (*APSCU v. Duncan*, 2012; Nolter, 2012). Other higher education rules, such as those dealing with admissions personnel's incentive-based compensation, have been challenged in court as well (see, e.g., Dundon, 2015). Aggrieved parties may also submit "petitions for reconsideration" to agencies, asking to have a rule altered or rescinded (Kerwin & Furlong, 2011, p. 85). Of course, many lawsuits are resolved before going to trial, and as Wagner et al. (2011) note, filing a lawsuit can benefit a party by getting an agency to negotiate a settlement.

Another postfinalization activity is congressional legislation to override a rule or certain aspects of a rule (Bryner, 1987; Kerwin & Furlong, 2011). Because the president must sign such legislation for it to become law, the White House has involvement in this process as well. Something else the White House might do after a rule is finalized but before it takes effect is to issue a request to postpone the effective date of a rule; this has occurred when a new presidential administration has come to power and agencies under the previous one had issued new regulations shortly before the previous president left office (O'Connell, 2011).

Moreover, the Department of Education may also take action with regard to higher education rules after they are finalized—for example, to provide information to institutions, lenders, and other interested parties as to how the rules should be interpreted or to clarify the meaning of a rule (Kerwin & Furlong, 2011). According to some respondents in this study, the Department of Education has replied to specific inquiries, sent letters to institutions, and explained regulations to attendees at financial aid conferences sponsored by the department across the country. The department may also take it upon itself to review its own rules and to clarify or begin a process to amend them (Kerwin & Furlong, 2011; Lubbers, 1998). In a move that fuses the first and final stages of the rulemaking process, the department sometimes initiates a new rulemaking to revise or repeal an earlier regulation. For example, the Department of Education—under a new presidential administration—revised the "safe harbors" rule for incentive compensation of college recruiters in a rulemaking that occurred about eight years after the previous "safe harbor" rule was finalized (see Federal Student Aid Programs, 2002; Program Integrity Issues, 2010a). Also, a new rulemaking was initiated in 2014 in a second attempt to define the "gainful employment" requirement for career-focused programs after key sections of the first Gainful Employment Rule were nullified by a federal court following a lawsuit (*APSCU v. Duncan*, 2012; Program Integrity: Gainful Employment, 2014).

[handwritten margin note: no definite start or finish!]

Additional Considerations

As Kerwin & Furlong (2011) note, "it is unwise to consider rulemaking as a process that has a definite start and finish" (p. 85). Indeed, as the last example in the previous section illustrates, the rulemaking process is fluid; the issuance of one final rule may mean the demise or substantial revision of another, and the initiation of rulemaking—phase 1 discussed above—may also serve as a postfinalization activity for an earlier rule. Additionally, some proposed rules may be formally withdrawn and therefore never become final (O'Connell, 2008, 2011). Some rules may never even reach the proposal stage. This was the case with the Accreditation and Student Outcomes Rule, in which negotiated rulemaking took place and the Department of Education indicated what it wanted to regulate. But owing to an outcry from congressional officials and interest groups alike, the rulemaking was abandoned (Lowry, 2009).

Moreover, in addition to the process described above, rules proposed by the Department of Education as well as other agencies are subject to the provisions and requirements of several federal statutes that have been issued over the years for the purpose of regulating bureaucratic policymaking (Anderson, 2006; Kerwin & Furlong, 2011; Lubbers, 1998). One such statute, the Paperwork Reduction Act, mandates that regulatory bodies analyze "paperwork burdens" that new regulations are likely to impose on stakeholders (Kerwin & Furlong, 2011, p. 60; see also Lubbers, 1998; Paperwork Reduction Act, 2012). This act also puts the OMB in charge of overseeing and approving the "collection of information" by agencies (Lubbers, 1998, p. 118; Paperwork Reduction Act, 2012; see also Kerwin & Furlong, 2011). Another statute imposing additional requirements on rulemaking is the Regulatory Flexibility Act, under which departments are required to be mindful of—and make efforts to decrease—any onerous obligations that a new regulation may impose upon "small businesses and organizations" and similar entities (Kerwin & Furlong, 2011, p. 61; see also Anderson, 2006; Lubbers, 1998; Regulatory Flexibility Act, 2012).

Over time, the rulemaking process has also been subject to several executive orders issued by presidents, some of which have later been revised or repealed by subsequent presidents (Kerwin & Furlong, 2011; Lubbers, 1998). For example, an executive order issued by President Bill Clinton—the same one that requires OMB review for "significant" regulations as explained above—also requires departments to weigh a prospective regulation's costs against its purported benefits (Executive Order No. 12866, 1993; Kerwin & Furlong, 2011). This executive order supplanted a similar one that President Ronald Reagan had issued, which also required weighing costs against benefits, as well as showing that the anticipated benefits of the rule would outweigh its expected costs (Executive Order No. 12291, 1981; Kerwin & Furlong, 2011; Lubbers, 1998). But Clinton's executive order also effectively repealed certain aspects of Reagan's executive order. For example, under Clinton's order, only "significant" rules (as described above) would be subject to OMB review (see Executive Order No. 12866, 1993; Lubbers, 1998). President Barack Obama also annulled, by executive order, some aspects of executive orders that had been issued by his immediate predecessor, including OMB review of agency guidance and a diminution in the role of the vice president in rulemaking (Executive Order 13497, 2009; Kerwin & Furlong, 2011). As these examples illustrate, a president can alter important aspects of rulemaking procedure with the stroke of a pen, and different presidents have held very different views regarding matters such as the extent to which OMB review should take place and how large a role the vice president should play in rulemaking.[6]

Summary and Conclusion

The procedural rules for creating regulatory policy affecting higher education are drafted by political and bureaucratic elites such as members of Congress, the president, and high-level Department of Education officials. However, these rules provide for some participation in the rulemaking process by interested parties who are not necessarily politically powerful. The regional meetings, the notice-and-comment period, and negotiated rulemaking all allow for members of the general public as well as higher education institutions, student-focused interest groups, and other organizations large and small to communicate directly with Department of Education officials about their perspectives on proposed rules. But as discussed in more detail in later chapters, there are costs associated with these forms of participation that may make meaningful participation in this process quite difficult for individuals or groups that have limited resources. Requirements set forth in the Higher Education Act that a broad range of different types of participants be included in regional meetings and negotiated rulemaking allow for the possibility of very diverse viewpoints to be considered during the process.

But some of the procedural rules are structured to favor actors that are already powerful in higher education policymaking. Congress has the power to review and, if so inclined, to rescind a final rule through the legislative process (Congressional Review Act, 2012; Kerwin & Furlong, 2011; Lubbers, 1998). The president and Congress can also use their lawmaking powers to change the procedural rules at any time. And while the Department of Education is required to include a wide variety of interested parties in negotiated rulemaking and regional meetings, it is also true that if one negotiated rulemaking participant—even the department's own representative—does not agree to consent to the proposed regulatory language, then the department writes the NPRM entirely on its own. This procedural rule gives the department an enormous advantage: although it is required to involve a wide array of actors in the negotiations, the department is the only participant in the proceedings that is empowered to draft the NPRM any way it wants if it withholds assent to the proposed language.

This chapter has described the procedural process of higher education rulemaking. Although the process described here is the conventional way higher education regulations are created, it is important to note that the process does not always follow this linear pattern. For example, as explained above, a rulemaking procedure for what would have become the Accreditation and Student Outcomes Rule was initiated but never finalized, and the NPRM for the first Gainful Employment Rule was issued separate from and later than other regulations that were negotiated together with gainful employment issues.

Our attention turns now to those various policy actors who participate in the higher education rulemaking process. Who are they? Do some actors play a consistently greater or more influential role throughout the process than others? These questions are addressed in chapter 4.

CHAPTER FOUR

Policy Actors' Influence

Since before the Gainful Employment and Accreditation and Student Outcomes rulemakings were initiated, various policy actors were forming opinions about the matters to be regulated by these prospective rules and were taking steps either to support or to oppose them. Who were those policy actors? And how much influence did they have on each rulemaking's ultimate outcome? Questions such as these relate to the "who" of higher education rulemaking: Which policy actors participate in and otherwise influence the process? How does actors' participation vary by phase in the rulemaking process? And which actors appear to have the greater influence over what happens during higher education rulemaking? This chapter addresses these questions.

Among the theories of the bureaucratic role in policymaking, discussed in chapter 2, are three different views about the types of actors who particularly drive bureaucratic policy processes and outcomes. The first one emphasizes the power of the bureaucracy, recognizing that bureaucrats possess a fair amount of discretion as to how they fulfill their tasks, owing at least in part to their expertise and a lack of substantial oversight by Congress (Anderson, 2006; Hill, 1991; Niskanen, 1971; Rourke, 1969; see also Moe, 2012). As outlined in chapter 2, there are various ways that bureaucracies can influence higher education policy and practice, and higher education rulemaking is one of them.

The second view sees the political branches—the president and Congress—as the actors who hold more power in bureaucratic policymaking. These actors exercise their power through a variety of mechanisms such as legislation, power over administrative budgets, and congressional investigations of bureaucratic activity (McCubbins et al., 1987, 1989; Moe, 2012; Wood & Waterman, 1991). The third view, which argues that agencies are ruled largely by outside interest groups, holds that powerful regulated entities can and do persuade agencies to promote policies that benefit the regulated entities' own interests (Bernstein, 1955; Laffont & Tirole, 1991; Makkai & Braithwaite, 1992; Niles, 2002; Stigler, 1971; see also Kerwin & Furlong, 2011). Regulated groups' influence may be the consequence of, for example, professional relationships and persuasion campaigns (Laffont & Tirole, 1991; Makkai & Braithwaite, 1992; Niles, 2002). There is some evidence of disproportionate influence of business organizations over rulemaking, particularly during the notice-and-comment phase (Golden, 1998; Wagner et al., 2011; West & Raso, 2013).

Many observers have rejected the notion that any one theory of bureaucratic activity is sufficient to explain entirely how the process works or who has the most power in the process (see, e.g., Bertelli, 2012; Carpenter & Krause, 2014; Moe, 2012; and see chapter 2 above). With regard to the higher education rulemaking process in particular, no previous study has documented the precise role and perceived amount of power that different policy actors hold in this process. This chapter provides an empirical analysis of the policy actors involved in higher education rulemaking, including a description of actors' participation in each phase of the process and the influence of different types of actors over the process as a whole.

Participants in Higher Education Rulemaking by Phase of the Process

As chapter 3 explains, there are distinct phases in the higher education rulemaking process, even though the process does not always include all of the phases and does not necessarily proceed in a linear fashion. Participation by the various actors differs by phase of the process, with some stages, such as regional meetings and the notice-and-comment period, having more widespread participation than other stages.

Pre-Rulemaking and Initiating Rulemaking

The US Department of Education plays a prominent role in the higher education rulemaking process even before rulemaking is initiated. The department makes the decision to commence a rulemaking in the first place. It determines whether circumstances warrant waiving negotiated rulemaking or the notice-and-comment period, and it posts notices in the *Federal Register* about forthcoming regional meetings and negotiated rulemaking. Personnel within the Department of Education also determine the locations where regional meetings will take place; the locations of those meetings can have consequences for how well the meetings are attended and what issues are discussed. For example, a former Department of Education employee described a situation in which a regional meeting was held at an institution where students did not receive a lot of federal financial aid: location matters!

> That particular school doesn't have a vibrant student aid program[;] they don't
> need one. . . . So we had a hearing at a school where the students didn't have any
> interest in how much a Pell Grant was and didn't really care. They don't have to
> care like what the Stafford Loan limits are or anything like that . . . so we didn't
> have anyone show up for the hearing. . . . So that can absolutely throw the agenda.
> Because if we had gone to a different school that would be directly influenced by
> the regulations that are getting ready to come out, we probably would have had
> greater participation.

Congress is also involved in the pre-rulemaking phase by enacting legislation that necessitates new regulations, as it did in the 1992 reauthorization of the Higher Education Act, when it required negotiated rulemaking for many new higher education regulations (see Hannah, 1996; Texas Guaranteed Student Loan Corporation, 2001). The Department of Education wrote in the preamble of a Notice of Proposed Rulemaking that sought to amend certain student financial aid regulations:

> Section 492 of the HEA [Higher Education Act] requires the Secretary, before
> publishing any proposed regulations for programs authorized by Title IV of the
> HEA, to obtain public involvement in the development of the proposed regulations.
> After obtaining advice and recommendations from individuals and representa-
> tives of groups involved in the Federal student financial assistance programs, the
> Secretary must subject all proposed regulations to a negotiated rulemaking pro-
> cess. All proposed regulations that the Department publishes must conform to
> agreements resulting from that process unless the Secretary reopens the process
> or provides a written explanation to the participants in that process stating why
> the Secretary has decided to depart from the agreements. (Student Assistance
> General Provisions . . . Notice of proposed rulemaking, 2002, p. 51036)

US senators are also involved in the pre-rulemaking phase by voting to confirm (or not to confirm) political appointees to the Department of Education. Such appointees can be very important players in the higher education rulemaking process, as discussed later in this chapter, so votes to confirm or not confirm someone to these positions play a crucial, if indirect, role in higher education rulemaking.

The White House participates fairly actively in the pre-rulemaking phase as well. Although the Senate plays a role in the appointment of political appointees to agencies such as the Department of Education, the president plays an even bigger role by selecting the individuals to hold these posts and sending them to the Senate for confirmation. Also during the pre-rulemaking phase, the White House communicates the administration's higher education policy agenda to the Department of Education. As explained by a Department of Education official: "I wouldn't say from the president we get any direction, but we certainly get some input from the White House in terms of what issues we put on the negotiating agenda. They don't typically get involved in the negotiations per se, so it's more that we get direction as to what issues. . . . It sets up the framework in which we negotiate."

The White House is also involved in this early stage when the president issues an executive order that shapes rulemaking procedures (Kerwin & Furlong, 2011). Executive Order No. 12866 (1993), for example, created several mandates that federal agencies (including the Department of Education) must follow during rulemaking, such as conducting a cost-benefit analysis, writing regulations that are easily comprehensible, and receiving Office of Management and Budget approval of "significant" regulations (Executive Order No. 12866, 1993).[1]

Interest groups and other interested parties also have the opportunity to influence rulemaking in the earliest phase. On occasion, the Department of Education will host a conference call with interested parties for the purpose of answering questions about a forthcoming rulemaking. In the case of the 2010 Program Integrity rulemaking, two conference calls were hosted by the department—one with for-profit institutions and one with financial analysts—in response to a flurry of questions the department had received after announcing the rulemaking (Program Integrity: Gainful Employment, 2011). As explained by a journalist familiar with the 2010 Program Integrity rulemaking, "the Department had to hold a separate call for analysts to explain what they were doing in rulemaking when they first announced that they were going to have a round of rulemaking that might touch on issues. . . . In addition to the normal press call, they had so many inquiries they wound up having to hold a separate call for Wall Street analysts." Another journalist noted: "They don't normally have those conference calls in advance but there was a lot of chatter on the street about, what does this mean for for-profit colleges? Are they really going to crack down on for-profit colleges? Is this going to be like really punitive? So everyone was all up-in-arms and so the policy folks in the Department [of Education] decided to do this to sort of calm the hysteria." Thus, on the more controversial rulemakings, interest groups and the Department of Education may be involved in the pre-rulemaking stage through conference calls.

Moreover, under the law, interested parties have the ability to petition the department to commence rulemaking (Administrative Procedure Act, 2012; Furlong, 1998; Furlong & Kerwin, 2005; Kerwin & Furlong, 2011; Lubbers, 1998). Naturally, this would occur during the pre-rulemaking stage. One such petition was submitted in 2006 by a group known as the "Project on Student Debt," which promoted the financial interests of college students. The petition sought student loan payment limits and debt forgiveness under specific circumstances (Huntley, 2006). However, such petitioning only rarely occurs in higher education rulemaking. Indeed, such petitions are so rare that some Department of Education officials could not recall any petitions being submitted. A former department official interviewed for this study said, "I'm trying to remember whether we had proposals for rulemaking changes. I don't recall whether we did or not." A different department official said, in response to the question of whether anyone had submitted a petition to commence a rulemaking, "Not that I can recall but there may have been somebody that has done that. I don't know."

Regional Meetings

Regional meetings are held at different locations across the country in anticipation of negotiated rulemaking in the Office of Postsecondary Education. The meetings involve widespread participation by many different policy actors. The Department of Education is responsible for organizing and moderating these meetings. Among this study's focal rulemakings, Department of Education representatives who attended regional meetings included two Office of Postsecondary Education personnel and a lawyer with the department's Office of General Counsel. A wide variety of interest group representatives, and even some individuals who are not formally associated with an organized interest group (such as individual students and taxpayers), attend regional meetings to provide input to the Department of Education about the topics they believe should be addressed by regulatory policy.

The interest groups that attend regional meetings include representatives of various different kinds of higher education institutions (and associations representing them), students and student associations, consumer rights groups, accreditors, lending organizations, guaranty agencies, TRIO program advocates, and state- and local-level public officials (such as state higher education officers), among others. When rulemakings have been expected to affect a particular area—for example, international institutions, students with disabilities, or campus safety advocates—representatives of those interest groups have

TABLE 4.1
Actors speaking at regional meetings associated with focal rulemakings

Higher education actors	Not higher education actors

Higher Education Institutions
  Four-year public institutions
  Two-year public institutions
  Nonprofit private institutions
  For-profit institutions
  Minority-serving institutions
  Vocational/technical institutions
  Professional schools
	Department of Education
	  Office of Postsecondary Education
	  Office of General Counsel
	
	State/local officials
	  State agencies
	  Local public officials
	  School district

Faculty/administration
  Faculty union
  Association representing college
    administrators
  TRIO / educational opportunity program
    administrators
	Business interests
	  Lending organizations
	  Guaranty agencies
	  Financial analysts
	
	Advocacy groups
	  Disability advocates

Accreditors
  Regional accreditors
  National accreditors
  Specialized accreditors
	Working women advocates
	  Campus safety advocates
	  Advocates for the financially needy
	  Consumer advocates
	  Legal aid societies

Students/consumers
  Students
  Student government representatives
  Parents
	International interests
	  Foreign embassy / consulate
	  International education representative

	Other
	  Information technology professionals
	  Entertainment industry representatives
	  Educational consultant
	  Nonprofit organization providing
	    financial aid information
	  Private citizen
	  Workforce training organization

attended and spoken at regional meetings as well. For example, a fire safety advocate spoke at a regional meeting following the enactment of the Higher Education Opportunity Act because the legislation required higher education institutions to disclose certain information about campus safety (*Public Regional Hearing on Negotiated Rulemaking*, 2008b). Table 4.1 indicates the various categories of actors who spoke at the regional meetings associated with this study's focal rulemakings, where records reflecting speakers were available.

Other actors may observe regional meetings even though they do not participate. For example, financial analysts have observed regional meetings where issues pertinent to the for-profit sector of higher education were discussed, such as the first Gainful Employment Rule and the related Program Integrity rulemaking, which were negotiated together (*Public Regional Hearing on Negotiated Rulemaking*, 2009; researcher's interviews). Journalists have also observed and reported on regional meetings. Interest groups or individuals who are not willing or able to attend a regional meeting in person may submit comments in writing to the Department of Education (Federal Perkins Loan Program, 2007c, p. 32411; researcher's interviews).

Negotiated Rulemaking

The negotiated rulemaking stage has involvement from a considerable range of policy actors, albeit smaller than the range of interest groups attending regional meetings. Once again, the Department of Education is involved at this stage— the department requests nominations for particular categories of actors to participate in negotiated rulemaking, selects negotiators from among those nominated, and participates via its own "federal negotiator" in the negotiations (see, e.g., Office of Postsecondary Education: Notice, 2006; researcher's interviews). Interest groups that have participated in negotiated rulemaking include different types of higher education institutions (e.g., four-year and two-year, for-profit and nonprofit, public and private, minority-serving, and religiously affiliated), higher education students, consumer advocates, lending organizations, guaranty agencies, higher education administrators (e.g., college business officers, financial aid administrators, and admissions officers), state-level agency employees, and accreditors. When a specialized issue (such as ability-to-benefit tests) is being regulated, representatives from a specialized group (such as test designers) are asked to participate in the negotiations. Often, interest groups are represented by an association at negotiated rulemaking, but sometimes representatives of individual organizations (such as accreditors or individual colleges or universities) participate.

In addition to those who participate in negotiated rulemaking, several other actors observe the proceedings. Congressional staff, journalists, members of the general public, consultants, Office of Management and Budget staff, and— when issues of particular importance to for-profit education are at stake— financial analysts have all observed negotiated rulemaking proceedings. Toward the end of negotiated rulemaking sessions, the facilitator asks whether anyone observing the proceedings would like to make a statement. At times, some of the observers do make statements; however, such statements do not appear to have much influence over the language of proposed regulations. Negotiated rulemaking meeting summaries for several of the focal rulemakings indicate that statements from the public were solicited but that few, if any, meaningful public statements were made at the time (US Department of Education, 2006d, 2007a, 2007c, 2008). A representative of for-profit higher education explained: "At the end of each session, there is an open mic and the facilitator will turn around and say 'Okay, anybody here from the general public want to get up and say anything?' . . . Every once in a while, somebody does. And usually the negotiators are packing up their bags and rustling their papers and you know, I don't know that it has a particular impact."

Noticeably absent from negotiated rulemaking are many of the interest groups that participate in regional meetings. Groups such as chambers of commerce, TRIO program advocates, the League of Women Voters, and fire safety advocates have attended and spoken at regional meetings, but this study has not found instances of such a diverse range of groups having representation at the negotiated rulemaking table. One reason for this may be that negotiated rulemaking participants must be limited in number, while anyone who so desires may speak at a regional meeting.

Drafting the Proposed Rule

As explained in chapter 3, the question of which policy actors will participate in the drafting of a proposed rule depends on whether negotiated rulemaking takes place and, if so, whether the negotiating team reaches consensus. When negotiated rulemaking does not take place, the Department of Education alone writes the proposed regulation. Also, the department writes proposed regulations on its own when negotiated rulemaking is conducted but negotiators do not reach consensus, defined as all parties at the negotiating table being in agreement about the proposed language (Lubbers, 1998; Pelesh, 1994; Pritzker & Dalton, 1995). This policy gives the Department of Education tremendous power over this phase of the process, because the department has its own negotiator taking part in negotiated rulemaking proceedings. If the department's negotiator is the only one dissenting, then consensus is not reached, and the department is free to write whatever proposed regulation it pleases (Pelesh, 1994). Although every participant in negotiated rulemaking has the power to block consensus of the language, the department is the only actor whose dissent results in the authority to write the proposed rules on its own.

Some interest groups also play a role in the drafting of proposed regulations, particularly when negotiated rulemaking is conducted. If negotiated rulemaking has taken place and the negotiating committee reaches consensus, then the interest groups involved in negotiated rulemaking have had an opportunity to make their positions known and have had at least some agreement with the proposed language ultimately developed by the committee. Even if the language is not perfect from a negotiator's perspective, the fact that consensus was reached indicates that all participants agreed that the negotiated language was likely preferable to having the Department of Education draft the Notice of Proposed Rulemaking on its own. However, participation in negotiated rulemaking can be effective even when consensus is not achieved. For example, in one of this study's focal rulemakings where consensus was not reached during negotiated rulemaking, the department considered suggestions from negotiators about numerous issues, including the burdensome nature of a certification requirement the department was considering. Ultimately, the department went into the final negotiating session and drafted the NPRM with a requirement that was more acceptable to stakeholders as a result of negotiators' suggestions (Federal Perkins Loan Program, 2007b, 2007c). Even when there is no negotiated rulemaking, outside groups may still influence the NPRM drafting process by communicating with Department of Education personnel as they are drafting the proposed rule. This may occur, for example, if an outside group is consulted as an expert in the field or in a matter being regulated (Kerwin & Furlong, 2011; Office of the Federal Register, 2011).

Notice-and-Comment Period

After an NPRM is published in the *Federal Register,* interest groups, the general public, and other actors are given time to submit written comments to the Department of Education regarding a proposed higher education rule. Participation at this stage is reminiscent of the wide participation observed during the regional-meetings stage. Indeed, participation may be even broader during the notice-and-comment period, given that even congressional officials sometimes submit written public comments and that it is less expensive and time-consuming for smaller interest groups and members of the public to submit a comment than to attend an in-person regional meeting.

Interest groups that have participated in the notice-and-comment period during higher education rulemaking include (either through their associations or individually) various types of higher education institutions, lending organizations, guaranty agencies, college administrators, higher education students, consumer advocates, higher education faculty, state-level public officials, accreditors, and others. Members of the general public—that is, individuals not affiliated with a formal interest group—also participate in the notice-and-comment phase; however, their participation is relatively rare. Moreover, as a congressional staffer interviewed for this study explained, "the public can submit their comments,

TABLE 4.2
Categories of actors commenting on two focal rules

"Safe harbors" rule	Post-9/11 student loan reform
Higher education institutions	Lending industry
Four-year public institutions	Lending organizations
Private nonprofit institutions	Guaranty agencies
Technical colleges	
For-profit institutions	Congressional official
Minority-serving institutions	
	College administrators
Higher education faculty/staff	
Higher education faculty	
College administrators	
Accreditors	
Lending industry	
Lending organizations	
Guaranty agencies	
Other	
Lawyers	
Consumer advocates	
Professional trainers	
Distance education providers / course designers	

but what's going to be paid most attention to is going to be stuff that comes on letterhead from the association."

A sample of the categories of commenters is displayed in table 4.2, which lists the categories of actors who submitted comments for two higher education rules, one that provided "safe harbors" for incentive payments to college admission staff and one that reformed student loan obligations for some 9/11 victims' families.[2] These rules present an interesting contrast: the "safe harbors" rule was quite prominent when it was being created, while the other was considered less prominent. Also, negotiated rulemaking occurred for the "safe harbors" rule but not for the student loan reform rule. It is important to note that the categories of actors who submitted comments on these rules' NPRMs are only samples of the many different types of actors who have submitted comments on higher education rules over the years.

There is one important exception to the broad participation of interest groups during the notice-and-comment phase. As negotiated rulemaking participants interviewed for this study explained, when a negotiated rulemaking committee has met and reached consensus on the language of a proposed rule, the negotiators themselves do not participate in the notice-and-comment period, at least insofar as they would be criticizing or otherwise negatively commenting on the NPRM.

Finally, the Department of Education also participates during this stage. The department collects the comments, reviews them, and decides—prior to the drafting of the final rule—whether to make changes to a rule proposal based on the comments. Importantly, the department is not required to make any changes based on comments submitted during this stage (Golden, 1998; Yackee, 2006).

Drafting the Final Rule

The Department of Education is the policy actor who most obviously and directly participates in this phase of the higher education rulemaking process. Department officials are the ones who determine whether to change the language of a rule based on public comments or for other reasons. Department officials also draft an "Analysis of Comments and Changes" that is published as part of the final rule, describing the number and general content of comments received during the notice-and-comment period and explaining why rule language was or was not altered in response to those comments. Also, as explained in chapter 3, the Office of Management and Budget is involved in this phase, since the OMB must give approval to virtually all final rules that are issued under the authority of the Higher Education Act (Executive Order No. 12866, 1993; researcher's interviews).

Although not necessarily directly involved, Congress and the president also have some involvement at this stage. First, the president is involved via the OMB and through the OMB's approval power at this stage (Executive Order No. 12866, 1993). Moreover, statutes and executive orders issued in advance may directly affect the Department of Education's actions during the drafting of the final rule. For example, Executive Order No. 12866 requires the department not only to seek OMB approval but also to provide a cost-benefit analysis in conjunction with "significant" rulemakings (Executive Order No. 12866, 1993, p. 645). And congressional statutes such as the Paperwork Reduction Act require the department to take certain steps—such as estimating anticipated "paperwork burdens" that new regulations will create—in advance of the publication of a final rule (Kerwin & Furlong, 2011, p. 60; see also Paperwork Reduction Act, 2012).

The Postrulemaking Period

Various types of activities may occur during the postrulemaking period. At this time the Department of Education may issue nonbinding regulatory guidance, explaining to stakeholders how to comply with new regulations (researcher's interviews). More adversarial activities may occur during this stage as well. Congress may review a rulemaking and pass legislation overriding it. Under the Congressional Review Act, final rules must be sent to Congress before they become effective, and Congress has the opportunity to pass a bill overriding the rule (Congressional Review Act, 2012; Kerwin & Furlong, 2011; Lubbers, 1998; Shapiro, 2007). In fact, Congress may pass legislation at any time changing the substance of a regulation. Whenever legislation is passed, the president is also involved by signing the override or other legislation that rescinds or alters a rule.

Interest group activity occurs during the postrulemaking period as well. One way an interest group might be involved at this stage is by filing a lawsuit challenging the rulemaking. For example, a lawsuit filed by the Association of Private Sector Colleges and Universities in January 2011 resulted in a court's striking down part of a final rule regarding distance education because of alleged procedural problems during the rulemaking process (American Association of Colleges of Nursing, 2011). Also, as explained more fully in chapter 1, a federal court in 2012 nullified part of the first Gainful Employment Rule as the result of a lawsuit brought by the same association representing for-profit colleges (Nolter, 2012). However, there is little interest group activity during the postrulemaking period as compared to regional meetings and the notice-and-comment phase.

Involvement That May Occur at Any Stage

Some actors engage in activities that can occur during any stage of the higher education rulemaking process. Congress may at any stage pass legislation or, short of that, pressure the Department of Education to cease rulemaking in a particular area (researcher's interviews; see also Lowry, 2009). This was done with regard to the unfinished Accreditation and Student Outcomes Rule, which would have tied institutional accreditation to student performance. Senator Lamar Alexander threatened to initiate legislation that would stop new regulations of higher education accreditors at least until the Higher Education Act was reauthorized (Lederman, 2007b; Office of Senator Lamar Alexander, 2007). Moreover, a House of Representatives appropriations subcommittee drafted a portion of legislation that forbade the department to use appropriations for the purpose of regulating accreditation (Lowry, 2009). And as noted above, when legislation influences rulemaking, the president becomes involved as well, by signing the legislation.

The Office of Management and Budget can also be involved at any stage of the higher education rulemaking process, because the Department of Education consistently keeps the OMB updated regarding rulemaking activity. A Department of Education official respondent confirmed, "We keep OMB informed as we're going along through the process." Interest group lobbying of Congress to pressure the Department of Education can occur during any stage of the process as well.

Policy Actors' Influence over Higher Education Rulemaking

Through interviews with higher education and policy actors, this study investigated perceptions of policy actors' power within the higher education rulemaking process. The actors who were perceived as having the most meaningful influence over higher education rulemaking include Department of Education officials, congressional officials, the White House (including not only the president but also the Office of Management and Budget), and certain interest groups.[3] Perhaps not surprisingly, these are generally the same actors who participate consistently in many stages of the higher education rulemaking process.

Department of Education Officials

Department of Education personnel have had a noticeable and often immediate impact on higher education rulemaking. The department—and more specifically, the Office of Postsecondary Education within the department—determines such matters as who participates in negotiated rulemaking, whether to agree to consensus in negotiated rulemaking, and, if consensus is not reached, what language to include in an NPRM. The department also decides whether to heed the recommended changes suggested during the notice-and-comment period, and department bureaucrats draft the language of final rules.

Many of this study's respondents identified the Department of Education as an actor with great influence over higher education rulemaking. One observer noted: "The Department, by the nature of how rulemaking works, they set the agenda and they set a tone too. But the department representative, the federal negotiator, it would be hard to argue that they're not the most important player at the table in every one."

In the negotiated rulemaking process, the department has particular power because it votes on consensus, and if there is no consensus, the department gets to write the proposed rule on its own. Although any actor at the negotiating table may withhold consensus, the department is the only one for whom withholding consensus means that the actor—and only that actor—gets to write the language

Dept of Ed has trem. power!

of the NPRM. A for-profit sector representative observed: "The Department [of Education] has the lion's share of the power. Because the department ultimately, if we do not reach consensus, they get to do what they want. They get to go forward with any proposed regulation they want to go forward with. And that gives them tremendous power." A department official confirmed that the department's power to participate in negotiated rulemaking and to withhold consensus gives this actor an edge in the rulemaking process: "The department always is like [the] gorilla in the room because at the end of the day, if we don't reach consensus, we can write any rules that the secretary wants us to. And so at the end of the day, we have a disproportionate influence on the process."

But to whom is the Department of Education's power attributable: the department itself, or the prevailing presidential administration? The professional positions of department officials fall under two categories: political and career personnel. Because political appointees are appointed by the president, they tend to align with the president's policy positions and remain employed by an agency for relatively short periods of time, whereas career bureaucrats tend to act on the agency's behalf, often through multiple presidential administrations (Carpenter & Krause, 2014; Gilmour & Lewis, 2006; Spiller & Urbiztondo, 1994). When describing the power of the department in the rulemaking process, many of this study's respondents did not distinguish between the two types of bureaucratic actors. However, this is an important distinction to make. To the extent that political appointees represent the president, their power over the rulemaking process might properly be attributed to the White House.

Nevertheless, this study finds that the Department of Education's career bureaucrats exercise many important powers in the higher education rulemaking process. Career bureaucrats have served as the department's negotiators during negotiated rulemaking (see, e.g., US Department of Education, 2002). They have attended regional meetings and have been at least occasionally the only representatives of the Office of Postsecondary Education at such meetings (see, e.g., *Public Regional Hearing on Negotiated Rulemaking*, 2006). In the words of a representative of for-profit higher education: "The bulk of what happens in rulemaking is going to be done by the career people. They're the ones that know the issues and understand the issues. And most of the issues are way too 'inside baseball' for the political people to get involved in. You're just not going to get the undersecretary focused on verification or satisfactory academic progress. It's not going to happen."

The first Gainful Employment Rule provides an example of the influence that career bureaucrats can have on higher education rulemaking, but also of the limitations of this influence. A congressional staffer surmised that a career staffer at the department may have wanted to pass some additional regulations of career-focused higher education programs "for a long time," and indeed, the Gainful Employment Rule did just that. But it was not until a Democratic administration came to power that a rule such as this was adopted. Moreover, as is discussed further below, the first Gainful Employment Rule as initially proposed by the department would have been more onerous for the career-college sector than the final rule ultimately was (Adams, 2011). Thus, the power of the department to influence regulatory policy in this instance was not unrestricted.

Congressional Officials

Numerous higher education rulemaking insiders interviewed for this study opined that Congress possesses substantial power over the rulemaking process. One reason why congressional officials have so much influence is that Congress provides funding to the Department of Education. A private college representative observed that "Congress has the ability through the appropriations process to prevent any rulemaking from going forward. They can reverse rules, and they do so on a somewhat regular basis." A negotiation expert familiar with higher education rulemaking remarked, "The department is tuned in to Congress because that's where the department ultimately gets its funding and so on, and they don't like to be crosswise with important committee leadership . . . in Congress." These observations about the "power of the purse" are supported by the literature on public administration (Bertelli, 2012, p. 40).

Another avenue for congressional influence has been through the ability of members of Congress to nominate individuals to participate on negotiated rulemaking committees. A state agency official speculated that nominations by congressional officials may "carry . . . some extra weight." A representative of for-profit higher education agreed, "There have also been representatives for seats at the table that were directly nominated by congressional offices. They're almost always approved, in fact." Thus, although congressional officials do not directly participate in negotiated rulemaking, their influence is nonetheless felt at that stage.

Members of Congress have also expressed their viewpoints on Department of Education actions by making statements, either directly or indirectly, to the department. As discussed above, congressional influence was instrumental in stopping the prospective Accreditation and Student Outcomes Rule from being issued: numerous senators openly opposed the rulemaking (at least for the time being), and a congressional subcommittee placed language into a budget bill to forbid the department to use funds to create new rules governing higher education accreditation. After these moves, this rule did not go forward (Lowry, 2009).

Although Congress possesses a great deal of legislative power over higher education rulemaking, this power does not always get exercised. For example, a for-profit institutional official observed about negotiated rulemaking: "Generally, my experience has been during negotiated rulemaking . . . most congressional members will stay away from that process. They will say, let that play out until a proposed rule comes. And if the secretary is doing something that we think is afoul of the law, then we'll interject ourselves at that time." Moreover, this study has found that congressional officials are less likely to scrutinize or to speak out about rulemakings that are uncontroversial or highly technical in nature. For example, the Distance Education and Teach-Out Plans Rule was relatively uncontroversial and involved a specialized subject matter relating to distance learning and accreditation (Institutional eligibility, 2009). This rulemaking received considerably less congressional attention than either the Gainful Employment Rule or the unfinished Accreditation and Student Outcomes Rule. Incidentally, the Distance Learning and Teach-Out Plans Rule was the only one of these three for which the negotiating committee reached consensus.

The White House

Representatives of the White House have had a very apparent influence on higher education rulemaking. As explained previously, the president can issue executive orders that mandate certain actions on the part of the department during rulemaking and can influence the rulemaking process through political appointees to the Department of Education. Political appointees have influenced the direction of, and the discussion surrounding, higher education rulemaking by championing certain policies or positions. When asked which personnel at the department had played a prominent role in supporting the Gainful Employment Rule, one congressional staffer interviewed for this study identified several political appointees within the Office of Postsecondary Education. A journalist also opined that the Gainful Employment Rule was "being driven by the Obama administration and his appointees in the Education Department." Political appointees are more likely to become involved in rules that are prominent, as opposed to those that are less controversial. A former department official stated, "If it is a situation where the program that's being discussed has high visibility, then the political appointees are going to have a lot more say in how things are written." Conversely, political appointees have been less likely to involve themselves with highly technical rules. As a representative of for-profit higher education observed, the "political people" in the Department of Education are "only going to get involved on these big contentious ones where one or more groups are on a major position about something the department is trying to do that is sufficiently big and broad and easy to understand that someone who doesn't have a background in higher ed. can get it."

Even when political appointees are not actively championing a particular policy, all new higher education rules must meet with the approval of high-level political appointees at the Department of Education, whose positions reflect the policies of the presidential administration. A federal employee who works with education issues observed: "Ultimately the appointed secretary has to sign off on the regulations. And the executive agencies are working toward the goals of the elected executive."

White House actors other than the president have also had meaningful influence over higher education rulemaking. The OMB—a White House office—has exercised both direct and indirect power over higher education rulemaking. Again, the OMB is involved via its review and approval power in the creation of rules deemed "significant" (Executive Order No. 12866, 1993; see also Kerwin & Furlong, 2011; Lubbers, 1998). The OMB may also affect appropriations to government agencies, a power that might persuade agencies to make rules as pleasing as possible to the OMB (Kerwin & Furlong, 2011). A policy actor in its own right, the OMB also often reflects the president's perspective.[4] An interest group leader stated: "The White House is always involved because regulatory packages before they're published as a Notice of Proposed Rulemaking or the final regulation [have] to be cleared by the Office of Management and Budget which very explicitly represents the White House's perspective."

Interest Groups

Interest groups exert influence throughout the higher education rulemaking process by participating in negotiated rulemaking, submitting comments during the notice-and-comment phase, meeting with Department of Education officials, and lobbying Congress to pressure the department about particular rules. Sometimes interest group preferences are clearly seen in proposed rules. Proposed regulatory language for the Distance Education and Teach-Out Plans Rule,[5] for example, achieved consensus during negotiated rulemaking and thus contained language that was acceptable to the interest groups represented at the negotiating table. But sometimes interest group influence is apparent even if rules do not on the surface appear to benefit those groups. For example, by reading the final text of the first Gainful Employment Rule, one may conclude that the rule disadvantages for-profit institutions and other career-education programs by placing new requirements and greater regulatory burden on them; and, indeed, the rule does this. But comparing the final rule to the proposed rule reveals that these institutions could have fared worse than they actually did under the final regulations (Adams, 2011; Program Integrity: Gainful Employment, 2010, 2011).

Interest group influence has varied over time, depending on such factors as what issues are prevalent in the higher education policy community and whose political allies hold public office. For example, during a business-friendly Republican presidential administration (Jacobe, 2004), the for-profit higher education sector enjoyed more influence over higher education rulemaking, as evidenced by the adoption of regulations that benefited for-profit institutions' recruiting practices, including the provision of "safe harbors" that allowed incentive compensation payments to admissions staff (Federal Student Aid Programs, 2002; see also Kantrowitz, 2010). When a new Democratic presidential administration came to power, these provisions were eliminated, and other regulations of the for-profit sector—including both of the Gainful Employment Rules—were put into place (Program Integrity: Gainful Employment, 2011, 2014; Program Integrity Issues, 2010a; see also Mettler, 2014). One congressional staffer observed that during the Obama administration, the focus on the Gainful Employment concept was "a reflection of the current administration and the players there. . . . Over time, if you look historically across, between the two parties, probably the Republican party has been a little more receptive to the [professional] schools and for-profits playing in higher ed than the Democrats have been."

Regardless of political context, there are certain characteristics of interest groups that may serve to provide some groups with more influence over higher education rulemaking than others. The subsections that follow describe the types of interest groups that have had particular influence in the higher education rulemaking process.

WASHINGTON-BASED INTEREST GROUPS

Washington-based higher education associations such as the American Council on Education (ACE) were identified by insiders as particularly powerful in the higher education rulemaking process.[6] One reason that such organizations may be viewed as having a lot of influence is the extensive experience their staff members have with rulemaking. A Department of Education official explained:

"I think that the large associational representatives on committees, people from like the American Council on Education and some of the other associational-type folks, play a huge rule, in some ways disproportionate, because they're used to negotiating."

Another reason the ACE in particular has been perceived as so influential is that the organization has a large membership (see also Gladieux & Wolanin, 1976). A higher education negotiator representing private institutions stated, "Certain people, I think, are influential like ACE because they tend to speak for a whole group." And a Department of Education official said, "There's certain associations, there's certain people like that that you kind of look for their comments because you know that they represent a lot of people, and they're generally well thought-out comments."

Given their geographic location, Washington-based associations have had a unique ability to attract personnel who had previously worked in the federal government (see also Cook, 1998). As explained by one representative of a Washington-based higher education interest group, that organization had "hired a[n employee] from the department . . . and [the employee] came with a great deal of depth and understanding and practical experience in the loan programs, which is something we were very concerned about. . . . I think we're better off, [the employee]'s better off and the department's better off because you know you've got somebody who knows how it works in the department." The news media have documented other instances of personnel from organizations with a Washington presence going to work for the Department of Education (see, e.g., Field, 2009; Selingo, 2006). Such employment situations may fuel the perception that interest groups with a presence in Washington, DC, are particularly influential.

INTEREST GROUPS WITH EXPERTISE
IN THE REGULATED SUBJECT AREA

Interest groups whose members have a great deal of expertise in the regulated subject area have also meaningfully influenced higher education rulemaking. Financial aid administrators and interest groups that represent them were perceived by several respondents as being particularly influential. A reason for this perception may be that persons with specialized knowledge of a substantive policy area have been accorded greater credence during the rulemaking process. A respondent who has worked for both the government and an interest group said: "Because [the] student aid delivery system is so much a part of what the law is, and therefore so much a part of what the regulations are, NASFAA [the

National Association of Student Financial Aid Administrators] over the years has tended to be very important. . . . [The other associations] try not to get into any big disagreements with NASFAA because we assume that NASFAA knows more about really how it operates on campus than anybody."

Another negotiator described a rule involving student testing that was negotiated during the same time as the first Gainful Employment Rule. During those negotiations, certain actors had particular influence precisely because of their specialized knowledge:

> One of the issues [in negotiated rulemaking] was on [tests], so the students who [do not] have a high school diploma or its equivalent, they can enroll in school after taking a . . . test that shows that they have some capabilities of handling college course work without that credential. . . . We didn't have anybody at the table who understood what [such] . . . testing was about. . . . They added somebody from the testing services as a stand-in for that discussion only, and a consumer advocate attorney who had some understanding of it. But the whole conversation was just between those two and the department representative. Everybody else kind of stood on the sidelines because . . . they didn't have an understanding of the issue and the impact of any change that would come out of it.

Because negotiators are selected at least in part based on their expertise in the matter being regulated, negotiated rulemaking provides an opportunity for specialized interest groups to have particular influence. But the type of specialty that has influence through negotiated rulemaking varies by the subject matter being regulated. Both the unfinished Accreditation and Student Outcomes Rule and the Distance Education and Teach-Out Plans Rule involved several different kinds of accrediting organizations, but no lenders or consumer groups, in their negotiated rulemaking sessions. Accreditors were involved in Gainful Employment negotiations, as were lenders and consumer advocates; however, fewer accreditors participated in Gainful Employment negotiations than in either of the other two negotiations.

INTEREST GROUPS WITH SUBSTANTIAL RESOURCES

Interest groups that have substantial resources have also had meaningful influence in higher education rulemaking. Respondents described numerous strategies that interest groups have used to influence higher education rulemaking, including lobbying Congress, holding meetings with various federal officials, and communicating their positions via the media. Pursuing any of these strategies costs money, and pursuing all of them takes significant finan-

cial resources. Also, participating in negotiated rulemaking is an expensive en-
deavor. Although the Negotiated Rulemaking Act (2012) provides that some of a
negotiator's expenses "may" be compensated by the agency conducting negotiated rulemaking, this is not required (§ 568[c]). As a former Department of Education official noted, "you've got to have resources to dedicate to have their impact. It's not a trip to Washington. It's at least four trips to Washington. It's a lot
of homework between the meetings and then three-day meetings. So if you're
going to be a negotiator, it's really hard to get in there."

Having financial resources also enables an interest group to hire professional staff who can be dedicated to regulatory policymaking work, as opposed
to making do with limited staff who must focus on all aspects of policymaking. Thus, having more resources leads not only to having more staff-hours devoted to working on regulatory policy matters, but also to having staff who are
more experienced at rulemaking. And experience with the rulemaking process
is another characteristic that has made some interest groups more influential
than others. As explained by a consumer advocate, "it certainly helps to have
some background in understanding how to write regulations, how to read regulations, how to understand the broader implications."[7]

COLLEGE AND UNIVERSITY STUDENTS

There is evidence that the Department of Education makes a point of paying
attention to feedback from the higher education students who participate in
rulemaking. A department official explained: "A couple of the voices that I tend
to listen to actually are the students, if they have something to say . . . because
they are, in fact, students and they haven't necessarily been tracking things a
long time, and they don't have a lot of time to do this[;] sometimes they're not as
well versed in the issues. But if they have something to say I really try to make
sure their voice is heard and I try to listen carefully to what they're saying
because they're the ultimate constituents of what we're doing." A former department official agreed: "When I was there, and I think it's still true, students had
a very substantial impact and it was sort of simply because it was partly they had
good leadership but it was not because they had resources. In fact, they had very
few resources. And it wasn't because they had a history of power. It was partly
sort of the moral persuasion that they brought. [The e]nterprise was about them
and they were often very influential in that regard."

But not all respondents agreed that students held much power in higher education rulemaking. A community college representative who also noted that
students bring "moral persuasiveness" to the table said: "When we got down into

more sort of arcane matters . . . they were not as well-versed in terms of just the process and how to read a law and how to read a regulation. So I think their bottom-line effectiveness was a little stunted in that way."[8] A Department of Education official said, "People who aren't so used to negotiating like students, for example . . . [are] not as effective." And a for-profit college representative opined, "There are always one or two student representatives there, but I wouldn't say they were particularly effective participants, usually, in the proceedings." Thus, although they are sometimes perceived as influential, higher education students are not the most powerful group in the process.

The influence that higher education students do have in the rulemaking process may largely be a result of the actions of Congress: specific language in the Higher Education Act (2012) recommends that students and legal groups representing them should be consulted during rulemaking. Moreover, the Conference Report of the 1992 reauthorization specifically stated, "It is the intent of the conferees that the Secretary [of Education] should include students and student advocates from all sectors of postsecondary education in the negotiated rulemaking process, including the regional meetings" (US House of Representatives, 1992, p. 516). Because students' status in higher education rulemaking is influenced by congressional will to include students as participants in negotiated rulemaking and regional meetings, should a legislative change remove or diminish students' role in the process, students' power is likely to diminish as well.

CONSUMER ADVOCATES AND LEGAL AID ORGANIZATIONS

Interest groups representing consumer interests, often in the form of legal aid organizations, also appear to influence higher education rulemaking. These groups may be perceived as influential for many of the same reasons students are—after all, they are representing consumer interests, which are aligned with student interests in higher education regulatory policymaking. In fact, a couple of respondents grouped students and consumer advocates together when describing these actors as influential. As was the case with students, the Higher Education Act specifically lists "legal assistance organizations that represent students" as a group that should be consulted during higher education rulemaking (Higher Education Act, 2012, § 1098a[a][1]). Moreover, the legislative history of the 1992 reauthorization shows that the Conference Committee specifically intended to involve legal aid organizations by "add[ing] legal aid representatives to those who will be in the process" (US House of Representatives, 1992, p. 516).

[margin annotation: recommendations are as good as policy]

Also, as is the case with students, there is evidence that department officials have made sure that consumer advocates receive attention at negotiated rulemaking sessions. One Department of Education official said: "And the other group that I try to—although . . . it depends on the issue, is the legal aid people because a lot of times they're kind of a lone voice also sitting out there versus everybody else around the table. So those are a couple of things that they kind of stand out as somebody I don't want to say I listen to, but I try to make sure that their voice gets heard in the group."

Summary and Conclusion

As this chapter demonstrates, the participation and influence of different types of policy actors in the higher education rulemaking process often vary based on the stage of the rulemaking process as well as the issue being regulated. While some actors participate in all or most stages of the process, others may participate in only one or two stages. Some actors consistently hold more power in the process than others. The level of influence exercised by different actors tends to vary by the subject matter and prominence of the regulation at hand. These findings support the argument from the literature implying that combinations of theories are essential to describing policy actors' roles and influence in administrative processes (see, e.g., Bertelli, 2012; Bertelli & Lynn, 2006; Carpenter & Krause, 2014; see also Moe, 2012).

It is evident that political actors are influential over every higher education rule and are active during all stages of the rulemaking process, as theories of political control would predict (see, e.g., McCubbins et al., 1987, 1989; Wood & Waterman, 1991). All higher education rules are authorized by legislation passed by Congress and signed by the president. Other legislation sets the Department of Education's budget and procedures that must be followed in the rulemaking process. Presidential executive orders have mandated that certain procedures be followed when issuing rules (see also Kerwin & Furlong, 2011). Political appointees to the Department of Education, who influence the agency's regulatory policy agenda, have been appointed by the president and approved by the Senate. The department has been mindful of the wishes of prominent members of Congress and has altered rulemaking following congressional pressure (see also Lowry, 2009). As this study's focal rules illustrate, the more prominent, costly, or controversial the rule, the larger the role that the political branches are likely to play in the rulemaking. This includes more direct involvement by the political branches in the rulemaking process itself. When a regulation is deemed "significant," the OMB reviews the rule (Executive Order No. 12866, 1993, p. 51738). Congressional representatives and White House offices have been vocal about their positions on prominent rules such as the Gainful Employment Rules and the Accreditation and Student Outcomes rulemaking. Thus, although political-branch involvement and influence is present in every rulemaking procedure, the degree to which the political branches exercise their powers varies depending on the issue being regulated.

However, as might be predicted by theories emphasizing bureaucratic discretion (see, e.g., Hill, 1991; Niskanen, 1971), the Department of Education itself also has meaningful influence over higher education rulemaking, particularly in the rule drafting process. The department is actively involved during all stages of rulemaking. It selects the actors that will participate in negotiated rulemaking and participates directly in negotiations. If even one negotiator—including the department's negotiator—disagrees with the proposed regulatory language, then the department drafts the language of the NPRM on its own (see also Pelesh, 1994). Also, during the notice-and-comment period, the Department of Education has the discretion to disregard any or all comments received (see also Golden, 1998; Yackee, 2006). But evidence also indicates that bureaucratic power is more likely to be tempered by other forces in cases of more prominent rules. For example, in the case of the controversial and scrutinized Accreditation and Student Outcomes rulemaking, there were protests and legislative threats from congressional officials, and the Department of Education ultimately retreated from creating the rule (see also Lowry, 2009). Yet consensus— including Department of Education approval—was achieved in the negotiation of the less prominent Distance Education and Teach-Out Plans Rule, which did not receive the same level of negative attention from political actors.

Some findings of this study support agency capture theory (see, e.g., Laffont & Tirole, 1991; Makkai & Braithwaite, 1992). Interest group personnel have gone to work for the department or vice versa (see also Cook, 1998; Field, 2009; Selingo, 2006). There is also evidence of interest groups' sometimes substantial influence over higher education rulemaking, particularly from organizations that are based in Washington, are well-resourced, and hold much expertise in the regulated subject area. Interest group influence is seen in both controversial and lower-profile rules. The first Gainful Employment Rule, although burdensome for career-education programs, was ultimately not as onerous as its NPRM had suggested it would be (Adams, 2011). This indicates a level of strong influence by interest groups representing institutions subject to those regulations.

But it is not only high-resource interest groups that have influence: this study also finds that Department of Education officials make a point of paying attention to feedback from higher education students and that consumer advocacy groups have some meaningful influence in the higher education rulemaking process. However, the fact that students and consumer advocates are influential in higher education rulemaking may be more of a testament to the influence of political actors, since it was Congress who drafted the legislation directing that students and consumers be involved in higher education rulemaking, and it was the president who signed that bill into law.

Figure 4.1 depicts the manner in which actors' influence in the higher education rulemaking process varies by rule subject matter. The issue being regulated and particularly whether the rule has a high profile largely determine which actors will hold meaningful influence over any given rule. Technical rules, which may require a certain amount of expertise in the subject matter to draft good regulations, are more likely to be influenced by interest groups with relevant technical expertise, such as financial aid administrators or test makers. When rules are prominent and controversial, such as the two Gainful Employment Rules and the unfinished Accreditation and Student Outcomes Rule, some interest groups have expended great resources attempting to influence rulemaking. Congress, the White House, and the Department of Education's political appointees have exerted more influence with regard to high-profile rules and those with subject matters that are easier for laypeople to understand. On the other hand, bureaucrats within the Department of Education tend to have more power over low-profile rules that receive little attention from political actors. Also, in the lower-profile Distance Education and Teach-Out Plans Rule, interest groups that participated in negotiated rulemaking reached consensus with the department on NPRM language, indicating interest-group satisfaction—at least for the groups involved in the negotiations—with the rule's proposed language.

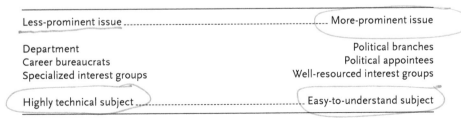

Less-prominent issue .... More-prominent issue

Department	Political branches
Career bureaucrats	Political appointees
Specialized interest groups	Well-resourced interest groups

Highly technical subject .... Easy-to-understand subject

Fig. 4.1. Policy actors with power by rule prominence and technicality

In sum, which actors hold meaningful influence over higher education rule-making depends greatly on the matter being regulated. Bureaucrats and specialized interest groups may have more influence over low-profile and technical rules; however, political actors appear to hold the reins a little tighter, and interest groups with resources tend to spend more money, when the rules are more high-profile and controversial. Specialized interest groups tend to have more influence when the prospective rules involve their areas of expertise, but those groups are observed participating less frequently with rules that less directly involve their subject area.[9] Washington-based interest groups and consumer advocates also have at least some meaningful influence in higher education rulemaking. The Department of Education does take students' viewpoints into account. However, students' current influence in the rulemaking process may largely be a result of the structure of higher education rulemaking put into place by Congress. Should that structure change, students' influence in this process may change as well.

This research complements the theoretical literature by confirming that no one category of policy actor consistently dominates the higher education rulemaking process. Rather, certain actors may be more or less influential depending on the matter being regulated. Indeed, this research illustrates the importance of understanding the details of rule subject matter—even within a broader category such as "higher education"—to understand which actors exercise meaningful power in the rulemaking process. A rule's substantive policy area, technicality, and level of prominence or controversy are all relevant to determining which policy actors are likely to exert influence over the rule's creation and final form.

This chapter has described the policy actors who participate and are influential in the higher education rulemaking process. But how, precisely, do policy actors go about influencing higher education rulemaking? What strategies do they employ? What powers do particular actors hold that may help them achieve their policy goals through higher education rulemaking? Chapter 5 addresses these questions.

CHAPTER FIVE

Strategies and Powers of Influence

After learning about the prospective Gainful Employment and Accreditation and Student Outcomes rulemakings, many policy actors sought to make their positions on these rules known to regulators and to influence the rulemaking process to achieve desired outcomes with regard to these rules. But how did policy actors go about doing this? Higher education interest groups have used a variety of methods—from communicating with Department of Education officials, to asking congressional representatives to intervene, to filing lawsuits after rules become final—in attempts to influence rulemaking. Moreover, government officials have used official powers to influence higher education rulemaking, whether it is Congress using legislation or budgetary authority, the president using the appointment power, the Office of Management and Budget using its review power, or the Department of Education exercising any of its numerous authorities over the higher education rulemaking process.

All of the strategies and other actions that have been employed to influence higher education rulemaking can be conceptualized as exercises of power—or at least attempts to exercise power—by interested parties who want to achieve particular regulatory outcomes. These exercises of power are often overt and participatory, such as lobbying efforts, participation in negotiated rulemaking, and comments to the regulating agency during the notice-and-comment phase (see, e.g., Cook, 1998; Golden, 1998; Pelesh, 1994). Steven Lukes (2005), who has written extensively about the characteristics of power, may categorize such "observable" influences over decision making (including "political participation") as "One-Dimensional" exercises of power (pp. 16, 19). He used a 1957 statement by Dahl to illustrate: "A has power over B to the extent that he can get B to do something that B would not otherwise do" (quoted in Lukes, 2005, p. 16).

But as Lukes explains, exercises of power can also involve less direct and more obscure influences. For example, an actor may exert power by controlling who will participate in policymaking, or by determining what particular policy changes will be up for debate (Lukes, 2005; see also Gaventa, 1980). Such exercises of power, in which actors control the participation of others in decision making, Lukes has labeled "Two-Dimensional" (2005, p. 20). An even more hidden exercise of power—dubbed "Three-Dimensional" by Lukes (p. 25)—involves the manipulation of others' "perceptions, cognitions and preferences in such a way that they accept their role in the existing order of things" (p. 28). In other words, powerful actors may control others' beliefs about such matters as what is good or bad policy, as well as whether something is inevitable or whether open participation in policymaking will have any effect at all (Gaventa, 1980; Lukes, 2005). Thus, it is important to be mindful that a policy actor may be influencing the higher education rulemaking process even though the actor is not directly participating in, or even noticeably influencing, any aspect of the process.

Policy actors have exercised power over higher education rulemaking in many different ways, overt and direct as well as indirect and obscure. Chapter 2 describes some theories about bureaucratic policy actors and which ones tend to exercise more power in policymaking. Of course, different types of strategies and powers are available to different types of actors. For example, as explained in chapter 2, theories focusing on bureaucratic discretion state that bureaucrats have a fair amount of autonomy in their professional decision making and that such decisions can influence policy and benefit bureaucratic actors (see, e.g., Hill, 1991; Niskanen, 1971; Rourke, 1969; see also Anderson, 2006). As political control theory notes, Congress and the president can use their lawmaking powers to shape rulemaking substance and procedures (see, e.g., McCubbins et al., 1987, 1989). Theories that highlight the power of influential organizations have identified several ways that such power can be exercised in regulatory policymaking: through communications or working relationships with regulators, participation in regulatory policymaking, or lobbying the political branches that oversee the bureaucracy (see, e.g., Laffont & Tirole, 1991; Makkai & Braithwaite, 1992; Niles, 2002). Each of these activities is an example of a strategy or power that a policy actor may use to influence bureaucratic policymaking processes, including higher education rulemaking.

This chapter explores the strategies and other exercises of power that various policy actors have used to influence higher education rulemaking and regulatory outcomes. More specifically, the chapter identifies, describes, and categorizes the various actions used by policy actors; presents a typology of the different strategies; and analyzes the ways various theories of power and of bureaucratic policymaking apply to these findings.

How Policy Actors Influence Higher Education Rulemaking

This study identified numerous strategies or other actions that policy actors use in attempts to influence higher education rulemaking. These strategies can be divided into four categories: use of official powers by governmental actors; participation in legally prescribed rulemaking procedures; informal strategies that actors employ within the rulemaking process; and persuasion of actors outside the public participation venues of rulemaking.

Official Powers of Governmental Actors

Governmental actors are empowered to influence policy and policymaking processes in various ways. Depending on the office that a governmental official holds, different official powers may be exercised to influence higher education rulemaking. For example, congressional officials, in conjunction with the president, have the power to pass legislation and the power to determine an agency's budget. Many of this study's respondents agreed that legislation can be a powerful tool. A representative of the student lending industry said: "Congress is the one that wrote the law. And sometimes Congress, if they see a regulation that comes up, and it really has missed what it was meant to do, Congress may subsequently write some type of amendment to clarify their position and to change what was done in the negotiated rulemaking process."

Legislation may contain either vague or specific language (Stone, 2002). The more specific the statutory language, the more influence the legislation has over the rules that are authorized through it. According to a former Department of Education official,

> Now I think as you sort of go down the hierarchy . . . whether that's the people who write the regulations in the department that's affected or whether it's the people who write the law and [guide] the writing of the regulation . . . If the law is vague then those people within the department . . . most people would call them bureaucrats . . . those bureaucrats have a tremendous amount of influence at that point. If it is a very tightly defined law, then the people who write the law have the most significant influence because . . . you have to write a rule that falls within the purview of the law. You can't go outside of what the law would allow. Your rule is intended to implement the spirit of the law. So if the law is very explicit then the

lawmakers have the most power. And if the law is not explicit, then the rule writ-
ers have tremendous stock.

Thus, by drafting the statute to be either vague or specific, lawmakers have the
power to determine how much influence another policy actor—the Department
of Education—is likely to hold in the rulemaking process.

Also, as shown in chapter 4, even preliminary steps or threats to use legislative power to override a rule can be effective in influencing higher education
rulemaking. While the prospective Accreditation and Student Outcomes Rule
was being considered, a prominent senator threatened legislation, and a House
Appropriations subcommittee took steps toward adjusting the following year's
budget to weaken the Department of Education's ability to connect accreditation
and student outcomes (Lederman, 2007b; Lowry, 2009). That rulemaking was
later stopped in its tracks, never proceeding to even the proposed rule stage
(Lowry, 2009; US Department of Education, 2007d). A short time later, Congress did legislatively forbid the Department of Education to link accreditation
standards to student outcomes, while at the same time establishing some accountability and reporting requirements for institutions (Lowry, 2009). But as
this case illustrates, the power to legislate is so great that even taking preliminary steps toward using this power can produce the desired results in the higher
education rulemaking process.

Another action that falls under the category of official powers used by governmental actors is the president's power to issue executive orders. Some examples of executive orders that have affected the rulemaking process include
Executive Order No. 12291 (issued by President Ronald Reagan) and Executive
Order No. 12866 (issued by President Bill Clinton), both of which mandated—
among other things—that agencies weigh the anticipated costs and benefits
of a potential regulation (Executive Order No. 12291, 1981; Executive Order No.
12866, 1993; Kerwin & Furlong, 2011). Similarly, presidential directives and
memoranda may instruct federal agencies to draft regulations in a particular
manner. One proposed rule references the "March 4, 1995 directive to every
Federal agency to reduce regulatory and paperwork burden and to eliminate or
revise those regulations that are outdated or otherwise in need of reform" (Student Assistance General Provisions . . . Notice of proposed rulemaking, 1996b,
p. 49875).

Another official power that has influenced higher education rulemaking,
and one that is shared between the president and the Senate, is the appointment
of high-level officials to Department of Education posts (researcher's interviews;

see also discussions of the appointment power in Anderson, 2006; Bernstein, 1955; Furlong, 1998; McCubbins et al., 1989). As explained in chapter 4, presidential appointees to certain Department of Education positions require Senate approval, giving senators as well as the president influence over which individuals will be making high-level decisions at the department (see, e.g., Lowrey, 2012). Who these political appointees are influences the rulemaking process. One negotiated rulemaking participant explained: "Who is president influences who is at the helm of the Department of Education. And who is at the helm of the Department of Education may influence who is in your Office of General Counsel and some of those other positions at the Department of Ed. But it may also influence a general policy . . . I think bias might be a fair term. There might be a greater interest in a particular outcome based on the administration."

Within the White House, the Office of Management and Budget also holds official powers that can be used to influence the rulemaking process. Specifically, the OMB screens certain proposed and final rules and has the authority to reject them or to recommend alteration if a rule does not meet the OMB's approval (see, e.g., Kerwin & Furlong, 2011). The OMB also has the power to make "recommendations on agencies' budgets" (Kerwin & Furlong, 2011, pp. 241–242). Given its official powers, the OMB has been able to exert considerable influence over the higher education rulemaking process. According to a congressional staffer, the "OMB does have the opportunity to have a pretty weighty impact if they choose to." Another congressional staffer explained that the OMB "can highly influence what's in the rule, because OMB has to clear all rules before they're published." And a former Department of Education official said: "OMB often is looking at issues of coordination and management and budget, and they're looking at the budget implication of different regs and so those kinds of concerns, in large part, come into play."

In practice, the OMB's review authority gives it considerable power over higher education rulemaking even before any action is taken by its representatives. One of this study's respondents observed: "You would hear a lot at meetings with the department that, 'We can't do that unless we can [get] OMB to okay it.' So they were an additional decision maker who was definitely not at the table. I mean they made their decisions behind closed doors." Thus, just the suspicion of whether the OMB would disapprove of a certain aspect of a potential rule may be enough for certain language to be stricken from a draft Notice of Proposed Rulemaking.

Finally, the Department of Education's own rulemaking authority is an official government power that clearly and directly influences higher education rulemaking. The department has the authority to commence a new rulemaking, to solicit nominations for and to select negotiators, to have its own representative participate in negotiated rulemaking, to draft proposed rules in the absence of negotiated rulemaking consensus, and to determine whether to alter rules based on the public comment phase (researcher's interviews; see also descriptions of these powers in, e.g., Kerwin & Furlong, 2011; Pritzker & Dalton, 1995). These powers undoubtedly affect rulemaking outcomes. West and Raso (2013) note that the mere fact that a topic was selected for rulemaking is significant, "because agencies typically lack the resources to pursue more than a fraction of the initiatives that are warranted by their legal mandates" (p. 495). The decision to regulate in a particular subject area can also set the tone for future rulemakings and force interested parties to pour resources into the development of those regulations rather than allocate those resources otherwise (West & Raso, 2013). Therefore, the department's authority to commence rulemaking in a particular subject area is an important power that contributes to the trajectory of federal higher education policy.

Moreover, the Department of Education's ability to select negotiators can influence the direction of negotiated rulemaking. A for-profit higher education representative explained:

> It makes a huge difference on who they pick for a given sector to sit at the table. So even though the for-profits always have a person and the [private nonprofit college] . . . constituency always has a person, the actual person they pick makes an enormous difference. And so they pick somebody who's more confrontational or less confrontational, a more confrontation-averse person or someone who is looking to get to agreement more, someone who they think will ultimately back down to their colleagues and not withhold consensus as opposed to someone who will stand their ground. . . . The fact that the department gets to select the person gives them tremendous, tremendous impact over the process.

Additionally, the Department of Education has a representative, known as the federal negotiator, who participates in negotiated rulemaking. The federal negotiator, like any negotiator, may withhold consensus on proposed rule language; however, the department's withholding of consensus allows the department itself to determine precisely what language will appear in the Notice of Proposed Rulemaking (researcher's interviews; see also Pelesh, 1994). This official power, held by no other negotiators, gives the Department of Education a great deal of influence over final rules relating to higher education. Moreover, according to one negotiated rulemaking participant, if a particular negotiator is difficult or irritates the federal negotiator during negotiated rulemaking, there is a decent chance that the difficult negotiator will not be invited back for future negotiated rulemaking sessions.

Participation in Legally Prescribed Rulemaking Procedures

The rulemaking procedures that are prescribed by law (and described in detail in chapter 3) provide for a variety of opportunities for actors to participate directly in the higher education rulemaking process and to engage in strategies and other influential activities via that legally prescribed process. One strategy that falls in this category is submitting a petition to commence rulemaking. This action is permitted by law (Administrative Procedure Act, 2012; Furlong, 1998; Furlong & Kerwin, 2005; Kerwin & Furlong, 2011; Lubbers, 1998), but it occurs so rarely with respect to higher education rulemaking that many of this study's respondents (including Department of Education officials) could not recall an instance of its happening.[1]

By contrast, an action that is taken by a much larger number of actors is attending and speaking at the regional meetings that precede negotiated rulemaking. This action allows interested parties to speak directly to bureaucrats at the Department of Education and to inform them of the issues that the parties would like to see on a negotiated rulemaking agenda. Regional meetings are held at various locations across the country, and the location of the regional meetings may influence what topics are discussed and, as a result, what topics wind up on the negotiated rulemaking agenda.

Another strategy for influencing rulemaking through formal procedures is submitting written public comments during the notice-and-comment period. Comments are submitted not only by numerous interest groups—both large and small—but also by congressional representatives, state government agencies, vendors (such as a company that designs and sells electronic courses to institutions), and members of the general public who are not formally associated with any interest group. Several of this study's respondents believed that submitting such comments was an effective way to influence rulemaking outcomes. According to a federal staffer who used to work in the Department of Education: "Every single comment that comes in is genuinely recorded and debated internally within the Department of Ed. So to the extent that any comment that comes in, whether it can have an impact, the answer is yes." And a financial aid officer noted that comments have made a difference in rulemaking outcomes in the past, particularly when no contrary comments are received: "I remember from years past, the department has even indicated that one or two comments on a particular rulemaking wording . . . influenced the result of that wording. . . . It's just because they bothered to respond[;] those individuals bothered to respond and there was no one responding to the contrary."

On the other hand, several respondents believed that while writing comments during the notice-and-comment phase could be a somewhat effective tactic, it was not tremendously effective, and certainly not as effective as participating in negotiated rulemaking or having other in-person conversations with Department of Education personnel. A representative of private higher education institutions said that it is sometimes "difficult" to influence rulemaking via written comments "because in some ways, they have already run all the traps. They have already checked with this person and that person and got sign-offs in order to put out the Notice of Proposed Rulemaking. . . . It's not like they're really looking for a new way to do things."

Some respondents suggested that a comment may be more or less effective depending on who submits it or how it is submitted. One public university representative opined that a single comment signed by a large group of actors may have more influence than numerous separate comments from individual organizations or people. Moreover, a Department of Education official explained that the department tends to "look for" comments from particular actors who are known to represent a lot of stakeholders, who are "very familiar with the issue" being regulated, or who generally submit "well thought-out comments."

There is also some evidence that comments submitted by particular members of Congress may be more influential than a typical comment. According to an interest group representative and former federal staffer: "Say a member of Congress chooses and say a speaker or Senate president or a chairman or an original sponsor of legislation, comments on proposed rules. Those have significant influence on the views of an administration implementing those rules."

Another action that may be taken within the rulemaking process is nominating individuals to participate in negotiated rulemaking. The Department of Education selects the negotiators who will serve on the committee; however, the department is limited to the pool of individuals nominated when making this selection (researcher's interviews). Numerous interest groups have used this strategy, including different kinds of higher education institutions and associations, lenders, guaranty agencies, students, accreditors, and associations representing college administrators. Congressional officials have also nominated individuals for negotiated rulemaking, and some respondents indicated that negotiators nominated by members of Congress may have a better chance of being selected than other nominees.

Finally, an influential tactic within the official rulemaking process is participation in negotiated rulemaking. Many different types of interest groups—as
well as the Department of Education—participate in negotiated rulemaking,
but the level of participation is not as widespread as in regional meetings. Several of this study's focal rulemakings—including both Gainful Employment
Rules and the incomplete Accreditation and Student Outcomes rulemaking—
involved negotiated rulemaking, and an array of policy actors participated in
these negotiated rulemaking proceedings (researcher's data set).[2] Many of this
study's respondents believed that participating in negotiated rulemaking could
be an effective way to influence higher education regulations. A former Department of Education official explained: "Simply writing your comments and sending those in, that's nice, but that doesn't have a lot of impact. What has impact is
being there to be able to be part of the process. So in this new federal process of
negotiated rulemaking, the negotiators have a substantial amount of influence
and those who are not tied closely to a negotiator and who are simply submitting
their comments, those will be considered, but they will not drive the process."

During negotiated rulemaking, consensus-based language becomes the
language of the proposed rule (Lubbers, 1998; Pelesh, 1994; Pritzker & Dalton,
1995). However, participation in negotiated rulemaking can be effective even
when consensus is not reached. For example, in one of this study's focal rulemakings where consensus was not reached during negotiated rulemaking, the
department considered suggestions from negotiators about how burdensome
the documentation requirement that it had originally proposed was, and ultimately, the department proposed a less burdensome requirement as a result of
negotiators' suggestions (Federal Perkins Loan Program, 2007b, 2007c).

Negotiated rulemaking is an official avenue for participating in—and
influencing—the higher education rulemaking process, but it is also a fairly
complex policymaking process in its own right. As such, there are various strategies actors may employ within negotiated rulemaking. The next category of
strategies and actions used to influence higher education rulemaking describes
less formal activities that occur within the negotiated rulemaking process.

Informal Strategies Employed within Negotiated Rulemaking

One informal strategy within the negotiated rulemaking process is to convene a
"caucus" or a "subcommittee." Caucuses are private meetings that take place
during negotiated rulemaking. A caucus may be called by any negotiator (even
the Department of Education's negotiator), and the negotiator calling the caucus may include or exclude anyone the person chooses. Caucuses are used as a

tool of negotiation and persuasion. A former Department of Education official stated: "If you are looking around the table at the negotiating session and you see four or five people that you think are leaning with you, you try to call a caucus and get those people in the hall and see if you can't reach some sort of deal with them." Caucuses are also used to gather information about where other negotiators stand on particular issues. A public university administrator explained the value of "knowing when to call a caucus when you needed to get people that may not be as educated on your issue . . . so that you're not having the discussion and debating them at the table. . . . In some cases, I needed to find out where schools were on an issue that was of great importance to me. So you would caucus to gauge where people's interests were before you delved into that topic that you knew was going to be controversial from the Department of Education's perspective."

Subcommittees (also known as subgroups) are similar to caucuses, but while caucuses occur during negotiated rulemaking meetings, subcommittees take place between meetings. A representative of lenders and guaranty organizations described subgroups as follows: "I think the concept of . . . and I think this was encouraged by the department . . . to have sub-groups cover more specifically, specific areas on the regulations, those that had experience in those areas or would be most impacted by those areas[;] they would try to work those in subgroups and those sub-groups would get together to try to iron out any differences or come up or review the language that the department had proposed to see where the issues were and to make suggested changes to the language which would make it better for students."

Another action that has been taken within the negotiated rulemaking process is to avoid or withhold consensus. Because consensus requires all negotiators to agree, any one negotiator may withhold consensus and block proposed language that other negotiators would like to put forth. Any negotiator may employ this tactic, but it is somewhat risky for nonfederal negotiators, because lack of consensus at negotiated rulemaking means that the Department of Education can write whatever proposed rule it wants (Pelesh, 1994). However, some negotiators may be willing to take that risk if they believe the department's version of the rule would be more favorable to them than the proposed negotiated rulemaking language. A former Department of Education official observed: "On occasion, somebody will say, 'I trust the department more than I trust my colleagues.' So sometimes they'll hold out and actually, intentionally concede the responsibility to the department."

Sometimes policy actors observe negotiated rulemaking in a strategic way. A wide variety of actors observe negotiated rulemaking. This includes public officials, representatives of interest groups and other rulemaking insiders. But it also includes members of the general public, journalists, and, where financial markets may be affected, financial analysts. Indeed, this study has found that financial analysts—who were concerned about the influence of gainful employment regulations on the for-profit higher education sector—observed the first Gainful Employment Rule's regulatory negotiations (researcher's data set).

Different types of actors have different purposes for observing negotiated rulemaking. For example, interest groups may observe to keep informed about the kinds of issues the Department of Education seeks to regulate and to understand the thinking and reasoning behind regulatory language. Congressional staffers may observe to gather information about whether, in the opinion of their Congress member, the rulemaking is beyond the scope of the department's authority, to determine whether legislative intent is being followed, or to understand how a statute is being implemented at the bureaucratic level. A congressional staffer explained: "From a congressional perspective, that's usually what it is that we look out for. Are they following the statute and the statutory intent or are they trying to create new law outside of the scope of what it is that we authorized? . . . If they try to go beyond the scope, that's usually when congressional offices start to get a little concerned." Another congressional staffer said: "As a staff person that actually worked on writing the law, I wanted to see how the one law was being perceived to how the department was interpreting congressional intent and kind of how they were going to be implementing the bill and see what the various community members thought of the provision and things. . . . Sometimes you kind of find out unforeseen examples or situations that you haven't thought about when writing the language."

Even Department of Education personnel observe some negotiated rulemaking proceedings. A representative of for-profit institutions said: "When you look back into the department's 'peanut gallery' . . . there's easily 15 people from the department sitting there . . . five days a week for three weeks doing nothing but sitting there in case they are called upon for one reason or another during negotiated rulemaking."

A final strategy that occurs within negotiated rulemaking is coalition building, which involves persuading other actors to join one's coalition for the purpose of promoting certain rulemaking outcomes. Although coalition building was observed occurring during negotiated rulemaking, it may occur at any point in the higher education rulemaking process. Thus, coalition building is discussed in more detail in the next subsection.

Persuasion of Actors outside the Public Participation Venues of Rulemaking

Policy actors may seek to persuade other actors—outside of the official participation aspects of rulemaking such as negotiated rulemaking and the notice-and-comment phase—to either take positions or take actions that would benefit the persuading actor's interests. Coalition building is one such strategy (see also Cook, 1998). As mentioned above, coalition building can occur at any stage in the higher education rulemaking process. For example, some higher education associations created a coalition in the form of a "task force" in 2012 to inform Congress about the associations' concerns regarding a forthcoming Notice of Proposed Rulemaking on teacher education programs, in an attempt to persuade Congress to pressure the Department of Education to address those concerns (Association of Teacher Educators, n.d.; Higher Education Task Force on Teacher Preparation, 2012).

Some particular kinds of actors that frequently form coalitions with one another during higher education rulemaking include students with consumer groups, lending organizations with guaranty agencies, institutions with accreditors, students with institutions, and institutions with other institutions. However, for-profit institutions have not infrequently been excluded from institutional coalitions. Some interest groups have even built coalitions with the Department of Education.

Coalition alliances tend to vary by issue in higher education rulemaking, and they can be fleeting. A congressional staffer explained: "In my experience watching it happen, I think they're very, I'm trying to think of the phrase, but that, you know, they're friends one day and enemies the next . . . alliances of mutual necessity at that moment."

Coalition building can be an effective strategy for influencing the higher education rulemaking process. Effective coalitions can be observed particularly during negotiated rulemaking, when policy actors are physically in the same room with each other and need each other to agree to their preferred regulatory language in order for it to become part of a Notice of Proposed Rulemaking. A former Department of Education official said that negotiators "need to always get people to join in with them to have any kind of power. Because it comes down to a vote, for all intents and purposes. I mean, people sit around a table and either agree or disagree. But if the majority of the people agree on something and the administration opposes it, it puts the administration in a tough spot." And a student representative said: "It doesn't help to go in and only, and sort of stay on your own and only advocate your own interest because . . . you have to reach consensus at some point. And so finding folks that have like-minded interests and trying to use that so the alliances are strength, I think is a really important part of negotiated rulemaking."

One example of coalition building involves "rallying the troops"—that is, motivating other individuals and groups with interests similar to one's own to get involved in, and to try to influence, rulemaking. In higher education rule-making, "rallying the troops" often involves encouraging members of an association or constituents of an interest group as well as others with similar interests to send comments to the Department of Education during the notice-and-comment period. According to a representative of college administrators, "The associations will through their usual communications with their members, give them talking points and urge them to write." A public university administrator similarly said, "Any number of associations do a good job drafting NPRM language, sharing it with membership and getting them on board as well as to send comments in."

"Rallying the troops" is not simply about getting like-minded individuals and organizations to send comments to the Department of Education. It also involves spreading information and, importantly, gathering information from actors with similar interests. Such information can be used in various ways in the higher education rulemaking process. For example, a student representative said that the information gathered while communicating with college students about a rulemaking helped the representative to prepare for participation in negotiated rulemaking: "Something that I did was have a small meeting with affected parties to ask them to take a look at this information, and let's have a meeting where we can come together and tell me your thoughts on this so I can take those thoughts back to Washington." A representative of one large interest group explained that the more significant the rulemaking, the more steps the organization will take to rally its membership: "The more important the regulations, in our opinion, to colleges and universities, the more efforts we would make to alert them in advance. So we would put articles on the web page, we'd put articles in our electronic newsletter, we might send our talking points to institutions and encourage them to file their own comments, we might talk to the press to try and get them to cover the issue and to call attention to our concerns."

Another form of coalition building involves expanding one's coalition to include actors who are not typically one's allies. This form of coalition building occurred when "safe harbor" provisions to allow certain incentive compensation for college recruiters were negotiated in 2002. With respect to that rulemaking, a representative of the for-profit higher education industry attempted to rally the support of the nonprofit sector:

> In 2002, it was interesting, we had—we started out as we often do with the . . . One Dupont crowd basically thinking that incentive comp was an issue that only applied to my sector and didn't affect them at all. . . . And through both sidebar conversations and mostly through conversation at the table, asked a lot of questions of the federal negotiators. . . . You could see the light bulbs going off in the heads of my fellow negotiators. . . . "Oh my gosh, we did that at my campus. Should we not being doing that?" So eventually they came to understand that, they engaged in a number of practices that would be covered by the incentive compensation rule and that maybe they did need to join forces with us and come to something.

Another persuasion strategy is lobbying Congress and encouraging congressional representatives to influence the Department of Education, either by threatening to stop or override a rulemaking, or by encouraging particular content to be included in a rule. A negotiator and for-profit industry representative described this strategy: "What I have observed over the years is that there are times when it appears the department is just dead determined to move ahead in a particular direction. . . . And so the only resort you have then, is to go political, which is go to the Congress, complain. . . . Try to bring pressure to bear, you know, outside really the rulemaking process itself to try to back them off. And you know, frankly I have seen that work."

Indeed, some higher education interest groups did just that in response to the prospective Accreditation and Student Outcomes rulemaking: they lobbied Congress to "rein the department in" with regard to the rulemaking, and members of Congress raised objections about the rulemaking a short while later (Lederman, 2007b). Another negotiated rulemaking participant and for-profit industry representative provided a different example, explaining how—with regard to the first Gainful Employment Rule—lobbying Congress could have indirect influence over the Department of Education: "To the extent that something controversial happens, constituency groups do go up to the Hill and complain and members of Congress do call the senior political leadership at the department and ask what's going on. . . . [When] Arne Duncan [then secretary of education] was up in Congress testifying at a House Education and Labor Committee hearing on the 2011 budget, four different members asked him about his Gainful Employment reg. Well, you better believe that Gainful Employment reg now has the attention of the senior political people at the department." Indeed, a congressional staffer identified lobbying Congress as "probably the most useful strategy that anybody has ever come up with."

When lobbying Congress for the purpose of influencing the rulemaking process, it is important to lobby key representatives, such as members on relevant congressional committees. One nonfederal negotiator explained:

> If we were in dispute with the Department of Ed on a particular position, we did sometimes get a letter from Congress, particularly from say then-Senator [Ted] Kennedy or from another senior member of the Education Committee. But it wouldn't be like we just go to anybody, like "Oh, I'll call my Congressman." If that wasn't his area of expertise, what was the point? . . . You would go to the chairman and ask for a letter saying, you know, "We respectfully disagree that the intent of Congress was X or Y or whatever[;] the department was trying to do something we didn't agree with."

Actors may also communicate directly with the White House in attempts to influence higher education rulemaking. For example, an actor or group of actors may write a letter to the president. In 2011, a coalition of interest groups representing students, consumers, minority groups, college faculty, and others sent a letter to President Barack Obama supporting the then-proposed Gainful Employment Rule (American-Arab Anti-Discrimination Committee et al., 2011). Interest groups may also meet with staffers in the Office of Management and Budget or Domestic Policy Council, two White House offices. A journalist interviewed for this study observed that some policy actors adopted the strategy of trying to persuade the OMB: "In the case of agencies, like for example, with this Gainful Employment Rule . . . OMB has to assess the economic impact of the Department [of Education]'s proposal. . . . So there for a while, people were lobbying OMB as well as the department." Around the time when the first Gainful Employment Rule was being developed, the OMB examined the potential economic impact of the proposed rule, and this was one of the contributing reasons for the delay in releasing its NPRM (Epstein, 2010).

Another persuasive strategy is to influence opinion via the media, which may include publishing opinion pieces or other information about rulemakings, posting information on one's website about rulemaking, or speaking with journalists in an attempt to get them to publish one's perspective. This strategy has often been used by interest groups. Numerous higher education associations post information and opinions on their websites about rulemakings (see, e.g., American Association of Colleges and Universities, 2007; Council for Higher Education Accreditation, 2011).[3] At least one interest group's website contained information instructing its members on how to employ such tactics as writing op-ed pieces (American Association of Community Colleges, 2011a) and using social media (American Association of Community Colleges, 2011b). Interest group members may take this advice in attempts to influence rulemaking. When this happens, interest groups use the media to influence rulemaking twice— once through the publication of instructive information on their websites and again if and when their members follow through by writing opinion pieces or utilizing social media to make a particular point.

Relatedly, sometimes interested parties will pen well-timed opinion pieces or other articles in newspapers or industry journals. Or representatives of interest groups will talk directly to journalists, attempting to get them to publish a particular point of view. One interest group representative remarked, "The press can carry your message. If you can't get it through some way, you can sometimes kind of help the public or the members of Congress or different people to see what's really happening, . . . You have to be careful, but you can talk to them and provide certain information."

Interest groups may also purchase advertising space in newspapers to make their position more widely known, as some proprietary school representatives did when the first Gainful Employment Rule was under consideration (Gorski, 2010). The use of such strategies may influence discussions during negotiated rulemaking. One negotiated rulemaking participant opined: "Comments made in *Inside Higher Ed* and *The Chronicle of Higher Education* in articles that are published during or in between negotiated rulemaking sessions will influence the conversation that's had. And inside those—there are op/ed's by consultants or academics."

Another strategy that should not be overlooked is communicating with Department of Education personnel outside of the legally prescribed rulemaking procedures. This may be done by writing a letter to the Department of Education about a particular rulemaking outside of the official commenting process, as some members of Congress did with respect to both the first Gainful Employment Rule and the unfinished Accreditation and Student Outcomes rulemaking (Lowry, 2009; Office of Representative Glenn W. Thompson, 2010; Office of Senator Bernie Sanders, 2010). Some interviewees for this study indicated that members of the public have employed this strategy as well (researcher's interviews). Interested parties may also call, e-mail, or privately meet with Department of Education personnel (researcher's interviews; see also Brown, 1994).

This strategy is easier to exercise if an interested party has a presence in Washington, DC, or personally knows staffers at the Department of Education. Although not always effective, this strategy might be more persuasive if it brings valuable information to the attention of the department, including—in the words of one negotiated rulemaking participant—"what the consequences of a rule are for actual individuals."

After the rulemaking process is complete, an actor may file a lawsuit against the Department of Education seeking to persuade a judge that a rulemaking is invalid. Lawsuits for the purpose of invalidating higher education rules have sometimes been successful (see, e.g., American Association of Colleges of Nursing, 2011; Nolter, 2012). Indeed, the first Gainful Employment Rule was substantially weakened, giving rise to the need for the department to develop the second Gainful Employment Rule, after litigation challenging the rule, brought by an association representing for-profit higher education, became quite successful (*APSCU v. Duncan*, 2012; Nolter, 2012). However, one public university administrator suggested that the threat of lawsuits challenging higher education rulemaking runs the risk of being ineffective: "We have had cases where we did not believe the department was correct in their interpretation of the law and you know sometimes the attitude of the department may be, well then sue us. They know you don't sue your regulators." While lawsuits challenging final rules may sometimes be effective, threats of filing lawsuits are not necessarily so.

A Closer Look at the Typology of Strategies and Powers Used to Influence Rulemaking

As described above, the strategies and powers used by interest groups, legislators, the Department of Education, the White House, and other actors in their attempts to influence higher education rulemaking can generally be divided into four categories: the use of official powers by government entities; participation in legally prescribed rulemaking procedures; informal strategies that actors employ within the rulemaking process; and persuasion of actors outside the public participation venues of rulemaking. Table 5.1 lists each of the specific powers and strategies falling under each category.

Not every policy actor with a stake in higher education rulemaking outcomes employs all or even most of these strategies. Many actors are constrained by limits on resources, knowledge, legal authority, and access to government officials that would permit them to pursue some of these strategies. For example, an individual college student or member of the public may be able to send a comment to the Department of Education during the notice-and-comment period

TABLE 5.1
Typology of strategies and powers employed in higher education rulemaking

Type of strategy	Strategies employed
Official powers of government	Congressional powers—legislation/budget Presidential executive orders Appointment power (president/Senate) OMB rulemaking review Department of Education rulemaking powers
Participation in legally prescribed rulemaking proceedings	Petitioning to commence rulemaking Regional meetings Written comments during the notice-and-comment period Nominating individuals for negotiated rulemaking Negotiated rulemaking
Informal actions within negotiated rulemaking proceedings	Caucuses/subcommittees Avoiding/withholding consensus Observing negotiated rulemaking Coalition building
Persuasion of actors outside the public participation venues of rulemaking	Coalition building Lobbying Congress Communications with the White House Using the media Litigation Communications with the Department of Education

but may not have the funding to travel to an out-of-state regional meeting and may not even be aware that the meeting is taking place. A small interest group without many resources may be able to attend and speak at a locally held regional meeting but may not have the funds to participate in or even to observe negotiated rulemaking. An interest group that has resources but neither a well-known reputation in the field nor connections with government officials is less likely to be selected for a seat at the negotiating table. And by definition, only governmental actors have official powers that may be exercised to influence the rulemaking process, and some governmental actors have more power over this process than others. Thus, some mechanisms of power over higher education rulemaking are simply off limits to many categories of policy actors.

Table 5.2 describes the various types of policy actors that have exercised the different strategies and powers over higher education rulemaking described in this chapter. Obviously, only governmental officials employ the powers falling under the first category of the typology, official powers of government. But nongovernmental entities—particularly interest groups—have been observed employing many strategies in the other three categories. Indeed, some interest group or other has been observed exercising every strategy in the categories of

TABLE 5.2

Strategies and powers used to influence higher education rulemaking, by policy actor

Strategy/tactic	Actors Identified as Using Strategy/Tactic					
	Dept. of Ed.	Congress	President	OMB	Interest groups*	General public
Official Powers of Government						
Rulemaking powers	X					
Legislation		X	X			
Appointment of Department of Education officials		X	X			
Executive orders / presidential directives / memoranda			X			
OMB powers of review and budget recommendations				X		
Legally Prescribed Rulemaking Procedures						
Speaking at regional meetings	X				X	X
Participating in negotiated rulemaking	X				X	
Nominating negotiators		X			X	
Submitting written public comments		X			X	X
Submitting a petition to commence a rulemaking					X	
Informal Actions during Negotiated Rulemaking						
Caucuses/subcommittees	X				X	
Avoiding or withholding consensus	X				X	
Observing negotiated rulemaking sessions	X	X		X	X	X
Coalition building	X	X			X	
Persuasion of Actors Outside of the Public Participation Venues of Rulemaking						
Coalition building	X	X			X	
"Rallying the troops"					X	
Expanding coalitions					X	
Lobbying Congress					X	
Communicating with White House officials					X	
Attempting to influence public opinion via the Internet or news media	X	X			X	
Communicating with Department of Education representatives		X			X	
Litigation					X	X

*For purposes of this table, "interest groups" refers to any organization, public or private, that has a stake in the outcome of a rulemaking. It includes such organizations as higher education institutions, lenders, guaranty agencies, associations representing such organizations, and state government agencies.

participation in legally prescribed rulemaking procedures, informal actions during negotiated rulemaking, and persuasion of other actors outside of the public participation venues of the rulemaking process. However, as noted above, not every interest group has the ability to exercise all or even most of these powers. An organization would need not only financial resources but also information, expertise, reputation, and access to governmental officials to be in a position to employ such strategies as communicating with government officials, using the media to spread a message, negotiated rulemaking participation, and—as would follow—all of the strategies that can be utilized within the negotiated rulemaking process. Thus, although this study has found that at least one interest group has exercised every identified strategy falling under all categories of the typology other than official powers of governmental actors, it is only the privileged few interest groups who have the ability to employ so many strategies.

Summary and Conclusion

Policy actors resort to various strategies and other actions to exercise power over the higher education rulemaking process and its outcomes (see table 5.2). The powers of these actors can be divided into four categories, displayed in table 5.1.

The strategies that various actors employed during the creation of the Gainful Employment Rules and in the period before the Accreditation and Student Outcomes rulemaking was halted are reflected in all categories of the typology. Official powers of government actors were put to use by the Department of Education's exercise of its official rulemaking powers and, less directly, by the political branches' lawmaking powers (legislation and executive orders). In the Accreditation and Student Outcomes rulemaking, threats of using official powers of legislation were also employed by congressional actors and seemed to have the desired effect (see Lederman, 2007b; Lowry, 2009). Participation in official rulemaking procedures, such as regional meetings, negotiated rulemaking, and the notice-and-comment phase, also occurred with respect to both of these rules. Observing negotiated rulemaking, communicating with Department of Education and White House officials, lobbying Congress, and conveying particular messages through the media were also used in attempts to influence one or both of these rulemaking procedures.

The strategies and other actions employed during the higher education rulemaking process may be viewed through the lens of Lukes's (2005) different "dimensions" of power. Strategies that employ obvious and participative first-dimensional powers include petitioning to commence rulemaking, speaking at regional meetings, serving on a negotiated rulemaking committee, nominating actors for negotiated rulemaking, submitting written comments, building or expanding coalitions, lobbying or communicating with public officials, avoiding consensus, and pursuing litigation. Each of these strategies represents an overt attempt to compel a particular response by other actors.

Strategies that seek to exercise second-dimensional power include the Department of Education's ability to select negotiators and Congress's ability to legislate rulemaking procedure and subject matter (see also McCubbins et. al., 1987, 1989). The appointment power shared by the president and one chamber of Congress also determines who will be in a position to make rulemaking decisions, both directly (the individuals actually appointed to political positions within the Department of Education) and indirectly (the career bureaucrats within that department who are hired by political appointees). Regional meetings, although identified as a form of first-dimensional power, also fall under the second-dimensional category, because the meetings help to set the negotiated rulemaking agenda and therefore help to determine the issues that will be discussed at negotiated rulemaking. Ultimately, however, it is the Department of Education that determines the negotiated rulemaking agenda. Therefore, this official power of the department is a potential form of second-dimensional power as well. Also, when rulemaking participants have knowledge of other actors' power—such as the OMB's review power or the president's policy preferences—this fact may be sufficient to limit consideration of alternatives to those likely to satisfy these actors, whether they are physically observing the rulemaking process or not.

Attempts to exercise third-dimensional power within the higher education rulemaking process are often made in conjunction with exercises of other dimensions of power. For example, expressing one's position through the media has the first-dimensional effect of overt persuasion, but it also may attempt to sway public opinion and personal beliefs. This may be particularly true if the media campaign is long-term and finds a way to connect its message to beliefs and values that people hold deeply.[4] Moreover, lawmaking has obvious coercive effects. But these actions may also serve to institutionalize certain values and priorities, which may—over the long term—have a third-dimensional effect by shaping people's values, beliefs, and perceptions (see Sabatier & Jenkins-Smith, 1999).

The specific strategies of the typology are ones that might be expected based on the theories of bureaucratic policymaking described in chapter 2. The powers that fall under the "official powers of government" category reflect both agency discretion (for example, in the Department of Education's decisions and management of the rulemaking process) and political-branch power (as through legislation, budgeting, and executive orders). These are precisely the types of powers that theories of bureaucratic discretion and political control would predict that these actors would exercise to influence the rulemaking process (see, e.g., Anderson, 2006; Hill, 1991; McCubbins et al., 1987, 1989; Niskanen, 1971; Rourke, 1969). And the various strategies and powers exercised by interest groups—scattered across the three remaining categories in the typology— are the types of activities that agency capture theory would expect powerful interest groups to use in attempts to influence their government regulators (see, e.g., Laffont & Tirole, 1991; Makkai & Braithwaite, 1992; Niles, 2002). These include lobbying Congress, communicating directly with Department of Education officials, and formally participating in the higher education rulemaking process (including negotiated rulemaking).

While the *who* of higher education rulemaking is described in chapter 4, the *how* of the process—the strategies and powers employed by different kinds of actors—is explained in this chapter. Largely unanswered at this point is the question *why*: Why do some actors participate in higher education rulemaking while others do not? And why do some actors choose to work with other actors in their attempts to influence the process? An examination of policy actors' perspectives on the higher education rulemaking process can help to answer these questions, as well as other questions about whether final rules reflect the beliefs of the policy actors that helped to create them. Chapter 6 delves into these issues.

CHAPTER SIX

The Role of Policy Actors' Beliefs

Because higher education rulemaking has been such an under-researched policymaking process, certain aspects of the process—including policy actors' beliefs about regulation and rulemaking and how their beliefs may play a role in the process—are likewise underexamined. But there is great value in understanding how policy and higher education actors' beliefs influence and shape the rulemaking process. The theoretical literature argues that beliefs may prompt actors to create coalitions and to advocate in favor of certain policies (see, e.g., Sabatier & Jenkins-Smith, 1999; Sabatier & Weible, 2007). However, a belief that one is largely powerless to create policy change may lead to political inaction on the part of a person (Gaventa, 1980; Lukes, 2005). Understanding how beliefs influence actors' activity in higher education rulemaking is important because, as explained by Lukes (2005), the beliefs of individuals are sometimes purposely shaped by other, powerful actors in order to further their own interests. Identifying beliefs that may lead an individual to act contrary to, or at least not in complete alignment with, that individual's own interests may indicate that an exercise of a less visible type of power has taken place (Lukes, 2005; see also Gaventa, 1980). Moreover, understanding the role of actors' beliefs in their rulemaking behavior is an important step toward achieving a greater comprehension of the motivations of individuals to become involved in important policymaking processes, such as higher education rulemaking. The beliefs and perspectives of policy actors are also important to understand because final policies often reflect the beliefs of their enactors, including "value priorities, perceptions of important causal relationships, perceptions of world states . . . and perceptions/assumptions concerning the efficacy of various policy instruments" (Sabatier & Jenkins-Smith, 1999, pp. 119–120). Identifying the extent to which an actor's beliefs are embedded in a final rule provides evidence of that actor's power in the higher education rulemaking process.

There are two categories of policy actors' beliefs that may play an important role in higher education rulemaking: beliefs about regulation and the rulemaking process itself, and beliefs about the substantive policy areas that are regulated through rulemaking. As is demonstrated in this chapter, both types of beliefs have played a role in some prominent higher education rulemaking procedures. Beliefs about the proper scope of the US Department of Education's regulatory powers surfaced in discussions about the unfinished Accreditation and Student Outcomes Rule, while the Gainful Employment Rules and other regulations primarily affecting for-profit higher education reflected some policy actors' beliefs about the role of market forces in higher education. This chapter examines the beliefs of policy and higher education actors as they relate to these two areas and discusses the role that such beliefs have played in actors' participation in higher education rulemaking, as well as in final rule outcomes. Understanding policy actors' beliefs may help to shed light on what motivates some actors to participate in the higher education rulemaking process, why some actors do not participate, and which actors' beliefs are reflected in final higher education regulations.

Beliefs about Rulemaking and Higher Education Rulemaking Involvement

A policy actor's beliefs about regulation—and about whether higher education rulemaking is appropriate in a given scenario—may have some bearing on the involvement an actor may have in the higher education rulemaking process. Such beliefs may influence the actor's decision to participate in rulemaking in the first place and, if the person chooses to become involved, how to participate (for example, through negotiated rulemaking or submitting written comments to the Department of Education). Policy actors who have been involved in higher education rulemaking (or who have observed it) have varying perspectives on the propriety or desirability of government regulation, including opinions about the amount of policymaking that the Department of Education should be able to conduct through rulemaking. For example, while some actors view the rulemaking that occurs within the Department of Education to be appropriate and necessary, other actors believe overregulation is undesirable and that agencies at times use the rulemaking process to legislate, which these actors view as improper. This study found that such beliefs have influenced policy actors' involvement in the higher education rulemaking process, although not always in the way that one might expect. Some actors holding antiregulation beliefs may eschew participation in rulemaking so as not to "enable" the government in this practice (in the words of one respondent), but antiregulation beliefs may influence other actors to become more involved in rulemaking. Based on experience with the higher education rulemaking process, a former Department of Education official explained: "People who believe least in it [regulation] are most likely to be aggressively involved . . . because they are there to protect their interests. . . . People who are 'against' whatever they're 'against' are engaged. Those who are 'okay' with what's going on are 'okay.' They all get involved."

Part of the reason for the greater involvement in regulatory policymaking of actors who hold more restrictive views of regulation may be that they wish to stop agencies from exceeding their policymaking authority through rulemaking. For example, some interested parties that hold antiregulation beliefs may nonetheless involve themselves extensively in rulemaking because not doing so might mean that the Department of Education will write a proposed rule entirely on its own. Having some input into the language of the rule is better than not participating and thus having no input at all, and there is a chance that the input of actors who prefer limited regulation may influence the department to regulate less extensively than it would otherwise. One journalist interviewed for this study remarked: "I think people are mostly driven by self-interest when it comes to rulemaking. So even if they philosophically dislike government regulation, if it's going to affect them, they want to have a say. . . . They are not going to sit it out just out of principle[;] they are going to try to shape it to be a form that is most favorable to them."

When some policy actors believe that the Department of Education is regulating inappropriately or excessively, they take actions within the rulemaking process to express those beliefs. For example, some community college officials at a regional meeting in 2006 stated that they were "offer[ing] testimony regarding the Department of Education's attempt to circumvent congressional authority with regard to the federal TRIO Upward Bound Programs" (*Public Regional Hearing for Negotiated Rulemaking*, 2006a, p. 121). At a different regional meeting discussing the same issue, an Upward Bound program director said: "My colleagues and I are here to address a notice of absolute priority for the classic Upward Bound Program. We both have substantial procedural problems with the proposed priority. We especially object to the fact that this process effectively changes a congressional priority for an administrative one, a practice we view as precedent-setting and disturbing" (*Public Regional Hearing for Negotiated Rulemaking*, 2006b, p. 34).

Some actors have submitted comments during the notice-and-comment phase of rulemaking to express their belief that a Notice of Proposed Rulemaking reflects an exercise of undue authority (researcher's data set; Student Assistance General Provisions . . . Final regulations, 2006). For example, in response to the NPRM for the 2002 rulemaking in which "safe harbors" were added to allow certain incentive-based compensation for college recruiters, some interest groups submitted comments indicating their belief that the proposed language would "rewrite" parts of the Higher Education Act and that such action would not be proper (researcher's data set). Additionally, in a regulation of the Academic Competitiveness Grant and National Science and Mathematics Access to Retain Talent Grant programs, "a number of commenters objected to the requirement that an eligible student must be receiving a Federal Pell Grant disbursement for the same payment period in which he or she will receive the ACG or National SMART Grant. They stated that the statute only requires that a student be eligible for a Federal Pell Grant, not receiving a Federal Pell Grant for the same payment period. These commenters believed that the Secretary exceeded her statutory authority and arbitrarily denied a Federal entitlement to otherwise eligible students" (Student Assistance General Provisions . . . Final regulations, 2006, p. 64406).[1]

Moreover, actors holding the belief that the rulemaking process should be limited to creating regulations that are closely tied to statutory law have worked to immobilize rulemakings that they believed the Department of Education did not have the authority to initiate. Several respondents cited the case of the unfinished Accreditation and Student Outcomes Rule as an example of a rulemaking in which some believed that the Department of Education was in danger of exceeding its authority. In that instance, the Department of Education commenced a rulemaking proceeding in an attempt to connect higher education student outcomes to accreditation and to instate new data gathering requirements (Lederman, 2007a; Lowry, 2009). Some congressional officials—most notably Senator Lamar Alexander—objected to the department's indication that it intended to regulate in this manner (researcher's interviews). A congressional staffer explained with regard to this unfinished regulation: "I think a lot of members were outraged just to begin with. I think, in part, because they were hearing from their schools, but sometimes Congress can get upset all on its own when the administration . . . goes too far in their view." As a result, some members of Congress expressed opposition to the rulemaking, including Senator Alexander, who said during a session of the Senate: "Congress needs to legislate first. Then the department can regulate" (Lederman, 2007b; Office of Senator Lamar Alexander, 2007). The senator also discussed his beliefs about regulation and higher education: "I believe the greatest threat to excellence of higher education is over regulation, not under-funding" (Office of Senator Lamar Alexander, 2007). This attempted-yet-never-completed rulemaking illustrates how beliefs that an agency should regulate less may prompt the actors holding such beliefs to become more involved in the higher education rulemaking process.

On the other hand, when congressional officials do not view the Department of Education as surpassing its authority through rulemaking, Congress may pay less attention to what the department is doing. For example, a congressional staffer, when asked about a particular student-aid-related regulation, replied: "I haven't paid close attention to it because in my . . . reading of what they've done, they've kept within the context of the statute. So, it's not been, they haven't aggressively tried to expand their authority." Thus, in some cases, policy actors (here, congressional officials) may have less involvement in higher education rulemaking if they believe the proceeding falls within the legitimate authority of the Department of Education.[2]

But it is also the case—as may be expected—that policy actors who view higher education rulemaking favorably and who do not possess strong antiregulation beliefs do participate actively in the process. For example, a representative of the National Association of Student Financial Aid Administrators, an organization that has participated in some way in multiple higher education rulemaking proceedings, made the following statement at a Department of Education regional meeting in 2008: "On behalf of the nearly 3,000 postsecondary educational institutions that are a member of the National Association of Student Financial Aid Administrators, I would like to express NASFAA's strong support for the negotiated rulemaking process. We believe that the community participation in the regulatory process allows us to work together to protect student access and choice in higher education, provide workable procedures, and ensure that statutory boundaries are maintained" (*Public Regional Hearing on Negotiated Rulemaking*, 2008c, p. 59). Far from being skeptical of the regulatory process, this statement reflects a belief in the value of negotiated rulemaking, particularly the participatory aspects of it. And this belief was expressed by a representative of a frequent rulemaking participant while participating in an early stage of the higher education rulemaking process. Likewise, several respondents in this study made statements reflecting a belief in the value of higher education rulemaking, or at least a belief that higher education has not been overregulated, and these same respondents have participated in some fashion in higher education rulemaking (researcher's interviews). So both actors holding beliefs that are skeptical of regulation or rulemaking and actors holding the opposite viewpoints have participated actively in higher education rulemaking. Both groups also have, on occasion, kept a less watchful eye on the proceedings, depending on the actor and the circumstances.

Beliefs about Self-Efficacy and Higher Education Rulemaking Involvement

Whether actors believe that their participation in higher education rulemaking will be effective—that is, will have some influence on the outcome of the rulemaking—can influence whether they become involved in the rulemaking process. It is important to observe whether this is occurring, because it may indicate that less visible forms of power, as described in chapter 5, are being exercised. Applying Lukes's (2005) theory of less visible exercises of power, Gaventa (1980) notes that a relatively less powerful party may neglect to take action against a more powerful party—even when such action would benefit the less powerful party—if the less powerful party believes that taking action would not change the situation. Gaventa further notes that this situation may indicate that the more powerful party has somehow acted to make the less powerful party believe its actions would be ineffective. This crafting of others' beliefs is evidence that an exercise of "Three-Dimensional" power may have taken place (Lukes, 2005, p. 25; see also Gaventa, 1980).

Although only a small number of respondents in this study discussed their beliefs about the efficacy of their own participation in higher education rulemaking, and therefore their views cannot be generalized to other policy actors, these few discussions can be informative about what actors in the higher education policy community think about their own ability to influence policy through rulemaking. Out of 20 respondents who made statements about such beliefs, 18 indicated that they felt they did have the power to effect change through rulemaking; 2 respondents stated their beliefs to the contrary.[3] Perhaps not surprisingly, all 18 of the respondents who believed in the effectiveness of their own participation have participated in higher education rulemaking. One of those—an interest group leader and regular rulemaking participant—described the belief that "if you want to affect public policy you have to participate at every stage of the process. But I think having limited resources doesn't preclude you from participating and, indeed, being effective. . . . If you want to influence public policy you have to participate in public policy across the board."

On the other hand, the two respondents interviewed for this study who did not believe their participation in higher education rulemaking would be effective were less likely to participate directly or more than minimally in the higher

[handwritten margin note: participate at every step to make a change!]

education rulemaking process. One institutional representative who did not feel qualified to do so did not participate in negotiated rulemaking. This respondent said, "[Rulemaking] didn't seem like something that I felt qualified for. . . . In retrospect, of course I'm going to affect things. And in the moment I probably would have said no because . . . I didn't feel like I had the knowledge."

Other respondents did not specifically state that their participation in rulemaking would be ineffective but did indicate their belief that it would be more effective to provoke policy change by lobbying Congress than by participating in rulemaking. These respondents either eschewed the higher education rulemaking process altogether or participated in it only to a minimal extent. One student representative who has participated in the notice-and-comment phase of higher education rulemaking but has otherwise not participated in the process believes efforts are better devoted to lobbying Congress. Another student representative who has focused on lobbying Congress and has not participated in rulemaking within the Department of Education said: "I don't know how much influence you have there [with the Department of Education]. . . . I don't know if your concerns are really going to be heard. I would say lobbying Congress directly you might have better luck, or finding out staffers on certain committees within Congress, who are assigned to that committee. That might be a better solution."

These findings provide evidence that, at least for some higher education stakeholders, actors' beliefs about the effectiveness of their own participation in higher education rulemaking may have some influence over those actors' decisions about whether to participate in the process. Respondents who believed that their participation would be influential were more likely to participate, and those who did not believe their actions would be influential (or who believed that lobbying Congress would be more influential) either have minimally participated in higher education rulemaking or have not participated at all. One interest group representative summarized the relationship between beliefs in the effectiveness of rulemaking participation and rulemaking involvement as follows: "If you didn't have some hope that you could influence them [the Department of Education's staff] about something, that's what makes the associations turn up. . . . They do have some hope that they can influence the department about a lot of things. . . . They think they can win enough of the time that they're willing to go over there and participate."

Evidence also suggests that actors' beliefs about the effectiveness of their own participation in higher education rulemaking may have some relationship with the coalitions that are formed during the process. Typically, coalitions based on these beliefs will take the form of joining or supporting a professional association or similar organization representing particular interests from which coalition members benefit or advocating for certain positions with which coalition members agree. In the higher education policy arena, there are a large number of professional associations that participate in politics and policymaking processes on behalf of higher education institutions, students, and employees (Cook, 1998). Many such organizations participate regularly and actively in the federal higher education rulemaking process. Such organizations are coalitions in their own right—they represent the joining together of various different constituents and often advocate for positions and causes that they believe will benefit their constituents. And some members believe that the organization may be better equipped to influence policy than a member would be, as an individual.

A few of this study's respondents suggested that the belief that one's own efficacy at influencing rulemaking is minimal may lead one to rely more heavily on an interest group or a professional association to represent one's interests in the higher education rulemaking process. An institutional representative described a belief that a professional organization representing this individual's interests might be more effective than the individual would be because the organization had "the power of multiple of voices. . . . They can represent multiple interests . . . [and] can be very effective through sort of the public comment space." Another institutional representative, who was active in an organization of institutions with similar interests, indicated a firm belief that the organization is more powerful in the policymaking process than an individual institution would be. This representative stated, "There's power in numbers" and suggested that "someone who's not attached to an organized interest group" would be among the least influential actors in the rulemaking process. Of course, there are many reasons to join a professional association, but these statements indicate that beliefs about the ineffectiveness of one's own, individual participation in a policymaking process such as rulemaking—and about the greater influence that participating as part of an organized coalition would have—may be one of them.

Some coalition-like behavior based on beliefs about the effectiveness of one's participation in the rulemaking process occurs outside the professional association setting as well. The institutional representative quoted above who did not feel knowledgeable enough to participate in rulemaking—and therefore did not personally participate—instead provided support for a colleague to participate in negotiated rulemaking. This respondent believed that the colleague would represent the same interests that the respondent would have represented and that the colleague would be a more qualified participant. This is an example of coalitional behavior—providing advocacy support for others with similar interests—performed as a result of beliefs about one's own ability to affect the rulemaking process. The Advocacy Coalition Framework contends that comparable beliefs about underlying policy issues and the instruments best suited to achieve policy goals may prompt actors to create coalitions with one another to advocate in favor of certain policies (Sabatier & Jenkins-Smith, 1999; Sabatier & Weible, 2007). This study indicates that coalitions among policy actors may also be formed based on different types of beliefs—beliefs about one's own efficacy in influencing policymaking and the belief that another actor in one's coalition may be more effective in prompting desired policy changes.

Beliefs about Substantive Policy Areas and Final Rule Content

Like other types of policies (see Sabatier & Jenkins-Smith, 1999), final higher education rules have reflected the beliefs of certain actors regarding the underlying substantive policy areas being regulated. Indeed, some final rules specifically state (typically in the Analysis of Comments sections) what actors' "beliefs" are regarding a particular matter and how those beliefs influenced the Department of Education to create a particular rule (see, e.g., Federal Family Education Loan Program, 1996; Federal Perkins Loan Program and Federal Family Education Loan Program, 1999; Student Assistance General Provisions: Final regulations, 1995; Teacher Quality Enhancement Grants Program, 1999a). A Notice of Proposed Rulemaking also sometimes states the beliefs of actors who were involved in the drafting of the proposed rule. For example, in a 1999 rulemaking that reformed student loan regulations for Peace Corps volunteers, the NPRM states: "The Peace Corps has requested that the Secretary provide a less burdensome means for borrowers who are not eligible for a statutory loan deferment or cancellation based on Peace Corps service to apply for economic hardship deferments of their federal student loans while serving in the Peace Corps. *The Secretary believes that the service performed by Peace Corps volunteers is important to the national interest, and is proposing to amend the economic hardship deferment eligibility criteria in the federal student loan programs in response to that request"* (Federal Perkins Loan Program and Federal Family Education Loan Program, 1998, p. 49798 [emphasis added]). In this case, the secretary of education's belief that Peace Corps personnel perform valuable work and should be entitled to an economic hardship deferment on federal student loans is plainly stated, and the final rule provides Peace Corps borrowers with eligibility for hardship deferments in keeping with the secretary's beliefs (see Federal Perkins Loan Program and Federal Family Education Loan Program, 1999).

Apart from expressly stating various policy actors' beliefs, some final and proposed higher education rules reflect beliefs in more subtle ways. For example, a series of rules regarding the payment of incentive compensation to recruitment and admission staff in colleges and universities demonstrates that varying beliefs about the role of free-market capitalism in higher education may influence the content of regulations. In the NPRM of a 1994 rulemaking regulating accountability for student loan servicers, the preamble states: "The Secretary is aware that some institutions pay incentives to recruiters or admissions office employees based on the success of those persons in enrolling students, provided that the enrolled students maintain satisfactory progress for and remain enrolled in the institution for a specified period of time. The Secretary considers this practice, which commonly is referred to as an incentive based on 'retention,' to be an example of an activity that is prohibited by the statute" (Student Assistance General Provisions and Federal Pell Grant Program, 1994, p. 9539). The position stated in this quotation reflects a belief that free-market, procompetition forces should be limited in the higher education admission process, as well as a belief about statutory interpretation. But later, in 2002, the Department of Education adopted a regulation that articulated circumstances—the "safe harbors"—in which the payment of incentive compensation to institutional recruitment staff would be allowed (Federal Student Aid Programs, 2002). This "safe harbor" rule reflects a different view from the one reflected in the previous statement, one that is more favorable toward free-market competition in the higher education student recruitment process. Even later, the department reversed course again and declared, via rule, that certain incentive-based payments to admission staff are no longer permitted, going back to a view that prefers more limited market involvement in higher education recruitment (Program Integrity Issues, 2010a). More recently, the Department of Education has again changed its stance; it will now not enforce incentive compensation prohibitions based on students' completion of their programs (Stratford, 2015). This latest change, which was made in reaction to lawsuits and a court decision, indicates a victory on the part of actors who believe in infusing competition and market forces into higher education policy and practice.[4]

The most obvious actor whose beliefs are seen in many higher education rules is the secretary of education. Indeed, many rulemaking materials (such as proposed and final regulations) plainly state that "the Secretary believes" certain things. Included are the secretary's beliefs about how government resources should be spent (see, e.g., Federal Family Education Loan Program, 1996), beliefs about the purpose of a congressional act (Teacher Quality Enhancement

Grants Program, 1999b), and—as exemplified by the Peace Corps regulation discussed above—beliefs about the value of certain programs "to the national interest" (Federal Perkins Loan Program and Federal Family Education Loan Program, 1998, p. 49798). In another example, in response to commenters who expressed a belief that guaranty agencies were better suited than the federal government to litigate certain student loan default cases, the final rule states: "The Secretary disagrees with the commenters. It is the Secretary's experience that the guaranty agencies are frequently inconsistent in pursuing and enforcing judgments. . . . The Secretary believes that centralized litigation by the federal government is the most cost-effective means of collecting these accounts. The Secretary believes that the number of defaulted accounts where the borrower has no income to be garnished but assets which could be attached will not be an overwhelming number and is convinced that the federal government has sufficient resources to litigate these accounts efficiently" (Federal Family Education Loan Program, 1996, p. 60483). This example illustrates how the beliefs of one powerful actor, the secretary of education, prevailed over the beliefs of others in the substance of a final rule.

Some of this study's respondents agreed that the beliefs of high-level Department of Education personnel have been reflected in higher education regulations. For example, one negotiated rulemaking participant has seen proposed rules that "reflected a very particular ideological perspective. . . . And it was clear that the rules were much more reflective of a particular secretary's vision, ideological vision, than any consensus-based vision that a negotiating team could have come up with."

Higher education regulations also reflect the beliefs of the presidential administration in power. The example of the addition and deletion of "safe harbor" provisions for paying incentive compensation to admission and recruitment staff indicates clearly that the beliefs of key personnel in the presidential administration can influence final rule content. As discussed above, higher education regulations went from barring incentive payments to admission staff under a Democratic administration, to permitting such payments in specified circumstances during a Republican administration, to prohibiting them once again under another Democratic administration, only to be partially walked back during the same Democratic administration in response to legal action by proponents of incentive compensation (see Federal Student Aid Programs, 2002; Program Integrity Issues, 2010a, 2010b; Stratford, 2015; Student Assistance General Provisions . . . Interim final regulations, 1994; Student Assistance General Provisions . . . Notice of proposed rulemaking, 2002; Student Assistance

General Provisions and Federal Pell Grant Program, 1994). These back-and-forth changes in substantive policy indicate a shift in the dominant viewpoint about the propriety of injecting an entrepreneurial element into college admissions. A higher education rulemaking observer noted: "It gets down into sort of biases and differences about how people think what education should be about. I think that there is really a strong point of view inside the Department [of Education] that admissions should just be around waiting for the phone to ring and you know it is this process by which students come to you and then you decide whether or not to accept them rather than the way the for-profit schools work, which is to go out and find the students. That is sort of a fundamental, philosophical difference." Another insider agreed, invoking—among other matters— the Gainful Employment Rule, which became a priority during the very early years of the Obama administration: "There was a very definite change, as you can imagine, between the Bush administration Department of Education and then the Obama administration Department of Education. . . . The Obama administration was concerned about gainful employment, incentive compensation issues and, perhaps, more unwilling to just say, 'The market is going to take care of this or this is only a few bad actors.' . . . And I think that difference in the political dynamic and how one views how much the federal government should get involved in things was obviously influential." And a negotiator said: "You're talking about rulemaking, but I can tell you there are lots of decisions that were being made in the department that were being held up by the political appointees and given a political or ideological slant. And so the staff's recommendations were modified to reflect that slant."

Given the power that the presidential administration and Department of Education personnel have over the content of final rules, it is unsurprising that their beliefs have been reflected in higher education regulations. One negotiated rulemaking participant commented, "I wouldn't say that . . . the administration's particular ideological orientation was a strong presence in the room, but it was something that everybody at the table was aware of, so it had, again, a kind of unspoken subtle effect, I felt, on the dynamic of the conversation."

Summary and Conclusion

Actors' own beliefs—about regulation and rulemaking, about their own ability to effect policy change through rulemaking, and about the subject matter of regulations—have influenced behavior in the higher education rulemaking process, as well as the outcomes of higher education regulatory policy. The theoretical literature predicts that actors' behavior in policymaking processes—

including whether and how much they get involved in the process—will be at least partially influenced by their beliefs (Gaventa, 1980; Lukes, 2005; Sabatier & Jenkins-Smith, 1999; Sabatier & Weible, 2007). Sabatier & Jenkins-Smith (1999) also suggest that policies, like beliefs, reflect the viewpoints, perspectives, and opinions of those who developed the policies. This study confirms that actors' beliefs do prompt them to act (or not to act) with regard to higher education rulemaking, although sometimes in a manner different from what might be expected given their beliefs. This study has also found that some actors' beliefs are reflected in final higher education rules.

Although actors hold differing beliefs about the desirability of regulation and about the propriety of some of the rulemaking that occurs in the Department of Education, antiregulation beliefs do not always mean that a party will avoid participating in rulemaking. To the contrary, such beliefs have been shown to prompt some parties to become involved, either to "rein in" a proposed regulation by working within the process or to speak from outside the process for the purpose of halting a rulemaking proceeding that the actor believes to be bureaucratic overreach, as was the case with the stalled Accreditation and Student Outcomes rulemaking (Lederman, 2007b; Lowry, 2009). Likewise, although actors with favorable beliefs about rulemaking do participate in the process with some frequency, other actors take a more hands-off approach when they believe that regulation is appropriate. Thus, although beliefs regarding regulation and the rulemaking process have motivated some actors to get involved in the rulemaking process, it is not always the case that those with antiregulation beliefs will avoid involvement, nor does it mean that those with favorable beliefs about regulation will necessarily participate in the process.

Additionally, this study's respondents who made statements indicating a belief that their actions would have some influence on at least part of the higher education rulemaking process had personally participated in the process. By contrast, respondents who did not directly participate in higher education rulemaking, or who participated only minimally, expressed beliefs either that their own participation in the higher education rulemaking process would not have had much, if any, impact on rulemaking outcomes or that their efforts would more likely be effective by lobbying Congress rather than participating in the rulemaking process. This study also provides evidence that some actors who believe they personally would be unlikely to influence rulemaking may be willing to participate in the rulemaking process via coalition formation—by joining with other actors (including professional associations) who they believe would be more effective at influencing rulemaking outcomes. Hence, actors who have little faith in their own ability to influence the higher education rulemaking process do not necessarily remove themselves from the process entirely.

Finally, this study finds that higher education regulations do reflect beliefs, sometimes by directly stating actors' beliefs in proposed and final rules, and sometimes by a subtle reflection of a particular view (for example, that market forces and competition should or should not play a role in college admissions staff compensation). Frequently, the beliefs reflected in final higher education rules are those of the Department of Education or the prevailing presidential administration, two very powerful actors in the higher education rulemaking process. But sometimes other powerful actors' viewpoints are reflected in regulations as well. The outcomes of final rules also tend to be in certain actors' best interests. For example, allowing incentive payments to be made to admissions personnel not only reflects procompetition beliefs but would also serve the interests of institutions, particularly those in the for-profit sector, that use this practice as a means to enroll more students.

This chapter describes how the beliefs held by policy and higher education actors have played a role in these actors' behavior and in the higher education rulemaking process, as well as in the content of final higher education regulations. What other, external factors may influence the process? Have political, economic, and other contexts that surround higher education rulemaking proceedings had any relationship to the rulemaking process and its outcomes? Chapter 7 explores these issues.

CHAPTER SEVEN

Higher Education Rulemaking in Context

Rulemaking does not take place in a contextual vacuum (O'Connell, 2008; West & Raso, 2013). Changes occur in the broader environment that affect higher education and grab the attention of policy and higher education actors. For example, both of the Gainful Employment Rules (which placed additional regulations on largely for-profit institutions) were issued under a Democratic presidential administration, and the Accreditation and Student Outcomes rulemaking (which sought to hold institutions accountable for student outcomes via accreditation) took place during a Republican one. All three of these rulemakings were initiated during periods of national economic growth, but much of the development of the first Gainful Employment Rule occurred during an economic recession. How do these and other contexts surrounding higher education rulemaking influence the process and its outcomes?

Some policy theories recognize the important role that context often plays in the policymaking process. The Advocacy Coalition Framework, for example, views certain contextual phenomena as important in that they influence coalitions' actions and, in some instances, lead to the creation or alteration of public policy (Sabatier, 1986; Sabatier & Jenkins-Smith, 1999; Sabatier & Weible, 2007). Some influential contexts are "quite stable" and include such matters as a nation's constitution and ecological resources; other influential contexts are "more dynamic"—including economic conditions and governmental leadership—and can change with some frequency (Sabatier & Jenkins-Smith, 1999, p. 120). Indeed, according to the ACF, developments in policy often occur following "shocks" occurring to or within a policy subsystem (Sabatier & Weible, 2007, pp. 199, 204), such as a catastrophic event, new leaders coming to power, or a substantial shift in the economy (Sabatier & Jenkins-Smith, 1999; Sabatier & Weible, 2007).

The ACF's view regarding the influence of context on policymaking accords with an important aspect of Kingdon's (2003) theory on policy agenda setting.[1] The "agenda-setting process" refers to the methods through which policy issues make their way onto "the list of subjects or problems to which government officials, and people outside of government closely associated with those officials, are paying some serious attention" (p. 3). An important aspect of Kingdon's theory is the "policy window," a period of time following the occurrence of a high-profile event or a shift in the political environment that allows for the consideration of new potential policies for addressing issues to which the changes in context draw focus (Kingdon, 2003; Zahariadis, 2007, pp. 73–74). The concept of the "policy window" (Kingdon, 2003)—like the ACF's "shocks" (Sabatier & Weible, 2007)—demonstrates that alterations in context can have a meaningful influence on policymaking.

Political, economic, and social contexts such as party control of the federal government, economic recessions, and the occurrence of major events all characterize the environment in which higher education rulemaking takes place. As West and Raso (2013) note, changes in surrounding contexts can influence the work done by bureaucracies, including the creation of regulatory policy. It should be expected that such contexts would influence higher education rulemaking in particular, because higher education policy is a political and often partisan issue (Ansell, 2010). It is also an expensive one—annual federal spending on higher education has recently exceeded $75 billion (Pew Charitable Trusts, 2015). This chapter explores how higher education rulemaking has unfolded differently in different surrounding contexts. More specifically, it examines whether such things as rulemaking activity levels, regulatory subject matter, and policy actors' participation in rulemaking have varied under different political parties' control of government, different national economic circumstances, and in the aftermath of a high-profile event.

Party Control of Government and Higher Education Rulemaking

As any observer of US politics knows, much ado is made of political party control of different governmental offices and shifts of such control from one party to another. Included, of course, is the presidency, which grants one political party control of the executive branch of the federal government. Although presidents have appointed members of the opposing party to important federal posts—and many appointments must be confirmed by the Senate, which is sometimes controlled by the opposing party—the president has a great deal of authority over which individuals will occupy these posts. Moreover, higher education rulemaking occurs within an agency that is overseen by the secretary of education, who is a member of the president's cabinet (White House, n.d.). This makes presidential partisanship particularly relevant to higher education rulemaking. A representative of for-profit colleges explained, "We have an election and a new administration comes in and we get a new secretary of education, we get a new under secretary and deputy secretary and an assistant secretary for postsecondary ed and you know they are the political leadership that the career people report up to. And they set the agenda and they say, 'This is what we want to do.'"

Party control of Congress may also be influential over higher education rulemaking (O'Connell, 2008, 2011). Congress passes the legislation that authorizes new regulations, and party control of this institution influences the content of statutes that are passed. Party control of Congress also determines leadership positions on key congressional committees, and committee members can provide certain legislative and economic advantages for some constituents, as well as steer the direction of policy discussions and legislative priorities (see, e.g., Gladieux & Wolanin, 1976; Rosenzweig, 2001). Another important consideration is whether Congress and the presidency are controlled by the same or different political parties. If these institutions are controlled by different parties—a circumstance known as "divided government"—regulatory policymaking may be influenced through legislation that, for example, may entrust less power and discretion to the executive branch (Epstein & O'Halloran, 1996; Huber, Shipan, & Pfahler, 2001).

This study found that higher education rulemaking has differed during different periods of party control of the federal government, in the level of higher education rulemaking activity, the subject matter of rules, and the amount of power held by different policy actors in the higher education rulemaking process.

Activity Level of Higher Education Rulemaking and Party Control of Government

Observing the number of higher education rules issued during different presidential terms and periods of different party control of Congress may shed light on how much rulemaking tends to occur during different political parties' control of government.[2] The figures discussed in this section are descriptive statistics only; the findings are not more broadly generalizable, nor may anything be concluded about the significance of the differences between them. Nonetheless, the differences in the amount of higher education rulemaking activity that

TABLE 7.1

Average monthly volume of final higher education rules by presidential term, 1989–2013

Presidential term	Average monthly number of rulemakings
George H. W. Bush term (1/1989–1/1993)	1.000
First Bill Clinton term (1/1993–1/1997)	2.333
Second Bill Clinton term (1/1997–1/2001)	1.146
First George W. Bush term (1/2001–1/2005)	0.188
Second George W. Bush term (1/2005–1/2009)	0.271
First Barack Obama term (1/2009–1/2013)	0.396

takes place under different parties' control of the presidency and Congress can contribute to a better understanding of how political context influences the higher education rulemaking process.

As table 7.1 demonstrates, there were more higher education rules issued per month on average during Democratic presidencies than under the presidencies of the immediate Republican predecessors, from the administration of President George H. W. Bush through the first term of President Barack Obama.[3] The greatest average monthly numbers of higher education rules were issued during President Bill Clinton's terms. Although there was a higher average monthly number of rulemakings during President George H. W. Bush's term than during President Barack Obama's first term, the smallest average monthly numbers of higher education rulemakings were during President George W. Bush's two terms. As of this writing, more than three-quarters of the way through President Barack Obama's second term, the average monthly number of higher education rules at this point in the term is 0.553. This is a higher rate than occurred in his prior term or in President George W. Bush's terms, but still lower than the rate that occurred in either President Bill Clinton's or President George H. W. Bush's term.

An examination of higher education rulemaking activity during different periods of party control of both the presidency and Congress also reveals some interesting descriptive patterns. As table 7.2 demonstrates, between 1991 and 2015, a higher average monthly number of final higher education rules (1.9) was issued during the period of united party control under Democrats (that is, Democratic presidents and Democratic control of Congress at the same time) than under any other type of governmental control. The smallest number of average higher education rulemakings per month (0.2) occurred under united Republican party control.

Nine of this study's respondents believed that political actors' ideologies regarding the desirability of regulation may influence the number of rulemakings

TABLE 7.2
*Average monthly number of higher education rulemakings by control
of federal government, 1991–2015*

Party control of the federal government	Average monthly number of final higher education rules
Democratic president, Democratic Congress	1.9
Democratic president, mixed-party Congress	0.5
Democratic president, Republican Congress	1.2
Republican president, Democratic Congress	0.7
Republican president, mixed-party Congress	0.3
Republican president, Republican Congress	0.2

Sources: Library of Congress, 2016; US House of Representatives, n.d.; US Senate, n.d.; researcher's data set.

that take place during their administrations, with Democrats being perceived as having more favorable views of regulation than Republicans. Considering that lenders and for-profit institutions are often the parties being regulated through the higher education rulemaking process, it makes sense that there would be increased regulatory activity during periods of Democratic control if Democrats tend to be more skeptical than Republicans of such industries. However, as 19 of this study's respondents pointed out, there was more significant legislation affecting higher education enacted during or just before Democratic presidential administrations, including Higher Education Act reauthorizations in 1992, 1998, and 2008. As depicted in figure 7.1, higher education rulemaking increased in the year or two following each of these three Higher Education Act reauthorizations.

Figure 7.1 also illustrates how dramatically the number of issued higher education rules has generally decreased between 1991 and 2015, and particularly between the Bill Clinton and George W. Bush administrations. Also interesting are the minor peaks in higher education rulemaking that occurred in 2007 and 2013–2014, which, unlike the other peaks shown in this graph, did not occur within a year or two following Higher Education Act reauthorizations. These peaks occurred during the latter part of the second term of Presidents George W. Bush and Barack Obama, at a time when Congress was controlled by a different political party than the president's. This might indicate action to set forth higher education policy through rulemaking just before the president leaves office, which would be unsurprising given that such action would not be unlike the phenomenon of "midnight" regulations that are often issued at the very end of a president's last term (O'Connell, 2011), even though the peaks observed in higher education rulemaking activity did not occur in Bush's or Obama's very last year in office.

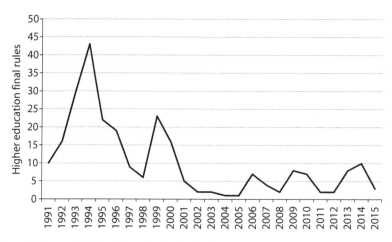

Fig. 7.1. Volume of higher education final rules by year, 1991–2015

It is important not to overstate the potential relationship between party control of the government and the amount of higher education rulemaking activity that took place during different presidencies. The fact that more higher education rules were issued under Democratic presidencies than by their immediate Republican predecessors is interesting and noteworthy because such an outcome would be expected, given similar observations in existing literature (Kerwin & Furlong, 2011). However, in the higher education policy arena, spikes in rulemaking activity seem to follow Higher Education Act lawmaking pretty consistently, which may confound any relationship between rulemaking volume and party control. Additionally, as figure 7.1 also demonstrates, the annual volume of higher education final rules has declined overall between 1991 and 2015, and Democratic president Barack Obama saw fewer higher education regulations during his tenure than Republican George H. W. Bush did. These facts indicate that factors other than a president's political party—such as the passage of legislation, economic factors, and the broader ideological climate—may influence higher education rulemaking activity as well.[4] Moreover, at least one study using advanced statistical analyses yielded mixed findings with respect to party control of various political institutions and rulemaking activity (O'Connell, 2008). Thus, the figures in this chapter describing the level of rulemaking activity during periods of different party control of government should be interpreted with caution.

Subject Matter of Rules and Party Control of Government

There have been some noteworthy differences in higher education rule subject matter under periods of different party control of the federal government (see also Mettler, 2014). Take the example of regulation of the for-profit higher education sector. Because deregulation of for-profit higher education tends to represent a more politically conservative, laissez-faire approach, rules that permit such compensation would be more indicative of conservative influence. As expected, this study's focal rules regarding the payment of incentive compensation to college recruiters differ vastly by party control of the federal government. A rule issued during the 1990s—while a Democratic president was in office and Democrats controlled Congress—prohibited incentive compensation paid to individuals who recruit students for higher education institutions (Student Assistance General Provisions . . . Interim final regulations, 1994).[5] A later rule, issued during the George W. Bush administration and during a period of mixed party control of Congress, permitted such compensation under specific circumstances (Federal Student Aid Programs, 2002).[6] Subsequently, under the Obama administration, with a Democratic Congress, a new rule removed the situations in which recruiter incentive compensation would be allowed (Program Integrity Issues, 2010a).[7]

In another example, the Gainful Employment Rule was adopted during the Obama administration with mixed party control of Congress, although this rulemaking procedure was initiated while Democrats held united party control of both branches (see Program Integrity: Gainful Employment, 2011). Given the focus of this rule on career-preparation programs, for-profit institutions felt the most targeted by this rule (researcher's interviews). After key aspects of the first Gainful Employment Rule were struck down by a court (see *APSCU v. Duncan*, 2012), the second Gainful Employment Rule was issued during the same presidential administration and still under mixed-party control of Congress (Program Integrity: Gainful Employment, 2014). Rules such as these, which predominantly regulate the for-profit sector, would be less expected under an administration that was more laissez-faire with regard to such institutions.

These differences in rule content are due at least in part to the influence of the presidential administration. Presidential vision and policy positions influence the higher education rulemaking agenda in that they determine what issues get put "on the table." As a journalist noted, "obviously the issues that are chosen depend in part on the administration that's in power." The Gainful

Employment Rules and the 2010 Program Integrity Rule are prime examples of the influence of presidential vision and policy positions on higher education rulemaking. About the Program Integrity and first Gainful Employment Rule, which were negotiated at the same time, a journalist said: "They have an agenda and they are trying to put it out there in rules. So this, you wouldn't have seen this rulemaking happening under George Bush. This is being driven by the Obama administration and his appointees in the Education Department." And a member of the for-profit sector said:

> Any proposed rule has to be vetted by, through OMB first. . . . So part of that vetting process is . . . where the department [goes] consistent with the general platform of the administration, and is it consistent with any other agencies that might have some similar interest or activity going on? . . . And I think especially during this round where you had, with gainful employment again, and also accreditation and even credit-hour [rules] to a lesser extent. But you've got some issues that certain members of the White House policy team have a very strong interest in, that's helping shape the Department [of Education].

Similar agenda-setting has happened during Republican administrations. According to a representative of nonprofit, private higher education, "there was a lot of sympathy for the for-profit sector" during a Republican administration, and for-profit institutions "were much more heavily represented in one way or the other than was the more traditional sector" at that time.

The political party of the president appears to be more closely related to higher education rule subject matter than congressional party control is. Table 7.3 lists the representative subject matters of this study's focal rules that have implications for for-profit and other nontraditional higher education during different periods of party control of the federal government. Rules that may be expected under Democratic leadership—namely, greater regulation of for-profit higher education programs and practices such institutions often use—occurred with regard to the focal rules under periods of Democratic control of the White House when there was both Democratic and Republican control of Congress. Similarly, rules that may be expected under Republican leadership—that is, relaxing regulations of the for-profit sector—occurred during times of Republican control of the White House and both mixed-party and Democratic control of Congress. Thus, the expected agendas of Democrats were reflected in focal rules issued during Democratic presidencies, and the expected agendas of Republicans were reflected in focal rules issued during Republican presidencies, regardless of which party controlled Congress.

TABLE 7.3

Representative subject matter of focal rules, by party control of federal government, for-profit and nontraditional higher education

	Subject Matter					
Party control of government	Limiting admissions incentive pay	Permitting admissions incentive pay	Broadening loan-providing authority for particular institutions	Setting standards for particular institutions	Eliminating disfavored regulations	None relating to for-profit higher education
Democratic president and Congress	X			X		
Democratic president, Republican Congress				X		
Democratic president, mixed-party Congress						X
Republican president, Democratic Congress			X			
Republican president, mixed-party Congress	X				X	
Republican president and Congress						X

Although these data are qualitative and therefore not necessarily representative of a broader population of regulations, the focal rules for this study were chosen carefully to reflect a broad range of rule subject matters, having different levels of prominence and occurring at different times throughout the observed time period. These rules therefore provide a snapshot of how the subject matters of certain higher education rules have differed by party control of the federal government, often in the ways one might expect.

Policy Actors' Power in Rulemaking and Party Control of Government

When the federal government is experiencing united control under a particular political party, actors whose interests are aligned with the controlling party's policy priorities can gain influence in the higher education rulemaking process. One reason this occurs is that one-party control of government can influence the content of laws to favor the policy preferences of the party in power, and the content of laws then has an impact not only on the content of regulations but also on the influence of actors whose interests align with the interests and ideology of the ruling party. Conversely, actors whose interests do not align with the interests and ideology of the party in power may see their influence dissipate.

For example, a once-powerful actor lost power based on actions taken during united party control during the early Obama administration, when the federal student loan program began to switch to a strictly direct lending model (Dynarski, 2015; Lederman, 2010). Before that time, while the federal government would guarantee some student loans, many loans were provided by private lenders; the Obama administration, with help from a Democratic Congress, changed this arrangement so that going forward, the federal government would be the direct lender for all federal student loans (Dynarski, 2015). Some of this study's respondents pointed out that as a result of this change, private lenders would have less influence over the higher education rulemaking process in the future. The direct lending policy also made other actors appear more powerful in the higher education rulemaking process. A representative of lenders and guaranty agencies expressed a belief that "the student group and Legal Aid had an incredible amount of power" around the time of the shift to direct loans. And a public four-year institutional official said of schools that advocated for the Direct Loan program, "I think Direct Loan schools right now do [have a lot of power] . . . because . . . Direct Loan schools represent a cheaper way to deliver loans, a more consistent way, and a much more student-friendly way than the alternative used to be."

Another reason actors with ties to the party in power have been more influential in the higher education rulemaking process is that congressional party control influences congressional leadership and congressional committee chairmanship. The most relevant congressional committees for higher education policy are the House Education and the Workforce Committee (and within it the Higher Education and the Workforce Subcommittee) and the Senate Committee on Health, Education, Labor, and Pensions (Hillman et al., 2015). These committees can influence the Department of Education and its implementation work, including rulemaking, and policy actors who have access to the Congress members who lead those committees may be able to influence higher education rulemaking through those committee members.

Thus, actors whose interests are aligned with a particular political party, or who otherwise have allies in the party, have more power in higher education rulemaking when that party is in control of the federal government at least in part because congressional leadership is based on party control, and congressional leaders have power over the Department of Education.

Economic Recessions and Higher Education Rulemaking

Another consideration is whether and how national economic conditions are related to the higher education rulemaking process. A majority of this study's respondents indicated that economic conditions are likely to have at least some influence on how higher education rulemaking unfolds. One way to determine the influence of economic conditions is to observe how, if at all, rulemaking occurs differently during economic recessions than during periods of economic growth. The National Bureau of Economic Research (n.d.) defines "recession" as "a significant decline in economic activity spread across the economy, lasting more than a few months, normally visible in real GDP, real income, employment, industrial production, and wholesale-retail sales." Recessionary periods occurred from July 1990 through March 1991, March 2001 through November 2001, and December 2007 through June 2009 (National Bureau of Economic Research, n.d.). This study found some interesting ways that economic recessions have influenced higher education final rule content, strategies employed to influence rulemaking, and policy actors' involvement in the rulemaking process.

Subject Matter of Rules and Economic Recessions

Economic conditions can influence the subject matter of final higher education rules in that during poor economic times, the Department of Education is more likely to pay attention to budgetary issues, and such issues may affect final rule content, even if in seemingly subtle ways. A former Office of Postsecondary Education employee explained, "Economics do drive the decisions that are made whether to make a rule a little looser or tighter . . . when you look at budget issues and you know well, if this is an 'and' or an 'or' it will make a difference. That certainly comes into play, absolutely." And an employee of an interest group representing college administrators said, "Generally as the department is doing it and putting things on the agenda, if . . . you are trying to get something on the agenda but it might have budget impact . . . they generally are under constraints that they can't entertain changes that would cost them more money, unless there is offsetting things in the regulatory package that would perhaps bring in money."

The economy may also influence the content of statutory law, which in turn influences the content of regulations implementing those statutes. As a representative of lenders and guaranty agencies explained, economic conditions have "a lot to do with what they do with the legislation itself," and rulemaking is prompted by that legislation.

But it is important not to overstate the influence that economic recessions may have on higher education rule content. A former Department of Education official explained that economic conditions "shouldn't matter. Laws get changed when you are in those kinds of times, and maybe the law gets changed to spend more money or to cut more money, which forces a rulemaking process. But the administration itself would be unlikely . . . to sit there saying, 'We need to change these regs because of economic conditions.'"

Actors' Involvement in Rulemaking, Strategies, and Economic Recessions

Economic conditions also play a role in determining which actors participate in the higher education rulemaking process and what strategies they employ to influence rulemaking. These two variables are discussed together because, when considered with respect to their relationship to the economy, they are related: in poor economic times, there is less actor involvement in certain aspects of the higher education rulemaking process, and this is so because fewer actors are employing certain expensive strategies to influence rulemaking.

Organizations with budgets that have been cut or that have been under pressure to save money will be less likely to participate in regional meetings or negotiated rulemaking, which often bear substantial travel costs (researcher's interviews). A representative of the Department of Education opined that economic conditions may have a greater influence over rulemaking participation than other contexts: "People representing states weren't nominated because state travel budgets had been slashed. And so I think that that's what's been interesting, is more than political party or more than anything else, it's the particular economic circumstance of a group that determines whether they feel that they can participate or not."

A financial aid officer agreed: "Negotiated rulemaking, I think that that's for the participants of it, you know of course the Department of Education can't subsidize any of this. . . . And so it's up to the individual or the individual's organization to support them to participate in negotiated rulemaking . . . depending on how the finances are for whoever the organization is. You know, someone may wish to participate but can't."

Along similar lines, the economy influences the strategies and other powers that actors employ during the higher education rulemaking process. According to a Department of Education official, strategies such as nominating individuals to serve on a negotiated rulemaking committee decrease because actual participation in negotiated rulemaking may become cost-prohibitive for some during times of economic recession. As a result there is a smaller pool of potential negotiators from which the Department of Education may select. Similarly, fewer actors are likely to employ the strategy of attending and participating in regional meetings during poor economic conditions. A representative of college administrators, for example, used to attend regional meetings but has not done so more recently. The reason? "It's just a matter of budgets."

An examination of records from regional meetings held in conjunction with the Gainful Employment and Accreditation and Student Outcomes rulemakings supports the argument that fewer actors participate in regional meetings during tough economic times. The series of regional meetings that preceded the Accreditation and Student Outcomes rulemaking was held in the fall of 2006 (Office of Postsecondary Education: Notice, 2007). During this nonrecessionary period, the number of speakers at each of these meetings ranged from 35 to 54, not including Department of Education personnel (US Department of Education, 2006a, 2006b, 2006c, 2007b). However, at a series of regional meetings held at the end of a recessionary period (June 2009), the number of speakers at each meeting ranged from 13 to 31, not including Department of Education personnel (Office of Postsecondary Education, 2009a, 2009b, 2009c). The first Gainful Employment Rule was one of the subjects of these June 2009 regional meetings (Program Integrity: Gainful Employment, 2010), and despite that rule's controversy, its regional meetings did not generate as many speakers as the regional meeting associated with the Accreditation and Student Outcomes rulemaking. The regional meetings that preceded the second Gainful Employment Rule—which took place during the nonrecessionary spring of 2013—had between 25 and 49 speakers (US Department of Education, 2013b, 2013c, 2013d, 2013e). Even though the subject matter was similar, there were more speakers at the meetings that discussed the second Gainful Employment Rule than the first; the meetings that preceded the first rule occurred during an economic recession, while the meetings that preceded the second did not. Although these numbers are descriptive only and this study found no direct evidence that these differences in the number of speakers at regional meetings was related to the surrounding economic context of each meeting, the patterns do support respondents' contentions that participation in aspects of rulemaking that require travel and attendance at meetings may occur less frequently during periods of fiscal constraint.

The differences in actor participation and strategies seen during economic recessions are consequential. With fewer actors attending regional meetings during recessions, owing to cost constraints, fewer constituent voices are heard during this crucial early phase of the higher education rulemaking process. Moreover, because well-resourced actors are more likely to be able to afford to employ these strategies in times of economic constraint, these already powerful actors take on even more influence during tough economic times, when actors with fewer resources will be less likely to participate and to be heard.

High-Profile Events and Higher Education Rulemaking

A social context surrounding higher education rulemaking that can influence the process is the occurrence of a high-profile event, one that captures at least a fair amount of media attention and that relates to higher education in some way, even if remotely. These occurrences may constitute one of the subsystem "shocks" leading to policy change as described by the Advocacy Coalition Framework (Sabatier & Weible, 2007; see also Sabatier & Jenkins-Smith, 1999) or a "policy window" described by Kingdon (2003), both of which often precede policy change. Specifically regarding higher education rulemaking, a wide majority of this study's respondents (41 out of 55) suggested that high-profile events at least somewhat influence the process. By drawing attention to an issue, a major event can—in the words of one respondent—"create[] a sense of urgency to address an issue, whether it's real or not."

In addition to drawing attention to certain issues, the occurrence of a major event can have more observable influences on higher education. This section describes how such events relate to the subject matter of higher education rules, as well as the amount of power certain actors have in higher education rulemaking and the use of certain strategies in attempts to influence the process.

Subject Matter of Rules and High-Profile Events

In recent decades, several high-profile events have affected the content of final higher education rules. These include events that affect the nation broadly (including military conflicts, terrorist attacks, and hurricanes) and events that affect higher education more directly (such as violence on college campuses). Rules involving student aid reform for some victims of hurricanes such as Katrina and Rita (Federal Student Aid Programs, 2006), an extension of special Pell Grant provisions to veterans of Operations Desert Shield and Desert Storm (Pell

Grant Program, 1992), and forgiveness of some federal student loans for 9/11 victims' families (Federal Perkins Loan Program, 2007a) have followed the occurrence of each of these national high-profile events. For example, a 2006 regulation waived a requirement that a student repay a need-based federal grant after dropping out of a higher education program—students would ordinarily be required to repay in such a circumstance—"if the student withdrew from an institution because of a major disaster" such as a hurricane (Federal Student Aid Programs, 2006, p. 45671). Rules such as these demonstrate how national disasters can affect a wide range of policy areas, from national security and defense, to emergency management, to higher education.

The timing of the regulations prompted by high-profile events has varied, from within a year or two after the event (see Federal Student Aid Programs, 2006; Pell Grant Program, 1992) to several years after the event (see Federal Perkins Loan Program, 2007a). Typically, rule content reflects a major event because rulemakings are spurred by new legislation that is prompted by the event (researcher's interviews). For example, the regulation reforming student financial aid for certain victims of hurricanes was prompted by the passage of such legislation as the Pell Grant Hurricane and Disaster Relief Act, the Student Grant Hurricane and Disaster Relief Act, and the Emergency Supplemental Appropriations Act for Defense, the Global War on Terror, and Hurricane Recovery (Federal Student Aid Programs, 2006). A congressional staffer said, "Usually when something like that happens, Congress responds." Then it becomes the Department of Education's job to issue the rules that implement the law, and those rules will invariably resemble the legislation.

But in addition to affecting rulemaking substance through legislation, major events can lead regulators to see regulations in a different light or to understand better how rules may need to be adjusted under certain circumstances. A former Office of Postsecondary Education employee explained:

> [Hurricanes] Katrina and Rita were such an impact and it impacted so many colleges that when you look at the postsecondary level, I mean I think that there's an eye towards flexibility. I think Katrina and Rita really opened the eyes to some of those individuals as to the level of flexibility needed at times, and that impacts regulation writing, absolutely. So fundamental watershed events like that [are] undoubtedly impact[ful]. I mentioned the flexibility, but also on the flip side, there was additional flexibility based on 9/11 that we tried to put into the regulations as much as possible, but then Katrina changed that even further.

Actor Participation in Rulemaking and High-Profile Events

High-profile events can cause certain actors to have more power in higher education rulemaking than they otherwise would. One way that this occurs is through increased participation in certain aspects of higher education rulemaking following certain high-profile events. Members of the general public do participate in higher education rulemaking, but they are typically not among the most influential actors in the process. In fact, one Department of Education official said that members of the public "rarely show up to make statements" and "rarely have impact" on negotiated rulemaking. However, after a high-profile tragedy on a college campus, statements made by members of the public who were personally affected by the event may carry more weight than public statements ordinarily would (researcher's interviews). An example of this occurred after the high-profile shooting event on the campus of Virginia Tech in 2007. The same department official who said that members of the public "rarely have impact" referred to this event and said: "We did a rulemaking a couple of years ago where we dealt with some campus security-related issues, and in that negotiated rulemaking process we had a conference call with the negotiators and the families of the victims of the Virginia Tech tragedy. And then some came—some of the Virginia Tech families came and spoke at one of the negotiating sessions. And I think that had an impact on softening the position of the some of the institutional advocates." Speaking of that same event, a representative of for-profit higher education expressed a similar sentiment: "There was a set of rules that dealt with public safety on campuses. . . . There were representatives from families of victims of the Virginia Tech situation and they came and presented to the committee and boy, you could have heard a pin drop. It was pretty powerful."

Major events can also prompt some actors to engage in certain strategies to influence rulemaking that they might not otherwise attempt. For example, a former Department of Education official said that major events can lead to a larger number of actors attending regional meetings, observing negotiated rulemaking, and submitting written comments during the notice-and-comment period. This respondent said that high-profile events can influence the employment of such tactics in these ways: "Particularly like for the public hearings . . . you would see lots more people show up for that kind of thing. And even sometimes maybe to sit through the rulemaking, but most of the time they don't have an audience. . . . If the public gets interested, the public might be more willing to submit comments." Thus, more individuals are likely to employ one of the strategies for public participation in higher education rulemaking if a high-profile event draws a great deal of attention to the rulemaking proceeding.

Summary and Conclusion

Higher education rulemaking occurs within various contexts, which may be political, economic, or social in nature. The higher education rulemaking process is not detached from the various contexts in which it occurs. Because the process itself is influenced by context, the outcome of the process—the content of final higher education rules—is also influenced by context.

Various policy theories acknowledge the influence of context on policymaking. As stated earlier in this chapter, the Advocacy Coalition Framework views certain contextual phenomena as important influences over advocacy coalitions' actions and, often, over the creation or alteration of public policy (Sabatier & Jenkins-Smith, 1999; Sabatier & Weible, 2007). This theory argues that developments in policy may occur following "shocks" hitting a policy subsystem, such as a high-profile event, shifts in economic circumstances, or new governmental leadership (Sabatier & Weible, 2007; see also Sabatier & Jenkins-Smith, 1999). This accords with Kingdon's (2003) theory that shifts in the political, economic, and social context may provoke the opening of a "policy window"—a relatively brief period during which certain actors have the opportunity to advocate for their favored policy choices to be placed on the government's "agenda" (see also Zahariadis, 2007). For example, when a new governmental administration takes office, actors who favor policies that may align with the new administration's ideology may step up efforts to promote their preferred policy to the new leadership (Kingdon, 2003).

The findings of this study support these conclusions from the theoretical literature in that certain policy contexts provide an opportunity for new higher education rulemaking to take place. The contexts analyzed by this study—party control of the federal government, economic conditions, and the occurrence of high-profile events—have all been found to influence the subject matter of higher education rules. High-profile events such as a war, a terrorist attack, or a hurricane have resulted in new rulemakings aimed at providing some sort of relief for victims of the event. With regard to the activity level of new rulemakings, from President George H. W. Bush through President Obama, a larger monthly average number of final higher education rules were issued during the presidential administrations of Democrats than of their immediate Republican predecessors. Moreover, between 1991 and 2014, there was a larger monthly average number of higher education rules issued during periods of united governmental control by Democrats than during any other type of united or divided government. During this same time period, the lowest average monthly number of higher education rules was issued during periods of united governmental control by Republicans. Because this is a qualitative study examining descriptive statistics only, and because of the timing of Higher Education Act reauthorizations (which tend to trigger waves of new rulemakings), the findings regarding the volume of rules should be interpreted cautiously. Nonetheless, these findings provide some interesting observations about how context may influence rulemaking, and they align with conventional wisdom that characterizes Republicans as generally holding more antiregulation views than Democrats.

The subject matter of higher education rules also relates to presidential administration. For example, the Gainful Employment Rule, which more heavily regulated for-profit higher education programs, was issued during a Democratic presidential administration, this following a period of somewhat looser restrictions on certain practices commonly adopted by for-profit institutions—for example, incentive compensation for college recruiters—that were granted via the rulemaking process during a Republican administration.

With respect to the power of particular actors over higher education rulemaking, this study confirms that some actors are more or less powerful in the higher education rulemaking process and employ different strategies to influence rulemaking in different contexts. For example, actors with ties to the political party in power and actors personally affected by high-profile events affecting higher education have held greater power in the process. Actors with fewer financial resources may participate less in higher education rulemaking during economic downturns and hence have a weaker voice than actors whose resources allow them to participate in many aspects of the process despite tough economic times. Indeed, there were fewer speakers at regional meetings held before the first Gainful Employment rulemaking than at regional meetings held before the either the second Gainful Employment rulemaking or the Accreditation and Student Outcomes rulemaking. The former were held during an economic recession, while the latter were not. In addition, if a regulation relates to a high-profile event, a larger number of individuals than usual are likely to attend regional meetings, observe negotiated rulemaking, and submit comments to the Department of Education during the notice-and-comment phase.

In sum, what happens during the higher education rulemaking process— and the content of the rules themselves—may differ in varying political, social, and economic contexts. These contexts include party control of government, economic conditions, and the occurrence of high-profile events. Another kind of context—one that seems ever present and tends to evolve more gradually over time—is technology. How has the evolution of information and communication technologies influenced the higher education rulemaking process and final higher education rules? How, if at all, has technology affected actor participation in higher education rulemaking? Chapter 8 responds to these questions.

CHAPTER EIGHT

The Use and Influence of Technology

Developments in information and communication technology have, in many ways, enabled people to more easily complete complicated tasks and to communicate quickly and remotely with people located anywhere on the globe. These technologies can be used in a variety of ways to influence and enhance policymaking. For example, policy actors and interest groups who favored or opposed the Gainful Employment and Accreditation and Student Outcomes rulemakings used technology to express their viewpoints regarding these regulations to a wide audience, wider than would have been possible before the Internet age. Just as the political, social, and economic contexts discussed in chapter 7 influenced the content of final higher education rules, developing technologies may be conceptualized as an evolving social context that itself influences final regulations, such as ones that govern student financial aid administration.

Moreover, as some have argued, the Internet and other advanced communications technologies have the potential to enable greater "grass roots" involvement in politics (Wheeler, 2006, p. 9; see also Johnson, 1998). Technology can enable the public to gather more information about government processes and laws and can enable government agencies and constituents to communicate more easily during the policymaking process (Johnson, 1998). However, the fact that technology has the potential to enhance democratic participation in policymaking does not necessarily mean that it actually will. As some scholars have pointed out, the know-how and wherewithal to employ new technologies often rest in the hands of a privileged few (Best & Krueger, 2005). Moreover, the mere fact that the public may use technology to participate in a government process does not necessarily mean that people will take the initiative to do so.

Studies have suggested that innovations in technology have had some noteworthy impacts on federal rulemaking in recent years (see, e.g., Balla & Daniels, 2007; Coglianese, 2004, 2006; Farina et al., 2011; Furlong & Kerwin, 2005;

Kerwin & Furlong, 2011; Stanley & Weare, 2004; US General Accounting Office, 2000). According to a study conducted by the US General Accounting Office (now known as the Government Accountability Office), several federal agencies were using communications technologies in connection with rules and rulemaking as early as the year 2000, ranging from posting "rulemaking information" on their Internet pages to receiving comments online (US General Accounting Office, 2000, p. 2). More recently, the federal government introduced "electronic rulemaking, or e-rulemaking" (Coglianese, 2004, p. 355; see also Coglianese, 2006; Furlong & Kerwin, 2005; Kerwin & Furlong, 2011; Schlosberg, Zavestoski, & Shulman, 2007; Stanley & Weare, 2004). This phenomenon includes the emergence of Regulations.gov, a website that permits anyone with an Internet connection to access electronic copies of Notices of Proposed Rulemaking and to send instant comments on an NPRM via the web (Coglianese, 2004, 2006; Furlong & Kerwin, 2005; Schlosberg et al., 2007). There have also been attempts to enhance rulemaking involvement through electronic social media (Farina et al., 2011). But has the proliferation of information and communication technologies actually led to increased or more diverse participation among policy actors in the higher education rulemaking process? Or has it simply provided a new way for largely the same types of participants to participate in higher education rulemaking and for powerful actors to influence it?

This chapter examines the various ways that developments in technology have influenced the higher education rulemaking process to make the process more efficient and to enhance participation, and it considers whether advances in technology have actually helped to bring more diverse perspectives into the process. The chapter also describes how—much like the various political, social, and economic contexts discussed in chapter 7—the emergence of new technologies has influenced the subject matter of higher education regulations.

Technology's Role in Efficiency and Participation in Higher Education Rulemaking

Technology has been incorporated into various aspects of the higher education rulemaking process, and as a result, the process has in many respects become more efficient and easier for policy actors to navigate. The Internet has provided a platform to communicate information about rules and rulemaking very broadly, making this information widely available and easy to obtain. Technology has also has promoted more avenues for participation in higher education negotiated rulemaking and has altered the way policy actors involve themselves during the notice-and-comment phase. But has technology served to expand or diversify the voices that are heard in this process? This section describes how advances in technology over the past two decades have influenced the higher education rulemaking process.

Sharing Information about Rulemaking with a Wide Audience

Technology has been used by public officials and interest groups alike to communicate information about higher education rulemaking with a wide audience, perhaps many times wider than the audience that received this information in the pre-Internet era. Policy actors have used e-mail, websites, and electronic social media to spread information and messages about higher education rulemaking.

E-MAIL

Because electronic mail has been around for a while now, it is easy to forget that in the years before e-mail, it was not nearly as easy or efficient as it is today to disseminate documents and other written communications. The ability to use e-mail (which was still fairly new in the early 1990s, at the beginning of the period examined by this study) and its increasingly widespread use over the years have contributed to efficiency in written communications and the dissemination of documents and other information in the higher education rulemaking process. For example, a for-profit higher education representative described how policy actors could subscribe to a Department of Education Listserv to receive notices about higher education rulemaking via e-mail. As this respondent pointed out, the fact that the department used this technology gave institutions little excuse to be unaware of the agency's rulemaking activities: "Theoretically, the financial aid person at every little college should be aware of the NPRM because the department does send out e-mail notifications if you ask them to. You can get on a Listserv where they will send you notifications that will tell you things like we've published an NPRM. So there's no reason you shouldn't know, if you're a school."

Interest groups have also made use of e-mail to send information about higher education quickly and easily to a large number of recipients. One interest group representative described how the widespread use of e-mail has made communicating about rulemaking more efficient:

The big difference now is of course being able to send out by e-mail, which really was not prevalent until—in terms of who was using it in the Washington circles—until I'd say around '96 or '97. Prior to that, it was pretty hard to get out draft copies of documents to people. You can call people, you could type up something in word processing and you could send it, but there wasn't a free exchange via e-mail where you could post stuff on a Listserv or send stuff. . . . You know, you had to fax stuff to people. So it was harder to get it out to your members, for them to review and then get back to you in a timely fashion.

WEBSITES

Similarly, over the past two and a half decades, policy actors' increased Internet presence, as more organizations maintain their own websites and more interested parties have become savvy Internet researchers, has influenced how information about higher education rulemaking is spread and received. Policy actors have put information, press releases, and position statements about higher education rulemaking on their own websites. The Department of Education's website contains information about proposed rules and forthcoming negotiated rulemaking sessions. Also available on the department's website is information about past negotiated rulemakings, including full transcripts of regional meetings, lists of regional meeting and negotiated rulemaking participants, negotiated rulemaking agendas and minutes, early drafts of NPRMs, and the dates and subject matter of proposed and final rules, with links to the full texts of the proposed and final rules (see, e.g., US Department of Education, 2010). Previously, much of this information could have been obtained only by addressing a specific request for documents to the Department of Education or by visiting the headquarters of document custodians. For information on forthcoming negotiated rulemakings or proposed and final rules, one could review a hard copy of the *Federal Register,* a specialized, government-produced periodical that is not routinely read by most citizens. Although many (but by no means all) libraries carry the *Federal Register,* a person would have to know where to find it and how to navigate its index. Now, in addition to the information available on the Department of Education's website, the *Federal Register* itself is available online, with electronic archives dating back to 1994 and, as of this writing, a plan to digitize the remainder of the *Federal Register* all the way back to its earliest issues in 1936 (Jordi, 2015).

Members of Congress also use their websites to communicate broadly about higher education rulemaking. Senators and members of the House of Representatives alike have posted information about certain higher education rules and regulatory proposals on their web pages, including press releases describing the member's position on the rule and actions that the member has taken to support or oppose a rule. This was done by Senator Bernie Sanders (Independent from Vermont) and Representative Glenn Thompson (Republican from Pennsylvania) when the first Gainful Employment Rule was being developed, with Sanders favoring a strong Gainful Employment Rule and Thompson opposing the regulation (Office of Representative Glenn W. Thompson, 2010; Office of Senator Bernie Sanders, 2010). In addition to individual members of Congress, congressional committees have used their websites to post position statements regarding higher education rules (see, e.g., House Education and the Workforce Committee, 2014).

Members of Congress can also use their websites to post their official speeches, which sometimes contain information or positions on regulation or subject areas covered by rulemaking. By doing this, congressional members make their speeches available, and even searchable on the Internet, for a wider audience. The text of the May 2007 floor speech of Senator Lamar Alexander about the unfinished Accreditation and Student Outcomes Rule, in which the senator criticized the Department of Education for the rulemaking and threatened to "offer an amendment to the Higher Education Act to prohibit the Department from issuing any final regulations on these issues until Congress acts," is available on the senator's website (Office of Senator Lamar Alexander, 2007).

Additionally, the White House website contains information about rulemaking and regulations in the form of press releases (see, e.g., White House Office of the Press Secretary, 2015) and blog posts (see, e.g., Muñoz, 2014). Like congressional websites, the White House's postings provide information about higher education rules and rulemaking but do not do so neutrally. Rather, they are written from the perspective of the White House and therefore reflect the administration's viewpoint on the rules. For example, a blog post about the second Gainful Employment Rule framed the rule as one that would "protect students" and help to "improve outcomes for students" in certain career-based training programs (Muñoz, 2014). This description reflects the favorable viewpoint of the Obama administration toward the Gainful Employment Rule. Based on remarks other public officials have made about this and the earlier version of the rule (see, e.g., House Education and the Workforce Committee, 2014; Office of Representative Glenn W. Thompson, 2010), it is fair to say that a different presidential administration may have chosen different language when describing such rules.

The White House's Office of Management and Budget also posts information about rules and rulemaking on several websites, including that of its own Office of Information and Regulatory Affairs (https://www.whitehouse.gov/omb /oira), Reginfo.gov, and Regulations.gov. As discussed in more detail later in this chapter, Regulations.gov in particular allows for enhanced participation in rulemaking by enabling interested parties to submit comments via the web to agencies during the notice-and-comment phase of rulemaking, as well as to review comments posted by others (see Office of Management and Budget, n.d.). The Obama administration also instructed federal agencies to develop plans that would increase the use of communications technologies to bring greater transparency and involvement to agencies' work and regulatory policymaking (Farina et al., 2011).

Interest groups also use their websites to spread information and to raise awareness about important issues that are the subject of higher education regulations. Like public officials, interest groups have posted information, press releases, and position statements about higher education rules and rulemaking on their websites. Also like public officials, these postings are often not politically neutral but tend to reflect the policy preferences and interests of the groups and their memberships. For all kinds of policy actors, having a web presence and making use of it to promote information and ideas about higher education rulemaking and regulatory subject matter is an important method in the current day not only to share information about higher education rulemaking, but also to educate others about the merits of one's position on the rules and to message that position to a potentially large audience.

SOCIAL MEDIA

Some policy actors also use electronic social media to send messages about higher education rulemaking to a wide audience. In particular, the social media site Twitter has been used by actors to express opinions and to provide information about higher education rulemaking. A simple search of Twitter produces numerous tweets from institutions and associations about higher education rulemaking. Institutions and governmental organizations frequently also have accounts on the social media site Facebook, which can likewise be used to transmit information about regulatory policymaking and other matters to a potentially very large audience. Some policy actors also post information and links to websites containing further information about higher education rulemaking and regulations on their Twitter or Facebook timeline, enabling other users who are following the page or are browsing it to view these messages. An interest group may also post instructions to its website readers about how to use social media effectively for the purpose of influencing policy, as the American Association of Community Colleges (2011b) has done.

The use of social media can spread a message to a lot of people very quickly and, if a web link is included, can potentially drive a lot of traffic to a user's website. Some interest groups may find such technology to be as useful or even more useful than e-mail in sending a message. A representative of a student interest group observed, "In terms of at least Twitter, I think Twitter and Facebook yeah, in terms of how many people you have following you or how many people are in that group or how many fans do you have or whatnot . . . putting out that call script or the 'Ask' or the 'Action Alert' or anything for your members to take action on, that definitely has had some impact." Because social media platforms such as these enable users to send messages to large numbers of people in an instant, a more active use of social media to send messages about rulemaking— even if only to provide a link to a webpage containing more information—is an effective way for policy actors to message about the process and about the subject matter under regulation.

Technology and Higher Education Negotiated Rulemaking

Interest groups have also used Internet technology to expand involvement in the higher education negotiated rulemaking process. During negotiated rulemaking, interest group negotiators can communicate in real time via text message and e-mail with their staff and members not present at the negotiating table, and they can incorporate those individuals' thoughts and comments into the negotiations. Thus there can be more direct participation by nonnegotiators in the negotiated rulemaking process than was feasible in the past (researcher's interviews). One interest group representative explained: "One nice thing now is you can send people electronically in minutes and you can get comments back the same day. So it makes for a much more participatory process. Because even those who aren't at the table can know the same day, maybe not the same minute, depending on whether or not somebody is texting, but they can certainly send it that evening saying 'Hey, we're working on this and we need to know what you think about this?' Or 'What would you recommend we do on something?'" Another interest group representative said, "You can sit with your Blackberry and find out anything from anybody and 10 years ago, that was not possible. . . . The ability to get information very quickly from people is just that much greater now than it was let's say 10 years ago in the process."

In addition to interest groups, members of the general public are able to have some additional involvement in higher education negotiated rulemaking, even if indirectly and only in a small way. Private citizens may use e-mail to communicate with interest groups and other parties involved in negotiated rulemaking. A representative of a state agency said that individual citizens "can send [negotiators] emails . . . which we can share with our colleagues on the panel."

However, this study found no evidence that because the public can e-mail their thoughts to a negotiator, the members of the public who do so have any more influence on higher education rulemaking than they would have otherwise. The potential for new perspectives to influence the higher education rulemaking process has increased through more widespread use of communication technologies, but that does not necessarily translate into more influence on the process from those new perspectives.

Technology in the Notice-and-Comment Phase

Internet technology has allowed for broader participation by nongovernmental actors during the notice-and-comment phase as well. Interest groups have posted on their websites suggested language for comments, which are then submitted to the Department of Education during the notice-and-comment period of the rulemaking process. As a result, the department receives a large number of form letters. Another important way in which technology is being used during the notice-and-comment phase is through the Regulations.gov website; interested parties—whether formal organizations or individual members of the public—may use Regulations.gov to submit comments on proposed rules. Many of this study's respondents indicated that Regulations.gov has made commenting on proposed rules much easier. A journalist said of Regulations.gov: "It does make it a lot easier to just shoot over a form letter. If you have to actually mail it in or e-mail it, even just click there and copy your letter in and then hit a button and then there it goes. It makes it easier, probably for interest groups to convince people to send letters because there is so little effort involved." And a representative of for-profit institutions said:

> I think it . . . [Regulations.gov] increased the number of comments that they get. I know we like it because we just submit comments and just hit that button. In the old days we were trying to get the copy in and run across DC to hand it to them by the deadline and hoping we didn't get stuck in traffic. . . . And I think it has also increased the number of general actors who are submitting comments. Now I think it's not just the associations. I think it is more some of the schools will be commenting. Some of the affected parties from students, things like that will comment more now that they can do it online. Because it's also there's a little more level of being anonymous when you do it online than when you actually have to write a letter and send it in. So it's just that degree of separation.

The advent of Regulations.gov coincided with an increase in the average annual number of comments received on higher education NPRMs. A review of the website and interviews with Department of Education personnel indicate that the Department of Education's Office of Postsecondary Education began receiving written comments via Regulations.gov around 2007. The department received a much larger average number of comments per rule in the five years following 2007 than in the five previous years. Leaving aside the two Gainful Employment Rules—each of which received more than 90,000 comments in response to its NPRM (Program Integrity: Gainful Employment, 2011, 2014)—as outliers, the department identified an average of 73.2 commenting parties per rule for which numbers were available from 2002 through 2006, and an average of 440.1 from 2008 through 2012—about six times the average for the five years preceding 2007.[1] This description should be viewed with caution because of the small sample size of rules, because these are descriptive statistics only, and because the analysis does not account for other variables that may have influenced the number of comments submitted. Nonetheless, these figures illustrate that a much larger volume of comments was received by the Department of Education on rule proposals in the few years after the department began accepting comments via Regulations.gov than in the few years immediately before it did so.

Regulations.gov also enables interested parties to view comments that other actors have submitted. Previously, comments were available to view by making a Freedom of Information Act request to the Department of Education, which took some time to fulfill, or by making a trip to the department's offices in Washington, DC. Now, only Internet access is needed to view electronically submitted comments in an instant. A for-profit sector representative said: "I always read through all the comments that are submitted electronically. Way back in 2002, they have to make the comments available for public viewing, and I actually had to go over the department and sit in a room and read the big Xeroxed book of comments."

It is important not to overstate the level of democratic participation in higher education rulemaking over the past several years as a result of Regulations.gov. Respondents were quick to point out that the increase in comments does not necessarily mean that commenters are having a greater influence on rulemaking than they had in the past. If many of the comments are form letters, the increase in the number of comments is not likely to indicate an increase of influence via commenting: several of this study's respondents characterized form letters as not very effective. Also, as one congressional staffer said, electronic commenting may have "increased the amount of comments" but may also have "decreased the effectiveness of it" by requiring Department of Education personnel to sift through large numbers of comments over a relatively short period of time. Other higher education rulemaking insiders shared this sentiment too (researcher's interviews). Indeed, the "Analysis of Comments and Changes" section of the first Gainful Employment Rule indicates that the Department of Education did receive a lot of form letters and that "the vast majority of the comments" received in response to that rule proposal "were similar, largely duplicative, and apparently generated through petition drives and letter-writing campaigns. Generally, these commenters did not provide any specific recommendations beyond general support of or opposition to the proposed regulations" (Program Integrity: Gainful Employment, 2011, p. 34390). Thus, once again, technology has helped nongovernmental policy actors to participate in and to learn about higher education rulemaking in a more efficient manner; however, it has not necessarily made these actors more influential in the process.

Technology and Higher Education Rule Subject Matter

Like the contexts described in chapter 7, the advancement of technology has influenced the subject matter of higher education rules. As technology changed and developed, the content of higher education rules began to reflect those changes, mainly by regulating the use of that technology. Among this study's focal rules, several reflect changes made relating to new technologies (see, e.g., Federal Student Aid Programs, 2002, 2006; Institutional eligibility, 1993; Student Assistance General Provisions . . . Final regulations, 1996a). An important addition to rule subject matter has been the regulation of distance learning programs in higher education. Online learning has become increasingly prevalent in higher education over the past few decades (Harasim, 2000), and some of this study's focal rules reflect how the Department of Education has regulated issues relating to distance education during that period. For example, a 2006 interim final rule redefined "telecommunications course" as "one that uses one or a combination of technologies to deliver instruction to students who are separated from the instructor and to support regular and substantive interaction between these students and the instructor, either synchronously or asynchronously" (Federal Student Aid Programs, 2006, p. 45667).

Another way in which technology has influenced the higher education landscape is through electronic delivery of student financial aid. Just as higher education rule subject matter has reflected changes to technology with regard to postsecondary instruction, the subject matter of regulations has also shifted to reflect technological changes in the federal student financial aid program. One example is a 1996 rule that changed regulations to allow emerging technologies to provide "an integrated student aid delivery system for students and institutions" (Student Assistance General Provisions . . . Final regulations, 1996a, p. 60586).

This study's respondents recognized the manner in which emerging technologies have influenced the subject matter of higher education rules, often through the discussions that occur during negotiated rulemaking. A representative of private, nonprofit institutions said that technology influences higher education subject matter in that it "brings up issues," such as distance learning and electronic funds transfer for student loans, that need regulatory attention from the Department of Education. Some respondents spoke of discussions among negotiators about how student authentication should be handled for distance learning courses. A representative of minority-serving institutions said: "One of the topics we had to discuss in our section was how do we account for a student that is enrolled at a distance? How do I know it's you taking that test when you are in Oklahoma, enrolled at a distance?"

Issues relating to the use of technology in financial aid delivery were also discussed during negotiated rulemaking. A representative of lenders and guaranty agencies reflected: "One of the challenges that was faced in rulemaking was, how do we write the language to pick up the new technology? For example, there's other ways to communicate. You can have electronic transfer of funds. There was a lot of discussion around that, how it should occur, when it should occur. . . . So those issues have now become a part of rulemaking."

Although these issues have arisen during the negotiated rulemaking process, they need not arise only in negotiated rulemaking. The need to update regulations to reflect changing technology is one that is faced throughout the higher education rulemaking process. Speaking of higher education rulemaking generally, a congressional staffer recognized the need for regulations to be up-to-date with modern technologies: "They want to update the regs so that they're current with the times. . . . If there's a more efficient way of doing something, you want to make sure that's allowed under the regs . . . student loan delivery, stuff like that." In short, as new technologies develop, industry makes use of them, policymakers become more aware of them, and the need to regulate their use in higher education arises.

Summary and Conclusion

Advancements in technology, particularly communication technologies such as the Internet, have influenced higher education rulemaking. Government officials, interest groups, and members of the public alike have utilized technology to advocate for their preferred rulemaking outcomes through e-mail, text messaging, their own websites, and governmental web portals such as Regulations .gov. Policy actors have used their websites to broadcast their positions about rulemakings such as those that created the two Gainful Employment Rules and that attempted to create the Accreditation and Student Outcomes Rule. Moreover, interested parties submitted many comments about the proposed Gainful Employment Rules and other proposed rules via the Regulations.gov portal. Developments in technology have also influenced higher education rule content in that regulations have been crafted to account for new technologies used in higher education, including distance learning and the use of electronics in financial aid delivery.

As explained at the outset of this chapter, advanced communication technologies have the potential to expand participation in policymaking processes such as higher education rulemaking (Johnson, 1998; Wheeler, 2006). This study has found evidence that technology provides more avenues for policy actors to participate in higher education rulemaking and makes participation more efficient. The Internet and widespread use of e-mail have made it easier for the Department of Education to provide information about forthcoming rulemaking proceedings as well as NPRMs and final rules, and to communicate with negotiators during negotiated rulemaking. The Internet has also made it easier for interested parties to view rulemaking-related documents. Technology has facilitated communication between interest groups and their constituents and has allowed people who do not participate in negotiated rulemaking to more easily learn what is occurring during negotiating sessions as well as to communicate their perspectives to negotiated rulemaking participants. Moreover, with Internet technology and the Regulations.gov website, interested parties can more easily and more efficiently submit and review comments during the notice-and-comment phase of rulemaking.

In a way, technology has contributed to leveling the playing field for groups that have fewer resources than the large associations. Although there are some costs involved in obtaining access to communications technologies, those costs are not as high as they used to be and the technologies are not out of the reach of many smaller organizations. A representative of a minority-serving institution suggested that advances in technology have provided for greater participation in the higher education rulemaking process on the part of interest groups that were previously too cash strapped to have much effect:

It doesn't cost a whole lot of money in today's society trying to get heard because of technology. I think that technology gives even those institutions with small pocketbooks like you say to get involved by communicating not only [with] the Department of Education on a federal level, but coordinating more to the state level. And then to communicate with legislators and their staff members . . . if you have something to say, I think you can be heard. . . . The blogs are perfect platforms for smaller institutions to get heard. . . . So if you have a small budget and you have something to say, I think if you want to do it, I think you can get your voice heard.

But it is important to recognize that even though technology may have increased efficiency in higher education rulemaking and made participation easier in some respects, there is little evidence that nongovernmental actors are having any more influence over higher education rulemaking as a result of advances in technology. Indeed, as one respondent pointed out, the fact that Department of Education personnel are reviewing so many additional written comments likely means that they have less time to consider any single comment. Moreover, although technology has allowed for indirect participation in negotiated rulemaking by individuals who are not sitting at the negotiating table, it has not necessarily prompted new categories of actors to participate in the process. Also, although technology has made information about rules and rulemaking more readily available, it remains the case that people must first understand what rulemaking is and be motivated to seek out that information. This study has not uncovered evidence that advances in technology have caused people to seek out information about rulemaking when they otherwise would not have, even if it is easier for those looking for information about rulemaking to find it. As has been indicated elsewhere in this book, certain categories of actors—government officials, experts in the regulated subject matter, and well-resourced interest groups—have been particularly powerful in higher education rulemaking. They remain the most powerful players in this process, even though advancements in technology have changed the way they exert their influence and the ability of other types of actors to communicate with them.

There are some additional ways that the Department of Education could use technology to broaden participation in and awareness of higher education rulemaking even further. For example, negotiated rulemaking proceedings could be televised or video streamed on the Internet, providing a much larger audience for these proceedings and contributing further to transparency in the regulatory policymaking process.[2] As technology continues to develop, there will be more new ways that policy actors can employ it to spread information about and promote greater participation in the higher education rulemaking process. Whether and how that will be done remains to be seen, and it is unknown whether such increased participation will lead to influence over higher education rulemaking on the part of any additional parties.

Technology continues to develop rapidly, just as actors continue to search for new ways to effectively influence higher education rulemaking outcomes. What does the future hold for the use of technology in higher education rulemaking? And what are the future prospects for higher education rulemaking more generally? The final chapter explores these matters. It also summarizes this study's conclusions and discusses its implications.

CHAPTER NINE

Conclusion

The Department of Education's Office of Postsecondary Education implements and administers provisions of the Higher Education Act through the creation of regulations. This regulatory policymaking process—higher education rulemaking—has been the subject of much controversy and political attention. It has been both praised and criticized by its participants and observers. At the same time, the process has managed to fly largely "under the radar" of many higher education actors and researchers. Important issues that have emerged in the course of investigating this under-analyzed process include the legal procedure that the process entails, the policy actors who influence the process and the methods they employ to do so, beliefs about higher education rulemaking and how those affect the process and its outcomes, and the influences of contextual factors and technology on higher education rulemaking. Two prominent and in many ways exemplary stories of higher education rulemaking—those of the Gainful Employment Rules and the never-finished Accreditation and Student Outcomes rulemaking—demonstrate the ways in which policy actors, their beliefs and powers, and surrounding political, social, and economic contexts have influenced the higher education rulemaking process and its outcomes.

Because it is a policymaking process that occurs within a department of unelected public officials, and because the process is attracting increasing amounts of attention from policy actors and journalists, higher education rulemaking (and the regulations resulting from it) will warrant continued observation, analysis, and criticism from policy actors, media observers, and researchers. This final chapter summarizes the findings and conclusions of each chapter, discusses the implications of the study for both theory and practice, and assesses some possibilities for the future of the higher education rulemaking process.

Summary of Chapter Findings and Conclusions
Chapter 1: Introduction

The first chapter introduced the higher education rulemaking process, defining it as the process of creating regulations that implement and administer aspects of the Higher Education Act of 1965 and its various amendments and reauthorizations (see also Hillman et al., 2015; Kerwin & Furlong, 2011; Pelesh, 1994). Some of the policies that have resulted from this process over the past several years include the controversial Gainful Employment Rules, which impose greater regulation on institutions providing career-focused education programs, including especially for-profit institutions. The restrictions could put these institutions' eligibility to receive federal student financial aid dollars at risk if certain standards are not met, such as their graduates' ability to meet federal student loan repayment obligations (Field, 2014a; Program Integrity: Gainful Employment, 2011, 2014). The first chapter also described some of the other policies that have resulted from the higher education rulemaking process, including rules that altered certain student aid obligations for some victims of Hurricanes Katrina and Rita and for some 9/11 victims' families (Federal Perkins Loan Program, 2007a; Federal Student Aid Programs, 2006) and a rule that revised regulations regarding accreditation of distance education programs and required higher education institutions to develop plans to assist students should an institution close before the students complete their programs (Institutional eligibility, 2009; see also Council for Higher Education Accreditation, 2009). There are many other subjects of higher education regulations, some of which are highly technical and some of which have the potential to profoundly affect an institution's operations, or even its very existence. Because the statute that authorizes higher education rulemaking is the Higher Education Act, chapter 1 also provided a summary of the main components of the Higher Education Act. Importantly, Title IV of this statute established federal financial aid programs, which have helped untold numbers of students pay for their postsecondary education (Higher Education Act, 2012, §§ 1070–1099c2), and is the subject of numerous higher education rules.

Chapter 2: The Federal Bureaucratic Role

Rulemaking is but one way in which the federal bureaucracy—defined as federal agencies managed by appointed (as opposed to elected) public officials that implement and administer governmental programs (see, e.g., Anderson, 2006; Howlett et al., 2009)—influences higher education policy and practice. There are several theories that purport to explain who has power over bureaucratic policymaking, as well as what occurrences in the contextual environment influence policymaking processes. One perspective, which emphasizes bureaucratic discretion, posits that bureaucracies and individual bureaucrats possess a substantial amount of discretion in how they fulfill their official tasks and thus are able to exert considerable authority in bureaucratic policy and operations (see, e.g., Hill, 1991; Niskanen, 1971; Rourke, 1969; see also Anderson, 2006). Another perspective emphasizes the influence of the political units—that is, the president and Congress—over federal bureaucratic policy, pointing to these branches' ability to construct the procedures that bureaus must follow to create policy and their power over bureaucracies' budgets and personnel as evidence of the political units' power (see, e.g., McCubbins et al., 1987, 1989; Wood & Waterman, 1991; see also Moe, 2012). Yet another theory posits that regulated entities can wield a fair amount of control over their supposed regulating agencies, owing to such factors as bureaucrats' close relationships with regulated parties, the movement of personnel back and forth between bureaus and regulated organizations, and some successful persuasion efforts on the part of regulated industries (see, e.g., Bernstein, 1955; Laffont & Tirole, 1991; Makkai & Braithwaite, 1992; Niles, 2002; Stigler, 1971).

Other theories focus less on which category of actors holds the most influence over bureaucratic policymaking, but instead combine perspectives to examine bureaucratic activities and practices (see, e.g., Bertelli, 2012; Bertelli & Lynn, 2006; Carpenter & Krause, 2014; Yackee, 2003; see also Moe, 2012). Still other theories take a step back and view policymaking (of which bureaucratic policymaking is an important part) as being influenced by factors in the surrounding environment such as economic conditions, who holds political power, the occurrence of a high-profile event, and the beliefs of influential policy actors (see, e.g., Kingdon, 2003; Sabatier & Jenkins-Smith, 1999; Sabatier & Weible, 2007; West & Raso, 2013).

Numerous federal agencies can influence higher education policy and practice. The most obvious is the US Department of Education, which implements the Higher Education Act, administers many higher education federal programs, collects data from colleges and universities, and provides funding for a variety of aspects of higher education. But other federal agencies—including the Department of Labor, the Department of Defense, the National Science Foundation, and others—all influence higher education policy and practice in some way (Cook, 1998; Hillman et al., 2015). The mechanisms of bureaucratic influence include funding decisions, inspections, investigations, adjudication, nonbinding rules and guidance, recognition of organizations (such as accreditors), and rulemaking (see, e.g., Anderson, 2006). Rulemaking may occur in two ways: "formal" rulemaking, which takes a form similar to adjudication, and "informal" rulemaking, the kind of rulemaking that routinely occurs in the US Department of Education to implement and administer provisions of the Higher Education Act (see, e.g., Kerwin & Furlong, 2011; Lubbers, 1998; O'Connell, 2008).

Chapter 3: The Procedural Process

Chapter 3 explained the procedure that the Department of Education follows to carry out higher education rulemaking. This procedure is based on a combination of various statutes and executive orders, including the Administrative Procedure Act, the Congressional Review Act, the Higher Education Act, the Negotiated Rulemaking Act, the Paperwork Reduction Act, and Executive Order 12866, among others (see, e.g., Kerwin & Furlong, 2011). In short, the process proceeds as follows (Kerwin & Furlong, 2011; Lubbers, 1998; O'Connell, 2008, 2011; Pelesh, 1994; Pritzker & Dalton, 1995):[1] The Department of Education decides to initiate a new rulemaking procedure, with authorization, in one form or another, from an authorizing statute. The department then drafts a Notice of Proposed Rulemaking, to be published in the *Federal Register.* Sometimes this is done through a negotiated rulemaking procedure, which involves some potentially affected parties in the drafting of the proposed rule. Negotiated rulemaking is generally preceded by regional meetings across the country of interested parties and Department of Education personnel to discuss the matters that should become the subjects of negotiated rulemaking and the eventual NPRM. If the negotiated rulemaking committee reaches consensus on proposed rule language, that language is typically used in the NPRM. But if no consensus is reached, then the Department of Education drafts the proposed language on its own.

After the NPRM is published in the *Federal Register,* the public may submit comments on the rule proposal for a specified amount of time, and the department considers the comments when drafting the final rule. Throughout the process, and certainly before a rule becomes final, the department keeps the Office of Management and Budget informed of rulemaking activity, and the OMB's Office of Information and Regulatory Affairs reviews all "significant" rules, which include those that would "have an annual effect on the economy of $100 million or more," among others (Executive Order 12866, 1993, p. 51738; see also US General Accounting Office, 2003, p. 23). A final rule, including a summary of the comments received and an explanation of why changes were or were not made in response to them, is then published in the *Federal Register*. The effective date of the regulation is either 30 or 60 days later (the latter time frame applies to "major" rules, to give Congress sufficient time to review and possibly override a rule via legislation).[2]

Chapter 4: Policy Actors' Influence

Chapter 4 described the policy actors who participate in and otherwise influence higher education rulemaking and discussed which actors participate in different stages of the process, as well as which actors are perceived to be particularly influential over higher education rulemaking and its outcomes. This study has found that the types of actors who are involved in the federal higher education rulemaking process, and who exert influence over it, tend to vary by the issue being regulated. More controversial and high-profile rules have seen more involvement and influence from Congress, numerous different interest groups, political appointees within the Department of Education, and the White House (including the OMB) than less prominent rules have. Rules that delve into very technical issues and those with low levels of prominence have seen more involvement and influence from interest groups whose personnel possess specialized knowledge of the topic under consideration as well as from career bureaucrats within the Department of Education.

Moreover, there are actors who have at least some influence over every higher education regulation. Congress creates the laws from which regulations and regulatory policymaking derive (Kerwin & Furlong, 2011). Congress also creates laws that delineate the procedures that agencies must follow when conducting rulemaking (McCubbins et al., 1987, 1989). The president signs such legislation into law and can also issue executive orders that affect rulemaking (Kerwin & Furlong, 2011). The OMB is involved (or at least informed) throughout the rulemaking process. And of course, the Department of Education has involvement in every stage of all federal higher education rulemakings because the department is the agency charged with issuing the rules. Interest groups do not have as much direct influence over higher education rulemaking as government entities, but some kinds of interest groups still have much involvement and influence at various stages of the process. Interest group involvement, in some form or other, appears during every stage of higher education rulemaking.

The influence of students in the higher education rulemaking process presents an interesting situation. Student groups typically lack the experience, expertise, and resources that are present in many of the interest groups that are widely viewed as influential over higher education rulemaking. Yet the Department of Education does take students' viewpoints into account during the rulemaking process, and some respondents in this study perceived student groups as being influential. The level of influence that students have is likely at least in part the result of the structure of the higher education rulemaking process put into place by Congress, which specifically includes students as a category of actor that should be consulted during the rulemaking process (Higher Education Act, 2012; US House of Representatives, 1992, p. 516). Should that structure change, students' influence in this process may change as well.

Chapter 5: Strategies and Powers of Influence

The fifth chapter detailed the strategies and other powers that different policy actors exercise in their attempts to influence the higher education rulemaking process. These strategies can generally be divided into four categories. The first category is official powers of government, which are exercised exclusively by public officials, whether elected or appointed. In this category are the powers to pass legislation (held jointly by Congress and the president); to issue executive orders (held by the president); to oversee rules (held by the OMB, a White House office); and to initiate, organize, and oversee a rulemaking procedure, as well as to draft proposed and final rules (all held by the Department of Education). The second category is participation in various rulemaking procedures; both governmental and nongovernmental entities can do this. Among the strategies are participation in negotiated rulemaking and in the regional meetings that precede them, nominating potential negotiated rulemaking participants, petitioning to commence rulemaking in a particular area, and commenting on proposed rules during the notice-and-comment phase.

The third category of strategies and powers used in higher education rulemaking is informal actions taken during negotiated rulemaking proceedings. These strategies include convening caucuses or subcommittees with other negotiators, avoiding or withholding consensus on proposed rule language, observing negotiated rulemaking, and coalition building with other policy actors who share one's interests in the rulemaking outcome. These strategies may be employed by public officials, interest groups, or members of the public. The fourth and final category of strategies and powers involves the persuasion of actors outside the public participation venues of rulemaking. This may take the form of communicating with the Department of Education, congressional representatives (including lobbying), or other public officials. It can also involve communicating with nongovernment officials, such as interest groups or journalists, in attempts to persuade them or others to support a particular regulatory outcome.

Chapter 6: The Role of Policy Actors' Beliefs

Chapter 6 discussed how actors' beliefs about higher education rulemaking, regulation in general, and regulated subject matters can influence the higher education rulemaking process, including participation in the process and the content of final rules. This study has found that actors' beliefs about rulemaking and regulation may influence their participation in the process, but that does not mean that those who oppose regulation or have negative opinions about the rulemaking process will necessarily avoid participating. Indeed, some actors who hold strong antiregulation beliefs participate in rulemaking for the purpose of influencing the Department of Education to regulate less, or to regulate only to the extent these actors believe that the law allows. Others, who hold beliefs that are more favorable toward regulation and rulemaking, also participate in the process, but some actors who hold such beliefs do not participate. Thus, policy actors' beliefs about regulation and rulemaking do influence their involvement in the higher education rulemaking process, but not necessarily in the manner one might expect.

Moreover, actors' beliefs about the effectiveness of their own participation in higher education rulemaking have influenced their participation in the process, at least in the case of actors interviewed for this study. Respondents who had not participated or had participated only minimally in higher education rulemaking indicated beliefs that their own participation in the higher education rulemaking process would have little to no effect on rulemaking outcomes, or that their actions would be more effective if they lobbied Congress rather than participate in higher education rulemaking. But some actors holding these beliefs have been willing to form coalitions with other actors who they felt would be more likely to influence higher education rulemaking, and therefore these actors have participated in the rulemaking process in an indirect way. Actors' beliefs about regulated subject matters are also influential in that the beliefs of powerful actors have been reflected in the content of higher education rules.

Chapter 7: Higher Education Rulemaking in Context

The seventh chapter examined the ways that higher education rulemaking has varied across different political, social, and economic contexts. One such context is party control of the federal government. Since 1989, more higher education rules were issued during the terms of Democratic presidents than during the terms of their immediate Republican predecessors; and since 1991, a greater volume of higher education rules were issued during united party control under Democrats (i.e., a Democratic president and Congress controlled by Democrats) than under any form of divided or any other form of united government. These figures are descriptive only, and owing to the small sample size and the fact that no statistical controls have been used in this analysis, nothing can be said of the significance of these differences in rulemaking volume, nor can the numbers obtained be generalized to any other populations or time periods. Moreover, upticks in higher education rulemaking also tend to occur in the year or two following a reauthorization of the Higher Education Act; this has happened over the past 25 years either during or just before a Democratic president's term. Thus, the volume of rulemaking activity may have less to do with a president's party affiliation than with the timing of reauthorizations. Still, as some respondents in this study pointed out, one might expect more rulemaking to occur during periods of Democratic control because Democrats often have more favorable views about government regulation than do Republicans.

The subject matter of higher education rules also differs by different party control of the federal government. Among this study's focal rules, those that tended to be more favorable toward for-profit higher education were issued more frequently during Republican presidencies, while those that were more restrictive of for-profit institutions—such as the Gainful Employment Rules—were issued during Democratic presidencies. Actors whose interests are aligned with the ideology of the party in power, or who have personal connections with members of Congress in the majority party, may have more influence over higher education rulemaking as well.

Economic conditions have also factored into higher education rulemaking. Regulatory content may be influenced by economic conditions in that rulemakers are more likely to be budget-conscious when drafting rules during tough economic times. Rules also may reflect authorizing statutes that themselves may have been influenced by economic conditions. Actor participation in rulemaking can also be influenced by economic conditions since participation in rulemaking (and particularly in negotiated rulemaking) can be expensive, and actors with fewer resources may be less likely to participate during a recession. Lower levels of participation can result in a "louder voice" for well-resourced policy actors during economic recessions.

Occurrences of high-profile events have also influenced higher education rulemaking. Some major events that have garnered a substantial amount of attention from the policy world have resulted in the passage of legislation to address an issue relating to the event. High-profile events can also affect final rule content by changing regulators' perspectives about how flexible regulations ought to be under certain circumstances. Such events can also influence actors' power and participation in higher education rulemaking. If a rulemaking procedure relates to the occurrence of a high-profile event, then individuals who were personally affected by the event may possess more power in the process than under ordinary circumstances. Also, there may be an uptick in public participation in rulemaking—such as during regional meetings and the notice-and-comment period—if a rulemaking procedure follows and relates to the occurrence of an event that has captured the public's attention.

Chapter 8: The Use and Influence of Technology

The eighth chapter discussed the influence on higher education rulemaking of recent advancements in technology, which have not only made participation in the process easier in many respects, but have also influenced higher education rule content. Internet technology has made it easier for policy actors to communicate with each other and with public officials about higher education rulemaking in numerous ways. Government officials such as Department of Education representatives and members of Congress have posted information about higher education rules and rulemaking on their websites. Participants in negotiated rulemaking have communicated with actors not present at the negotiating table via text messaging and e-mail, which may in effect allow nonnegotiators to influence the negotiations in a time-efficient manner. Moreover, since about 2007, the Department of Education has accepted online public comments on NPRMs via the Regulations.gov website, and there was a spike in the number of comments received on higher education NPRMs in the five years that followed 2007 as compared to the five previous years. Although nothing can be said about the significance of those differences, and these descriptive statistics did not account for other factors that might have also contributed to the increase, respondents in this study indicated that Regulations.gov has made it much easier for interested parties both to comment on NPRMs and to review the comments that other actors have submitted—something that, earlier, could be done only by making a specific request or visiting the headquarters of the custodians of submitted comments.

Also, much like the surrounding contexts discussed in chapter 7, advanced technologies have influenced higher education rule content. As new technologies emerge and higher education institutions, as well as student loan delivery organizations, find ways to incorporate technology into their operations, the Department of Education has altered rules to reflect and to regulate these new technologies. Regulations of distance learning higher education programs and the use of electronic student financial aid delivery are some examples of the subjects of higher education rules that reflect developments of technology (see Federal Student Aid Programs, 2006; Student Assistance General Provisions . . . Final regulations, 1996a).

Exemplary Higher Education Rulemakings

The higher education rulemaking procedures that are chronicled throughout this book—the Gainful Employment Rules and the unfinished Student Outcomes and Accreditation Rule—are in many ways emblematic of the findings of this study. The first Gainful Employment Rule, which focused largely on the accountability of for-profit institutions, was initiated after a new administration came to power—a Democratic administration following eight years of a Republican presidency. The for-profit sector mobilized to oppose the rule, and in doing so it actively sought information about the rule, participated in negotiated rulemaking, and made its position widely known (Gorski, 2010; Program Integrity Issues, 2010b; researcher's interviews). As a high-profile rulemaking, the first Gainful Employment Rule garnered the attention of members of Congress (Office of Representative Glenn W. Thompson, 2010; Office of Senator Bernie Sanders, 2010; researcher's interviews). A very large number of comments were made in response to the NPRM during the notice-and-comment phase of the rulemaking via the Regulations.gov Internet site, which had been in use by the Office of Postsecondary Education for only a few years at that time. Some policy actors felt that the final Gainful Employment Rule reflected beliefs that the involvement of business interests in higher education should be limited (see, e.g., Nolter, 2012). After the rule became final, it was legally challenged, and part of the rule was ultimately nullified in court (*APSCU v. Duncan*, 2012; Nolter, 2012). Later, the same presidential administration underwent another rulemaking procedure to develop the second Gainful Employment Rule (Program Integrity: Gainful Employment, 2014), which faced its own court challenge (Devaney, 2014).[3]

The Accreditation and Student Outcomes rulemaking resulted in significant part from the findings of the Department of Education's Commission on the Future of Higher Education. It sought to connect higher education student outcomes to institutional accreditation, as well as to establish certain data-gathering requirements (Lederman, 2007a; Lowry, 2009). But policy actors who opposed this type of regulation or believed that the Department of Education was overstepping its authority vocalized their opposition both quickly and emphatically. Members of Congress who disagreed with what the department wanted to do through this rulemaking took steps via their legislative powers and ability to speak from the floor of Congress to prevent the department from regulating in this manner (Lederman, 2007b; Lowry, 2009; Office of Senator Lamar Alexander, 2007). Regional meetings were held and a negotiated rulemaking committee was convened to discuss a proposed rule, but ultimately, the Department of Education chose not to issue an NPRM at that time (Lowry, 2009; US Department of Education, 2007d).

These cases demonstrate how policy actors, their beliefs, and surrounding contexts can influence the initiation of rulemaking, the behavior of actors in the higher education rulemaking process, and the ultimate outcome of the rulemaking procedure, whether it be the particular content of the final regulations or if a regulation gets issued at all. But these rulemakings also underscore another important point: that the outcomes of the higher education rulemaking process can have enormous stakes for postsecondary students as well as institutions. The Gainful Employment Rules and the unfinished Accreditation and Student Outcomes Rule sought to help students by improving educational quality and enhancing the value of a degree through different types of accountability incentives for institutions. Meeting these new standards is crucial to some institutions' financial well-being because their eligibility to receive Title IV federal student financial aid funds would hang in the balance. Ineligibility for Title IV participation has been associated with lower student enrollments for some institutions (Darolia, 2013), so this is a legitimate concern. As this book demonstrates, when the stakes are high, powerful policy actors will participate actively in the higher education rulemaking process and employ numerous different strategies to influence it.

Implications of This Study

This study has important implications. In the case of theory, there are implications for the literatures both of higher education policy and of bureaucratic policymaking. The findings of the study also provide some lessons for rulemaking practice.

Implications for Theory

This book has provided a detailed, empirically based account of the federal rulemaking process for higher education from start to finish. It is a process that has been under-analyzed in the research literature. The findings of this study portray not only the various stages of the higher education rulemaking process and the actors who participate in each, but also the strategies and other powers employed in the process, the manner in which actors' beliefs influence their involvement in the process, and the relationships between higher education rulemaking and certain surrounding political, economic, and social contexts.

This study also adds to existing rulemaking literature by applying theories of power and policymaking that other authors have not applied to rulemaking processes. These findings accord with the argument of the Advocacy Coalition Framework that beliefs motivate policy actors in the policymaking process, that beliefs are reflected in final regulatory policies, and that contexts such as presidential administration, economic conditions, and the occurrence of high-profile events can affect the nature of regulatory policymaking, which actors participate in rulemaking, and the strategies they use to influence rulemaking (see Sabatier & Jenkins-Smith, 1999; Sabatier & Weible, 2007).

Similarly, this research confirms Kingdon's theory that alterations in context—such as leadership change or the occurrence of a high-profile event—can prompt the consideration of new policies (Kingdon, 2003; Zahariadis, 2007). Kingdon (2003) contends that such contextual shifts can induce the opening of "policy windows," defined as "short periods" during which "opportunities for action on given initiatives" become available (p. 166). Although Kingdon's theory applied specifically to the setting of policy agendas, the present study shows that shifts in context can result in the adoption of new types of regulatory policies at the implementation level as well. Specifically, many of the "policy windows" of which Kingdon writes in the agenda-setting context have also been associated with differences in the nature of higher education rulemaking (including the volume and content of higher education rules), the actors involved in higher education rulemaking, and the strategies actors use in their attempts to influence the process.

This study's findings also support aspects of the conceptions of power discussed by Lukes (2005) and Gaventa (1980) by demonstrating that some individuals avoid participation in higher education rulemaking because they believe themselves powerless to influence rulemaking outcomes. Some of these actors join coalitions with other actors who they believe would be more effective at influencing rulemaking, and therefore do not opt out of the process entirely. However, these individuals have avoided participating in those aspects of the higher education rulemaking process in which they believe their own participation would not be effective at influencing the content of final rules.

This study also supplements the theoretical literature by demonstrating that no one category of policy actor consistently dominates the higher education rulemaking process. Bureaucratic discretion theory is accurate under some circumstances, usually for rulemakings that are low-profile and generally noncontroversial. But given the influence that Congress and the president have over the higher education rulemaking process, political control theories are at least as accurate and in some cases perhaps more applicable. This would be particularly true for rules that are high-profile and contentious. Moreover, there appears to be some degree of agency capture in that powerful interest groups have been successful, to a certain extent, in seeing their preferred policies come to fruition though higher education rulemaking, or at least in seeing policies adopted that are less detrimental than they potentially could have been. Specialized interest groups can be influential in the creation of highly technical rules. However, regulated groups are not always successful in getting their policy preferences adopted through higher education rulemaking. In sum, neither bureaucratic discretion theory, theories of political control, nor agency capture theory is completely accurate or completely inaccurate in all cases of federal higher education rulemaking. Instead, certain aspects of each of these theories may apply, depending on the levels of prominence and technicality of the rule being created.

Implications for Practice

This research also has several implications for practice. For policymakers and other rulemaking participants, the knowledge gained from this study's detailed, evidence-based description of the actors, strategies, beliefs, and contexts that influence higher education rulemaking can play an important role in the political branches' oversight of higher education rulemaking, as well as in the Department of Education's self-assessment as to how its regulatory policymaking process is proceeding. For interest groups and others seeking to influence rulemaking outcomes, the results of this research may aid in the development of new strategies and planning for future rulemaking and other policymaking participation (Matthews, 2012). This volume has described, in detail, the strategies used to influence the higher education rulemaking process, as well as the manner in which actors' beliefs motivate their participation in higher education rulemaking. It has also explained how higher education rules and rulemaking differ under different contextual circumstances. Actors seeking to influence higher education rulemaking may find these facts and explanations useful in deciding which strategies to employ and in motivating interest group members and other policy allies to act in the higher education rulemaking process.

This study also has practical implications for the higher education institutions and other stakeholders in higher education rulemaking outcomes who have thus far remained largely "on the sidelines" in this process. By bringing the details of the higher education rulemaking process to light, as well as by noting its importance to higher education practice and to such vital matters as the details of student financial aid programs, the analysis presented here can raise awareness about this policymaking process. Also, by providing a detailed description of the stages of the process and the strategies and powers that have been used in the past to influence it, this research can provide ideas for how to get started participating in higher education rulemaking to stakeholders who have participated in the process very little, if at all, in the past.

Finally, this study has practical implications for all of the higher education policy community—policymakers and nongovernmental stakeholders alike—in that it can provide insights into rulemaking patterns and practices that may be useful in preparing for a forthcoming Higher Education Act reauthorization, which is due to occur in the near future, and for the rulemaking that is sure to result from it (Matthews, 2012).

Future Prospects for Higher Education Rulemaking

What does the future hold for higher education rulemaking? As this study has made clear, the answer to that question is highly dependent on the answers to other questions relating to the surrounding context of rulemaking. Who will future presidents be, and what will be their viewpoints on rulemaking, regulation, and the substance of higher education policy? Will the federal government be controlled by Democrats or Republicans, or will there be mixed party control at the federal level? Will economic conditions allow for much rulemaking activity, including participation in expensive rulemaking processes by organizations and individuals that have few resources? Will high-profile events affect the higher education community, and will those events have ripple effects that influence rulemaking outcomes? How will technology continue to evolve, and how will those changes infiltrate higher education and financial aid delivery, as well as the ease of participation in policymaking processes? To the extent that these questions are not yet answerable, the future of higher education rulemaking remains somewhat unclear. However, there are several things that can be said about the future of higher education rulemaking based upon the findings of this study.

The Future of the Executive Branch and Higher Education Rulemaking

Under a president who holds an antiregulation ideology, or who doesn't believe that the federal government should have an active role in regulating higher education, there would likely be little use of the higher education rulemaking process to create new regulations; rulemaking would probably be used to ease existing regulations on higher education and related sectors. During the term of a president who is more open to using the Department of Education's bureaucratic authority to create and implement policy relating to higher education, there would likely be more higher education rulemaking activity, particularly if the president is working with a Congress controlled by a different political party. (It is worth noting that, toward the end of the final terms of both George W. Bush's and Barack Obama's presidencies, there was an uptick in higher education rulemaking volume while each president dealt with a Congress controlled by a political party different from his own [see chapter 7]).

As this study has also shown, rule subject matter has differed by party control of the federal government in the past. Through the powers to shape the federal higher education policy agenda and to appoint high-level political leadership to the Department of Education, a president can be influential over the subject matter of higher education rulemaking. There is likely to be vastly different regulatory content depending on whether a president holds, for example, a laissez-faire view toward the higher education marketplace as opposed to a view that regulating student loan markets would provide a societal good. A president who strongly supports career-related education may advocate for higher education rules that promote the interests of such programs and the institutions that provide them. A president who would like to rein in college costs may promote the use of the rulemaking process to issue regulations tying college costs to institutional eligibility for federal financial aid programs. Indeed, by linking financial aid eligibility to a higher education policy agenda item, a presidential administration (through its appointees to the Department of Education) can attempt to use rulemaking to regulate a wide range of higher education issues. Of course, as this study has also shown, employing the higher education rulemaking process frequently, or even infrequently but to regulate new areas of higher education policy that have not previously been the subject of rulemaking, will meet opposition from those who believe the department is overstepping its authority, or whose interests would be adversely affected by the rule. Individuals and groups opposed to such rulemaking may voice their opposition during regional meetings and negotiated rulemaking, submit critical comments during the notice-and-comment phase, attempt to pull together coalitions to oppose the rulemaking, make statements to the press or to public officials (including Department of Education officials) in opposition to the rulemaking, lobby congressional representatives to oppose the rule, and even file a lawsuit challenging the final rule's legality.

Future Legislation and Higher Education Rulemaking

Because an authorizing statute is critically important to rulemaking and influences the volume and content of regulations, the next reauthorization of the Higher Education Act will have a profound influence on higher education rulemaking. Last reauthorized in 2008, the act was due for another reauthorization after 2013 (Camera, 2015), but as of this writing, no new reauthorization has occurred. However, the Senate's Health, Education, Labor, and Pensions (HELP) committee has convened "working groups" and held hearings with regard to reauthorization, and interest groups have made public statements about what topics they believe should be included in the legislation (Camera, 2015; see also "Broad Coalition's Goals," 2015). The specific provisions of the new reauthorization, which remain to be seen, will have substantial implications for higher education rulemaking. The reauthorization is expected to cover student aid and debt repayment reform, issues related to teacher preparation programs, information provision to students and prospective students, and TRIO program restructuring. The chair of the HELP committee, Senator Lamar Alexander, has hinted that deregulation may be part of the reauthorization, saying that "weeding the garden" in the form of "eliminating unnecessary red tape" will be prioritized, as will "saving students money, and removing obstacles to innovation" (Camera, 2015).

Even beyond the next reauthorization, amendments to the Higher Education Act can take place at any time, and these may trigger new rulemaking as well. Thus, the composition of Congress and whether Congress and the White House are controlled by the same political party—and which political party that is, since ideology toward rulemaking and higher education policy both play crucial roles in the volume and content of regulations—will be important determinants of the future of higher education rulemaking.

Looking at the regulatory landscape more broadly, there are indications that rulemaking reform may be coming soon via congressional legislation. The Senate Judiciary Committee recently held a hearing to investigate the possibility of regulatory reform, at the beginning of which the chair, Senator Chuck Grassley

(Republican from Iowa), expressed concerns about administrative overreach and a perceived low impact of comments from the public (Grassley, 2015). If Grassley's sentiments are representative of a general mood in Congress—which would not be unexpected, given Republican control of the institution—then legislation to reform and streamline rulemaking procedures may be on the horizon.

Technology and the Future of Higher Education Rulemaking

Chapter 8 described ways that advancements in technology have influenced the higher education rulemaking process. As new technologies continue to develop, and as higher education institutions and student aid providers continue to find new ways to incorporate technology into their everyday operations, the Department of Education will need to adjust regulations to account for these changes in technology, as it has done in the past. Moreover, although the Department of Education has used technology to spread information about rules and rulemaking and to communicate more efficiently with rulemaking participants, there are still ways that technology can be used to enhance rulemaking participation even further. One such way is for the department to make greater use of electronic social media to confer with stakeholders about proposed regulations. For example, a group of scholars at Cornell University has partnered with some federal agencies to develop the Regulation Room website, which promotes increased participation in rulemaking and enhanced dialogue between stakeholders and regulating agencies through electronic social networking and moderated online conversations (Cornell University, n.d.; Farina et al., 2011). The Department of Education could employ similar social networking technologies to enhance participation and discussion in the higher education rulemaking process.

Another technology that could be used to spread more awareness and perhaps increase participation in higher education rulemaking is podcasting. A podcast functions like an online radio program, permitting subscribers and other interested parties to hear "digitally recorded audio shows" via the Internet, a smart phone, or a similar device (Flanagan & Calandra, 2005, p. 20). One may download a podcast as soon as it is posted or may do so sometime in the future, as long as the podcast remains available online. Subscribers may also have podcasts "automatically downloaded" onto their electronic devices (p. 20). Federal agencies such as the Government Accountability Office have produced podcasts that discuss important information about matters under their purview, and access to those podcasts is provided freely on the Internet (see, e.g., US Government Accountability Office, n.d.). Podcasting technology has existed for some time now, but this technology is not currently being used by the Office of Postsecondary Education in connection with higher education rulemaking. It could be used to improve public knowledge about the rulemaking process.

Another technology that has existed for a while but has not yet been used in higher education rulemaking is television or video streaming via the Internet. Although open to the public, such rulemaking practices as regional hearings and negotiated rulemaking are not yet televised or video streamed, even though verbatim transcripts of regional hearings and notes regarding negotiated rulemaking are routinely made available via the Department of Education's website. The department could increase access to and public involvement in higher education rulemaking by employing this technology in the future.

This book has provided an extensive and evidence-based account of the federal higher education rulemaking process, including an analysis of the policy and higher education actors who influence the process, the strategies and powers they employ to do so, and the ways in which actors' beliefs and various surrounding contexts—such as party control of government, economic conditions, high-profile events, and advances in technology—have influenced both the process and the substantive rules that result from it. Higher education rulemaking, like most federal agency rulemaking, is paradoxical in that it remains a subject of great controversy, while at the same time being a mysterious or hidden process from the perspective of many who are likely to be affected by its outcomes (see, e.g., Farina et al., 2011; Mettler, 2014). As time has progressed, the higher education rulemaking process has gained increased attention from stakeholders and the media, and it is likely to be the subject of continued observation, scrutiny, and critique in the future.

But amid the often tumultuous politics that surround policymaking, it may be easy to lose sight of the ultimate goal of the federal programs regulated by higher education rulemaking: to assist individuals with financing a postsecondary education that will ultimately prove to be valuable and worth each student's investment. Hopefully, the results of this research will be used by policy actors to continue to promote financial access to quality higher education for students in need.

This appendix explains the research methodology that was used to conduct this research. It lists the research questions and describes the study design, the data sources, and the data analysis techniques. It also contains a table listing all of the focal higher education rules and rulemaking procedures that were analyzed in the study.

Research Questions

This study examined three research questions, each of which contained subquestions that, together, were designed to answer each of the broader research questions. Following are the research questions and subquestions.

1. How are different types of policy actors involved and influential in the rulemaking process for regulations affecting federal higher education policy? Specifically,
   a. What categories of actors (including public officials as well as potential stakeholders in the outcomes of rulemaking) are directly or indirectly involved—and which categories of actors are noticeably not involved—at each stage of the rulemaking process for federal higher education policy? For example, which actors are more or less involved in the decision to commence a rulemaking, the decision as to what language will be included in the proposed and final rules, and other key decision points in the process?
   b. What strategies or tactics do policy actors use to influence rulemaking for federal higher education policy?
   c. What policy actors are perceived by participants and observers of federal higher education rulemaking to have the most influence over the rulemaking process? Why?
   d. What policy actors, if any, are consistently benefited by federal higher education final rules?
2. How, if at all, do policy actors' beliefs about rulemaking and the subject matters of rules relate to their involvement in the rulemaking process for federal higher education policy and to higher education rule content? Specifically,
   a. How, if at all, do policy actors' beliefs about government regulation or about rulemaking as a process relate to actors' involvement in the higher education rulemaking process? How, if at all, do such beliefs relate to the formation of

coalitions among various actors? For example, if actors hold antiregulation beliefs, how do such beliefs relate to the actors' involvement in the higher education rulemaking process or actors' coalition formation?

b. How, if at all, do policy actors' beliefs about the effectiveness of their participation in rulemaking relate to actors' involvement in the higher education rulemaking process? How, if at all, do such beliefs relate to the formation of coalitions among various actors?

c. How, if at all, do policy actors' beliefs about the subject matters of specific rules relate to the content of higher education regulations? How, if at all, do such beliefs relate to the formation of coalitions among various actors?

3. How, if at all, are various political, economic, and social contexts related to the nature of federal higher education rulemaking, to the actors that participate in federal higher education rulemaking, and to the strategies or tactics that actors employ to influence federal higher education rulemaking? Specifically,

a. How, if at all, does party control of the federal government (that is, of the presidency and Congress) relate to the nature of federal higher education rulemaking, to the actors that participate in federal higher education rulemaking, and to the strategies or tactics that actors employ to influence federal rulemaking for higher education? What are the reasons for such a relationship or nonrelationship?

b. How, if at all, do national economic conditions relate to the nature of federal higher education rulemaking, to the actors that participate in federal higher education rulemaking, and to the strategies or tactics that actors employ to influence federal rulemaking for higher education? What are the reasons for such a relationship or nonrelationship?

c. How, if at all, do high-profile events affecting higher education relate to the nature of federal higher education rulemaking, to the actors that participate in federal higher education rulemaking, and to the strategies or tactics that actors employ to influence federal rulemaking for higher education? What are the reasons for such a relationship or nonrelationship?

d. How, if at all, have developments in technology (such as the formal introduction of Internet technology into rulemaking) relate to the nature of federal higher education rulemaking, to the actors that participate in federal higher education rulemaking, and to the strategies or tactics that actors employ to influence federal rulemaking for higher education? What are the reasons for such a relationship or nonrelationship?

Study Design

This study employed a case study methodology. More specifically, it conducted a particular form of case study known as the "embedded case study" (Scholz & Tietje, 2002; Yin, 2003, p. 43; see also Merriam, 1998). An embedded case study analyzes "more than one unit of analysis" (Yin, 2003, p. 42; see also Merriam, 1998; Scholz & Tietje, 2002). According to Scholz and Tietje, "In an embedded case study, the starting and ending points are the comprehension of the case as a whole in its real-world context. However, in the course of analysis, the case will be faceted either by different perspectives of inquiry or by several subunits" (p. 2).

This study examined multiple cases embedded within a broader, overall case. As rulemaking takes place in numerous federal agencies, governs many different policy areas, and implements a variety of large pieces of legislation, the overall case that is analyzed in this embedded case study is the higher education rulemaking process, as a "case" of rulemaking at the federal level. The higher education rulemaking process is defined, for purposes of this study, as the process of creating regulations under the Higher Education Act and its amendments. Because the higher education rulemaking process is the overall case for this analysis, data were sought that would be relevant to the process in its entirety over time.

Embedded within this larger unit of analysis are several cases of individual higher education rules, for which additional, specific data were also sought. Individual federal higher education rules were studied in two different manners. First, a purposefully sampled (Maxwell, 2005) subset of 32 focal rulemaking procedures issued since 1991 was selected for a more detailed focus, and documents related to these rulemaking procedures and the rules that resulted from them were analyzed qualitatively. These rules were sampled with an eye toward obtaining diversity on the following three criteria: (1) time period during which the rule was published in the *Federal Register* (to examine rules that occurred across different time periods and different surrounding contexts), (2) their subject matters (to investigate whether policy actors' influence varies by rule subject matter), and (3) levels of prominence (to ensure adequate representation in this analysis of both more and less prominent rules). Table A.1 lists this study's 32 focal rules and provides the date of issuance, the *Federal Register* citation, and a brief description of each rule. Some of the rules are described in further detail in chapter 1. Three of these 32 focal rulemaking procedures—the 2011 Gainful Employment Rule, the unfinished Accreditation and Student Outcomes Rule, and the Distance Education and Teach-Out Plans Rule—were purposefully selected using the latter two sampling criteria described above for even further in-depth analysis, to gain detailed insights about actors' involvement in the higher education rulemaking process (the findings of which are discussed in chapter 4).

Second, the universe of federal higher education final rules from 1989 through 2015 was identified by the researcher and coded for certain characteristics about the rulemaking. The date each of these rules was published in the *Federal Register* was recorded, as was information about who was president and which political party controlled Congress at the time of issuance. In most cases, information about how many official comments were received regarding the rule's Notice of Proposed Rulemaking (according to the final rule's text), rule subject matter, and information about whether the rule was issued during an economic recession were also recorded. Counts of rules that were issued during different contextual eras (such as different periods of party control of government) were examined to identify patterns of rulemaking activity using descriptive statistics and qualitative analysis (these findings are discussed in chapter 7).

Data Sources and Data Collection

A valuable quality of case study research is that such studies tend to extract data from various different sources (Creswell, 2007; Yin, 2003). This is beneficial because gathering data from a variety of sources—a procedure known as "data triangulation"

TABLE A.1
This study's focal rules

Date rule issued	*Federal Register* citation	Brief description
August 14, 1991	56 Fed. Reg. 40442	Minority Teacher Training Project
June 25, 1992	57 Fed. Reg. 28568	Pell Grant regulations
March 10, 1993	58 Fed. Reg. 13336	Regulates administrative proceedings
June 8, 1993	58 Fed. Reg. 32188	Comprehensive regulation, including certain eligibility provisions
August 11, 1993	58 Fed. Reg. 42665	Regulates Byrd Scholarship
November 5, 1993	58 Fed. Reg. 59144	Regulates Talent Search
April 29, 1994	59 Fed. Reg. 22250	Regulates accreditors
April 29, 1994	59 Fed. Reg. 22348	Regulates lending issues
November 29, 1995	60 Fed. Reg. 61424	Requires reports on men's/women's athletics
December 1, 1995	60 Fed. Reg. 61760	Rule aimed at reducing student loan default
December 1, 1995	60 Fed. Reg. 61830	Regulates student financial aid eligibility
November 27, 1996	61 Fed. Reg. 60478	Regulation of lending industry
November 29, 1996	61 Fed. Reg. 60578	Regulates student loan administration
August 6, 1999	64 Fed. Reg. 42837	Administers Teacher Quality Enhancement Grants (TQEG)
October 25, 1999	64 Fed. Reg. 57528	Regulates student loans of Peace Corps workers
April 11, 2000	65 Fed. Reg. 19606	Regulates TQEG
June 26, 2001	66 Fed. Reg. 34038	Regulates Federal Work Study / other programs
November 1, 2002	67 Fed. Reg. 67048	States "safe harbors" for incentive pay
March 21, 2005	70 Fed. Reg. 13371	Regulates TQEG
August 9, 2006	71 Fed. Reg. 45666	Loan reform for victims of major hurricanes
September 22, 2006	71 Fed. Reg. 55447	Regulates Upward Bound
November 1, 2006	71 Fed. Reg. 64402	Regulates ACG / National SMART Grants
September 28, 2007	72 Fed. Reg. 55049	Loan reform for certain 9/11 families
November 1, 2007	72 Fed. Reg. 61960	Comprehensive student loan rule requiring student counseling
November 1, 2007	72 Fed. Reg. 62014	Regulates loans in nontraditional programs
October 23, 2008	73 Fed. Reg. 63232	Loan regulation
October 27, 2009	74 Fed. Reg. 55414	Distance education and teach-out plans
December 11, 2009	74 Fed. Reg. 65764	International consortia
October 29, 2010	75 Fed. Reg. 66832	Financial aid program integrity regulation
June 13, 2011	76 Fed. Reg. 34386	First Gainful Employment Rule
October 31, 2014	79 Fed. Reg. 64890	Second Gainful Employment Rule
N/A (unfinished)	N/A (unfinished)	Sought to tie student outcomes to accreditation

(Yin, 2003, pp. 98–99)—enhances the validity of a study's findings (Maxwell, 2005; Merriam, 1998; Miles & Huberman, 1994; Scholz & Tietje, 2002; see also Malterud, 2001). Data analyzed in this study derived from the following sources: (1) in-depth, semistructured interviews with various categories of policy and higher education actors, (2) archival rulemaking data including the texts of final and proposed rules, negotiated rulemaking materials (where applicable and available), and the texts of written comments submitted on proposed rules (where applicable and available), (3) news articles regarding higher education rulemaking, and (4) websites relating to higher education rulemaking of relevant government offices as well as higher education and lending industry interest groups. Each of these data sources is described in detail below.

Data Source 1: Interviews

In-depth, semistructured interviews were conducted with 55 individuals who participated in, otherwise possess insider knowledge about, or have been noticeably absent from the higher education rulemaking process despite having a stake in the outcome of rulemaking. Interviewees included US Department of Education officials, congressional staff, higher education association representatives, personnel at higher education institutions, members of other interest groups, and journalists. Some interviewees were personally involved with one or more of the focal subset of final higher education rulemakings selected for more detailed analysis. Some interviewees were not involved in any of the focal rulemakings but nonetheless provided important information relating to the overall case of higher education rulemaking.

Table A.2 illustrates the professional positions relevant to the higher education rulemaking process held by this study's respondents. Because some respondents have held multiple relevant positions and were therefore able to speak about rulemaking from a variety of perspectives, all relevant positions held by all respondents are reflected in table A.2. Thus, both current and former positions of respondents are listed, and table A.2 reflects 79 positions held by 55 respondents.

A "purposeful sampling" (Maxwell, 2005, p. 88; see also Creswell, 2007; Merriam, 1998) procedure was employed to select interviewees, in three parts. First, "key informant sampl[ing]" (Marshall, 1996b, p. 523) was conducted, through which interviewees were sampled based on their experience with and knowledge of the rulemaking process and/or federal higher education policy (see, e.g., Heckathorn, 1997; Marshall, 1996a, 1996b; Richards & Morse, 2007 regarding this type of sampling). These individuals were identified through an analysis of relevant, publicly available documents and websites. Additional interviewees were identified by gathering a "snowball sample," another purposeful sampling method (Marshall, 1996b, p. 523; see also Creswell, 2007; Heckathorn, 1997; Merriam, 1998; Richards & Morse, 2007). Such sampling involves locating "cases of interest from people who know people who know what cases are information-rich" (Creswell, 2007, p. 127). Finally, a "theoretical sampling" (Strauss & Corbin, 1998, p. 78) strategy was also employed. This technique involves identifying theoretical concepts within collected data and sampling additional participants based on whether they are likely to supplement, substantiate, or invalidate these concepts (see, e.g., Corbin & Strauss, 2008; Creswell, 2007; Marshall, 1996b; Merriam, 1998; Richards & Morse, 2007).

Data Source 2: Archival Rulemaking Documents

The second data source was archival rulemaking documents, meaning the texts of proposed and final federal higher education rules as published in the *Federal Register*, a sample of public comments submitted on proposed rules (where applicable and

TABLE A.2
Current and former positions held by interview respondents of this study (n = 55)

Position	Number of interview respondents who have held this position
US Department of Education Office of Postsecondary Education staff	7
Other US Department of Education staff	5
Congressional staff	6
Office of Management and Budget staff	1
Other federal staff	2
State-level government agency	3
Private nonprofit higher education institution / association representing same	5
Public four-year higher education institution / association representing same	7
Public two-year higher education institution / association representing same	4
For-profit higher education institution / association representing same	5
Minority-serving higher education institution / association representing same	4
Professional school / association representing same	2
Other higher education association	3
Association representing college administrators	4
Accreditor / association representing same	3
Association representing higher education students	4
Legal aid organization / consumer advocacy group	2
Lending organization / guaranty agency / association representing same	6
Negotiation expert	3
Financial analyst	1
Journalist	2

available),[1] and negotiated rulemaking materials (where applicable and available). Negotiated rulemaking materials include records of negotiated rulemaking sessions, transcripts of testimony at relevant regional meetings, texts and marked-up texts of potential proposed rule language, and lists of participants in negotiated rulemaking and regional meetings. Legislative histories of the Higher Education Act reauthorizations in 1992, 1998, and 2008 were also analyzed.

The texts of proposed and final rules were obtained from the *Federal Register* via the Lexis-Nexis Academic and HeinOnline databases. Archived negotiated rulemaking records as far back as the year 1999 were available on and downloaded from the US Department of Education's website. Public comments for rules whose NPRMs were issued since 2007 were available on the Regulations.gov website. I also obtained public comments for two earlier focal rules during a visit to the Office of Postsecondary Education's Washington, DC, office. Even though public comments were not available

1. Where more than 50 public comments on a given focal rulemaking were available for review, I selected a random sample of 50 comments to analyze. Where 50 comments or fewer on a given rulemaking were available for review, I analyzed all of that rulemaking's available public comments.

for all of the focal rules, this did not pose a major threat to the integrity of this data source. In the "Analysis of Comments" sections of final rules, the Department of Education provides summaries of the main points of comments received and then responds to them. Thus, much of the data that would have been obtained from a review of those comments was ascertained by analyzing the "Analysis of Comments" sections of the focal rules.

Data Source 3: News Articles

A qualitative analysis of news reports of federal higher education rulemaking activities provided insight into the politics of the process, specifically with regard to the actors involved, the strategies used, the beliefs expressed, and the contexts that surround higher education rulemaking. There were a total of 1,057 news articles between 1991 and 2010 returned at the time I conducted a search in a Lexis-Nexis Academic "US Newspapers and Wires" database for the following terms: higher education and (rulemaking or rule making) and department of education.

Broken down by time periods during which notably different types of contexts were affecting higher education, the total number of news articles on the date of my search was as follows:

1991–1994: 36
1995–2000: 115
2001–2006: 212
2007–2010: 694

Using a random number generator, I selected a random sample of 10% of news articles within each of the three time periods from 1995 to 2010 and 20% of news articles within the 1991–1994 time period. The 1991–1994 time period was oversampled because a relative few news articles containing these keywords were published during that time period, and oversampling would allow an analysis of more than just four news articles (which is all that would have been reviewed from that time period otherwise). To assure that my study would account for the most up-to-date news regarding federal higher education rulemaking, I also included a random sample of 10% of news articles published in 2011, even though 2011 was not included as a year in my study for purposes of selecting focal rules.

Using this search strategy, many news articles were collected that were not relevant to the purposes of this study (e.g., articles describing state-level education departments' rulemaking or articles that simply provided a synopsis of Department of Education *Federal Register* entries). Such articles were not coded, and a new random number generator search was conducted to find suitable replacement articles.

Data Source 4: Websites of Relevant Organizations

The fourth and final data source was Internet pages of organizations that are or could be involved in federal higher education rulemaking. Internet pages of relevant organizations often contain statements about higher education rulemaking that range from informational (for example, stating the dates of upcoming negotiated rulemaking sessions) to promotional (such as a statement applauding the Department of Education for issuing a particular rule or arguing for or against a proposed rule).

A total of 143 websites were reviewed, including websites for governmental entities, higher education interest groups and associations, and student lending industry organizations. These organizations were identified by a review of certain publications and websites reflecting the actors involved in higher education policy activity. Specifically, I reviewed the websites of many of the policy actors identified in Cook's (1998) analysis, many of the organizations listed in some of those actors' websites, some of the higher education associations listed on the then-existing website of the National Teaching and Learning Forum, and, to ensure that the lending community was well represented in this sample, many of the organizations that appeared in the member directory of the National Council of Higher Education Resources (n.d.) during the period of this study's data collection.

Data Analysis

Interview transcripts, archival rulemaking data, news articles, and websites were analyzed and coded using the "constant comparative method" (Glaser & Strauss, 1967, p. 105; see also Corbin & Strauss, 2008; Strauss & Corbin, 1998, regarding this technique). This method is commonly used in grounded theory research (Corbin & Strauss, 2008; Glaser & Strauss, 1967; Strauss & Corbin, 1998), but it has been used in the data analysis phase of some qualitative case studies as well (see, e.g., Goodman, 1985; Hamill, 1995; see also Eisenhardt, 1989). The constant comparative method involves analyzing data as it is in the process of being collected (as opposed to waiting until after data retrieval has concluded to begin analysis) and comparing incoming pieces of data with those already collected (Boeije, 2002; Corbin & Strauss, 2008; Creswell, 2007; Glaser & Strauss, 1967; Strauss & Corbin, 1998). Using this method, I reviewed new data while recalling points and patterns that had emerged in prior data.

A coding scheme was developed based on a combination of identification codes, codes derived from the literature, and "open coding," which refers to the discovery of "salient categories of information" within the data set (Creswell, 2007, p. 160). I constructed an outline of the coding scheme based on concepts derived from the theoretical literature. The initial coding scheme also included identification codes for the interviewee's or commenter's professional positions (for interview and comment data), the type of document being analyzed (for documentary data), and references to focal rulemakings. I then employed an open coding exercise in which I reviewed two early interview transcripts and one archival rulemaking document. A colleague knowledgeable about higher education policy and qualitative research also reviewed these same items as part of an interrater reliability exercise, during which multiple individuals review and code the same data to determine the extent to which consensus is reached on what codes should be used (Armstrong et al., 1997). My colleague and I saw many of the same codes emerging from the data. Where we saw different codes, we discussed our reasoning for identifying these codes, and I determined whether to include those codes based on our discussion. In most cases, those codes were also added to the coding scheme.

After the initial coding scheme was developed, the same colleague and I separately reviewed four additional interview transcripts and two additional archival rulemaking documents, using the initial coding scheme to code these data. We identified similar codes for many of the items in these documents, and for the remaining items, we discussed why we chose to code in a different manner. Based on this discussion, I determined ultimately how to code the items. I took notes during these discussions, and I considered and employed the coding reasoning discussed with my colleague as I coded the remaining data. The coding scheme was enhanced again with new, emergent open codes following this review as well.

The final coding scheme was entered into qualitative data analysis software, which I used to code interview, archival document, and news article data. Because of the ever-changing nature of website data, websites were not entered into the software's database. Instead, I reviewed the 143 identified Internet sites online, took detailed notes regarding their content, and then analyzed those notes.

Based on this study's research questions, I developed analytic tables to organize coded data and to assist with identifying patterns emerging from the various data sources (Miles & Huberman, 1994). The purpose of the analytic tables was to identify points and concepts emerging from the data that might help to answer the research questions, to compile a list of data sources that corroborated similar points and concepts, and to illustrate those points and concepts through quotations extracted from the data sources. After I finished coding data in the electronic database, I used the software to run queries identifying data that were coded in particular ways (for example, data that were coded for identifying influential actors, or data that were coded as reflecting certain beliefs). I then reviewed the query reports, identified points and concepts relevant to each research question, and included those points and concepts in the relevant analytic tables. I followed each point or concept with the interviews' or documents' identifying codes and, where the data presented descriptive quotations, I included the quotations in endnotes linked to the data source's identifying code. After I had run all coding queries and completed all of the analytic tables, I reviewed each table for the emergence of patterns of data that address each research question.

Chapter 1 · Introduction

1. Throughout this book, this agency is variably referred to as the "US Department of Education" or the "Department of Education."

2. Other authors have similarly categorized rules. Lubbers (1998) describes "Substantive rules," "Interpretative rules," and "General statements of policy" (p. 58). Anderson (2006) identifies "Substantive rules," "Interpretive rules," and "Procedural rules" (p. 223).

3. Throughout this book, references to data obtained by me in the course of conducting this research are made to "researcher's data set." When the data are specifically drawn from interviews, the citations specify "researcher's interviews."

4. An example of a federally funded merit-based scholarship is the (currently unfunded) Robert C. Byrd Honors Scholarship program (Higher Education Act, 2012, §§1070d-31–1070d-41), through which the federal government sets general parameters for the scholarship and provides funding for state agencies, which in turn award the scholarships to students "who have demonstrated outstanding academic achievement and who show promise of continued academic achievement" (§ 1070d-33[a]).

5. Title IX of the Higher Education Act is different from the more widely known Title IX of the Education Amendments of 1972, which addresses discrimination on the basis of sex at postsecondary institutions (Gladieux & Wolanin, 1976).

6. Although described in shorthand as a "rule" in this book, the Student Outcomes and Accreditation Rule was never finalized (Lowry, 2009). The reasons for this are explained later in this chapter, as well as in chapter 4.

7. The notice-and-comment stage, as well as the other stages of higher education rulemaking, are described in detail in chapter 3.

8. Among these 32 rules, 3 were selected for even more in-depth analysis to examine research questions relating to policy actor influence in the higher education rulemaking process (see Natow, 2015).

Chapter 2 · The Federal Bureaucratic Role

1. The other categories in Lowi's (1972) typology are "distributive policy," "redistributive policy," and "constituent policy" (p. 300; see also Smith & Larimer, 2013, p. 35).

2. A bureaucrat's history of employment in industry and/or desire to become employed by industry has been labeled "the revolving door" (Johnson, 1983; Makkai &

Braithwaite, 1992). Although a relationship between "the revolving door" and bureaucracy capture by industry has been empirically documented, this relationship has been characterized as only "modest" (Makkai & Braithwaite, 1992, p. 68). Nonetheless, the US government places some constraints on government personnel's employment in industry shortly after ending their government employment (US Office of Government Ethics, 2007).

3. See also Lindblom & Woodhouse (1993) regarding the influence of business organizations in policymaking.

4. An organizational chart depicting these and other offices within the US Department of Education appears in the US Department of Education website at www2 .ed.gov/about/offices/or/index.html.

5. Indeed, some have made the point that "valid interpretative rules are binding to the extent that they 'merely interpret' already existing legal duties," but the binding nature of such interpretive rules arises from the binding laws they purport to interpret (Gersen, 2007, p. 7).

6. One way adjudications and formal rulemakings differ is that, in some instances, the evidence may be submitted in writing in formal rulemaking; there is less leeway for allowing this in adjudications (Administrative Procedure Act, 2012, § 554(d); Lubbers, 1998).

Chapter 3 · The Procedural Process

1. This procedure is described at various points in numerous sources (Higher Education Act, 2012; Higher Education Opportunity Act, 2008; Kerwin & Furlong, 2011; Lubbers, 1998; Negotiated Rulemaking Act, 2012; 1998 Amendments, 1998; Pelesh, 1994; Pritzker & Dalton, 1995; and descriptions provided by some of the respondents interviewed for this study).

2. Negotiated rulemaking "consensus" has also been described as "the absence of dissent by any member" (Pelesh, 1994, p. 156) and as the "unanimous concurrence among the interests represented unless the committee agrees on a different definition" (Lubbers, 1998, p. 130). The Negotiated Rulemaking Act (2012) similarly defines "consensus" as "unanimous concurrence among the interests represented on a negotiated rulemaking committee," but the act also allows individual negotiating committees to redefine consensus as they see fit (§ 562[2]).

3. This finding is based on statements made by this study's interviewees, as well as a review of some written comments submitted to the Department of Education during the notice-and-comment phase for numerous higher education rules.

4. Further discussions of exceptions to the notice-and-comment practice appear in Kerwin and Furlong (2011) and Lubbers (1998).

5. Litigation as a strategy to influence higher education rulemaking is addressed in more detail in chapter 5.

6. The role that various political contexts, including the prevailing presidential administration, have played in higher education rulemaking is discussed in detail in chapter 7.

Chapter 4 · *Policy Actors' Influence*

1. As explained in chapter 3, a "significant" rule is one that could impose "an annual effect on the economy of $100 million or more or adversely affect" economic conditions "in a material way . . . , create a serious inconsistency . . . with an action taken or planned by another agency . . . , materially alter the budgetary impact of entitlements, grants, user fees, or loan programs . . . , or . . . raise novel legal or policy issues" (Executive Order No. 12866, 1993, p. 51738).

2. Both of these rules are described in further detail in chapter 1.

3. "Meaningful influence" in this context refers to a contribution to the higher education rulemaking process in such a way that the entity's policy objectives are at least partially achieved through regulation or lack thereof.

4. Indeed, West and Raso (2013) argue that OMB review has been "the most significant extension of presidential influence over the administrative process in recent decades" and that it has permitted the White House "to identify, modify, and occasionally block initiatives that are inconsistent with the priorities of the White House and its key constituents" (p. 501).

5. This rule is described more fully in chapter 1.

6. Washington-based higher education associations are sometimes collectively referred to as "One Dupont Circle," because that has been the address of several such associations (Cook, 1998; Gladieux & Wolanin, 1976; Natow, 2015; Parsons, 1997).

7. These findings are consistent with Wagner et al.'s (2011) observation that "information costs that are high in rulemakings . . . can also work as a barrier to diverse participation by all affected parties and allow the more informed and better resourced to effectively dominate the proceedings" (p. 117).

8. The viewpoint that students provide "moral persuasion" to the rulemaking negotiations, combined with the Higher Education Act's provisions requiring public input and recommending student involvement in regional meetings and negotiated rulemaking, may indicate a favorable "social construction" of college students as a "target group" of higher education rulemaking (Ingram, Schneider, & deLeon, 2007, p. 97; see also Schneider & Ingram, 1993).

9. It is worth noting that the ability of an interest group to provide technical expertise is itself a valuable resource, and one that may be disproportionately available to organizations that already possess a great deal of financial and other assets (Wagner et al., 2011).

Chapter 5 · *Strategies and Powers of Influence*

1. Although it is possible that other petitions have been submitted to commence a higher education rulemaking, this study has identified one such instance: in 2006 an organization representing higher education student interests submitted a petition that sought student loan reform to make college loans less burdensome for debtors (Huntley, 2006).

2. Indeed, the fact that negotiated rulemaking took place with respect to these and other higher education regulations indicates not only that interest group representatives made use of the strategy of participating in negotiated rulemaking, but also that the Department of Education employed its official rulemaking powers in these rulemakings

as well. From a broader perspective, the official lawmaking powers of Congress and the president can also be observed here, albeit indirectly, because the Higher Education Act was the authorizing statute for these rules, and the rulemaking procedure that includes negotiated rulemaking was created through legislation and executive orders.

3. These are just two of several examples of higher education interest groups posting information about higher education rules and rulemaking procedures on their websites (researcher's data set).

4. As explained more fully in chapter 2, the Advocacy Coalition Framework examines the role of beliefs and values in the policymaking process (Sabatier & Jenkins-Smith, 1999; Sabatier & Weible, 2007).

Chapter 6 · The Role of Policy Actors' Beliefs

1. See chapter 1 for a detailed description of these rules.

2. Other higher education actors interviewed for this study expressed that they do not hold antiregulation beliefs but nonetheless have not been involved (or at least not actively involved) in higher education rulemaking (researcher's interviews).

3. Because it was easier to identify and to obtain interviews from rulemaking participants than nonparticipants, I interviewed many more individuals who have participated in higher education rulemaking than individuals who have not. Therefore, there was a much smaller number of respondents who could personally speak about beliefs related to not participating in higher education rulemaking. The beliefs of the few respondents who have not participated in the higher education rulemaking process are nonetheless interesting.

4. In addition to displaying a particular view, the incentive compensation rules also represent some actors' best interests. Higher education institutions—most notably but not limited to those in the for-profit sector—were able to look upon the safe harbors as legitimate ways to compensate or to reward admissions personnel without risking a lawsuit (Epstein, 2009). As this example illustrates, higher education rules reflect interests as well as beliefs.

Chapter 7 · Higher Education Rulemaking in Context

1. Several scholars have applied the Advocacy Coalition Framework in conjunction with Kingdon's agenda-setting theory to analyze and explain policymaking (see, e.g., Dougherty et al., 2013; Dougherty, Nienhusser, & Vega, 2010; Mintrom & Vergari, 1996).

2. This study defines a "higher education rule" as one issued by the US Department of Education through its authority to implement provisions of the Higher Education Act and its various amendments and reauthorizations.

3. This study's data set included final priorities but did not include rules that merely made corrections or clarifications to existing rules.

4. Kingdon (2003) has identified contexts such as the passage of legislation, economic factors, and the broader ideological climate as influential over policy agenda setting. Thus, it would not be surprising if such factors influenced a policy phenomenon such as higher education rulemaking activity as well.

5. This rule was issued based on the authority of the 1992 Higher Education Act reauthorization (Kantrowitz, 2010), which was enacted by a Democratically controlled Congress and signed by a Republican president.

6. Although this rule was issued during a period of mixed-party control of Congress, it is worth noting that the Democrats held only the slimmest majority in the US Senate during this time because a former Republican had changed his affiliation to Independent (but caucused with Democrats), giving Democrats an advantage of one senator (US Senate, n.d.). The House of Representatives was controlled by Republicans at that time (US House of Representatives, n.d.), and the Democrats lost control of the Senate a short time later (US Senate, n.d.).

7. More recently, still during a Democratic administration but during a period of Republican control of Congress, the Department of Education indicated it would relax certain incentive compensation regulations. This illustrates the importance of another branch of government—the judiciary—because this announcement was made in reaction to a court decision (Stratford, 2015).

Chapter 8 · The Use and Influence of Technology

1. These averages were determined based on the number of commenting parties that were identified by the Department of Education in the "Analysis of Comments and Changes" section in final higher education regulations.

2. Concepts such as these are explained more fully in a discussion of future prospects for higher education rulemaking in chapter 9.

Chapter 9 · Conclusion

1. The brief description of the higher education rulemaking procedure that appears in this subsection is supported by the sources identified in this parenthesis and by the statutes and the executive order listed in the preceding text sentence. This procedure was confirmed by the research interviews conducted for this study.

2. But higher education rulemaking does not always follow such a neat and linear process. Sometimes rules are withdrawn or halted before becoming final (as was the case during the Accreditation and Student Outcomes rulemaking), and sometimes negotiated rulemaking and/or the notice-and-comment period is waived (Kerwin & Furlong, 2011; Lowry, 2009; Lubbers, 1998; O'Connell, 2008, 2011).

3. Mettler (2014) also describes some of these policy actors, strategies, and political contexts that influenced the unfolding of the Gainful Employment Rule.

Academic Competitiveness Grant Program and National Science and Mathematics Access to Retain Talent Grant Program: Final regulations, 72 Fed. Reg. 61248 (2007) (to be codified at 34 C.F.R. pt. 691).

Adams, C. J. (2011, June 15). "Gainful employment" rules leave many disappointed. *Education Week, 30*(35), 20.

Administrative Procedure Act, 5 U.S.C. §§ 500 et seq. (2012).

Ali, R. (2011, April 4). *Dear colleague letter.* Washington, DC: US Department of Education, Office for Civil Rights.

American-Arab Anti-Discrimination Committee et al. (2011, January 26). *GE regulation letter to Pres Obama January-26-2011.* Retrieved from http://images2.americanprogress .org/campus/GE_Regulation_Letter_To_Pres_Obama_January-26-2011.pdf.

American Association of Colleges & Universities. (2007, May 16). *AAC&U board alerts members about proposed accreditation changes.* Retrieved from http://archive.aacu.org /About/statements/accreditation5_16_07.cfm.

American Association of Colleges of Nursing. (2011, July). DoEd rules concerning state authorization voided. *AACN Policy Beat, 3*(7), 1. Retrieved from www.aacn.nche.edu /government-affairs/Policy_Beat_11July.pdf.

American Association of Community Colleges. (2011a). *Op-ed guidelines and sample text.* Retrieved from www.aacc.nche.edu/Advocacy/toolkit/Documents/2011_AACC_op -ed_FINAL.pdf.

American Association of Community Colleges. (2011b). *Social media how-to guide.* Retrieved from www.aacc.nche.edu/Advocacy/toolkit/Documents/2011_AACC-Social -Media_Guide_Fin.pdf.

American Council on Education. (2011). *New U.S. Department of Education regulations for gainful employment programs.* Retrieved from www.acenet.edu/news-room/Documents /Final-Gainful-Employment-Regulations.pdf.

American Council on Education. (2014). *Summary of 2014 gainful employment regulation proposed by the U.S. Department of Education.* https://www.acenet.edu/news-room /Documents/Gainful-Employment-2014-Proposed-Rule-Summary.pdf.

Anderson, J. E. (2006). *Public policymaking* (6th ed.). Boston, MA: Houghton Mifflin.

Ansell, B. W. (2010). *From the ballot to the blackboard: The redistributive political economy of education.* New York: Cambridge University Press.

APSCU (Association of Private Sector Colleges and Universities) v. Duncan. Memorandum Opinion. Civil Action 11-1314 (RC) (D.D.C. 2012).

APSCU (Association of Private Sector Colleges and Universities) v. Duncan. Opinion. Civil Action 14-277 (RMC) (D.D.C. 2014).

Armstrong, D., Gosling, A., Weinman, J., & Marteau, T. (1997). The place of inter-rater reliability in qualitative research: An empirical study. *Sociology, 31*(3), 597–606.

Association of American Universities. (2011, January). *University research: The role of federal Funding*. Retrieved from https://www.aau.edu/WorkArea/DownloadAsset.aspx ?id=11588.

Association of Teacher Educators. (n.d.). *Higher education task force on teacher preparation formed*. Retrieved from www.ate1.org/pubs/Higher_Education_T.cfm.

Balla, S. J., & Daniels, B. M. (2007). Information technology and public commenting on agency regulations. *Regulation & Governance, 1*(1), 46–67.

Basken, P. (2007, September 28). A year later, Spellings Report still makes ripples. *The Chronicle of Higher Education, 54*(5), A1.

Bernstein, M. H. (1955). *Regulating business by independent commission*. Princeton, NJ: Princeton University Press.

Bertelli, A. M. (2012). *The political economy of public sector governance*. New York: Cambridge University Press.

Bertelli, A. M., & Lynn, L. E. (2006). *Madison's managers: Public administration and the Constitution*. Baltimore: Johns Hopkins University Press.

Best, S. J., & Krueger, B. S. (2005). Analyzing the representativeness of Internet political participation. *Political Behavior, 27*(2), 183–216.

Boeije, H. (2002). A purposeful approach to the constant comparative method in the analysis of qualitative interviews. *Quality & Quantity, 36*(4), 391–409.

Borrego, A. M. (2001a, January 29). Computer Learning Centers files for bankruptcy. *The Chronicle of Higher Education* [online].

Borrego, A. M. (2001b, February 16). How a computer-training chain crashed in plain sight. *The Chronicle of Higher Education* [online].

Broad coalition's goals for the Higher Education Act. (2015, November 4). *Inside Higher Education*. Retrieved from https://www.insidehighered.com/quicktakes/2015/11/04 /broad-coalitions-goals-higher-education-act.

Brown, S. K. (1994, January 7). Proposed federal rules alarm colleges, "an extraordinary example of bureaucracy run amok." *St. Louis Post-Dispatch*, p. 1A. Retrieved from Lexis-Nexis Academic.

Bryner, G. C. (1987). *Bureaucratic discretion: Law and policy in federal regulatory agencies*. New York: Pergamon Press.

Burd, S. (2014, June 10). Despite previous failures in court, APSCU takes aim at incentive compensation rule again. *New America Ed Central*. Retrieved from www.edcentral .org/despite-previous-failures-court-apscu-takes-aim-incentive-compensation-rule/.

Camera, L. (2015, May 27). Higher Education Act reauthorization: What you need to know. *Education Week*. Retrieved from http://blogs.edweek.org/edweek/campaign-k -12/2015/05/higher_education_act_reauthori.html.

Carpenter, G., & Krause, G. A. (2014). Transactional authority and bureaucratic politics. *Journal of Public Administration Research & Theory, 25*, 5–25.

Clewell, B. C., Darke, K., Davis-Googe, T., Forcier, L., & Manes, S. (2000, September). *Literature on teacher recruitment programs* (Report No. DOE-2000-06). Washington, DC: US Department of Education.

Coglianese, C. (1997). Assessing consensus: The promise and performance of negotiated rulemaking. *Duke Law Journal, 46*(6), 1255–1349.

Coglianese, C. (2004). E-Rulemaking: Information technology and the regulatory process. *Administrative Law Review, 56*(2), 353–402.

Coglianese, C. (2006). Citizen participation in rulemaking: Past, present, and future. *Duke Law Journal, 55,* 943–968.

Congressional Review Act, 5 U.S.C. §§ 801 et seq. (2012).

Cook, C. E. (1998). *Lobbying for higher education: How colleges and universities influence federal policy.* Nashville, TN: Vanderbilt University Press.

Corbin, J., & Strauss, A. (2008). *Basics of qualitative research 3e: Techniques and procedures for developing grounded theory.* Los Angeles: Sage.

Cornell University. (n.d.). *History—Regulation Room.* Retrieved from http://regulationroom .org/about/history.

Council for Higher Education Accreditation. (2009, November 12). *Federal update: Final regulations implementing accreditation provisions in the Higher Education Opportunity Act of 2008 (HEOA).* Retrieved from www.chea.org/pdf/Fed%20Update_Chart_11.09.pdf.

Council for Higher Education Accreditation. (2011, September 28). CHEA urges repeal of credit hour and state authorization regulations. *Federal Update, 18.* Retrieved from www.chea.org/Government/FedUpdate/CHEA_FU18.html.

Council of the Inspectors General on Integrity and Efficiency. (2014, July 14). *The inspectors general.* Retrieved from https://www.ignet.gov/sites/default/files/files/IG_Authorities _Paper_-_Final_6-11-14.pdf.

Creswell, J. W. (2007). *Qualitative inquiry & research design: Choosing among five approaches* (2nd ed.). Thousand Oaks, CA: Sage.

Darolia, R. (2013). Integrity versus access? The effect of federal financial aid availability on postsecondary enrollment. *Journal of Public Economics, 106,* 101–114.

Devaney, T. (2014, November 6). Colleges sue feds over "gainful employment" rule. *The Hill Newspaper.* Retrieved from http://thehill.com/regulation/court-battles/223218 -private-schools-challenge-unlawful-college-rules-in-court.

Dougherty, K. J., Natow, R. S., Bork, R. H., Jones, S. M., & Vega, B. E. (2013). Accounting for higher education accountability: Political origins of state performance funding for higher education. *Teachers College Record, 115*(1). Retrieved from www.tcrecord.org (ID Number 16741).

Dougherty, K. J., Nienhusser, H. K., & Vega, B. E. (2010). Undocumented immigrants and state higher education policy: The politics of in-state tuition eligibility in Texas and Arizona. *The Review of Higher Education, 34*(1), 123–173.

Dundon, M. (2015). Students or consumers? For-profit colleges and the practical and theoretical role of consumer protection. *Harvard Law & Policy Review, 9,* 375–401.

Durant, R. F. (2015). Whither power in public administration? Attainment, dissipation, and loss. *Public Administration Review, 75*(2), 206–218.

Dynarski, S. (2015, September 29). No, student borrowers don't need to worry about loan market turmoil. *The New York Times.* Retrieved from www.nytimes.com/2015/09/30

/upshot/no-student-borrowers-dont-need-to-worry-about-loan-market-turmoil.html?
_r=0.

Eisenhardt, K. M. (1989). Building theories from case study research. *The Academy of Management Review, 14*(4), 532–550.

Ensuring Continued Access to Student Loans Act, Pub. L. No. 110-227, 122 Stat. 740 (2008).

Epstein, J. (2009, December 11). Unity on "incentive compensation." *Inside Higher Education*. Retrieved from www.insidehighered.com/news/2009/12/11/compensation.

Epstein, J. (2010, June 16). Partial "program integrity." *Inside Higher Education*. Retrieved from https://www.insidehighered.com/news/2010/06/16/regs.

Epstein, D., & O'Halloran, S. (1996). Divided government and the design of administrative procedures: A formal model and empirical test. *The Journal of Politics, 58*(2), 373–397.

Executive Order No. 12291, Title 3 C.F.R. 127 (1981 comp.).

Executive Order No. 12866, Title 3 C.F.R. 638 (1993 comp.).

Executive Order No. 13497, Title 3 C.F.R. 218 (2009 comp.).

Fain, P. (2014, October 30). Gainful employment arrives. *Inside Higher Education*. Retrieved from https://www.insidehighered.com/news/2014/10/30/final-gainful-employment-rules-drop-loan-default-rate.

Farina, C. R., Miller, P., Newhart, M. J., Cardie, C., & Cosley, D. (2011). Rulemaking in 140 characters or less: Social networking and public participation in rulemaking. *Social Networking & the Law, 31*(1), 382–463.

Feal, R. G. (2016, January 9). *Item no. 8(b): Report of the executive director*. Retrieved from https://www.mla.org/content/download/39395/1741149/rpt-execdir-J16.pdf.

Federal Family Education Loan Program, due diligence requirements: Final regulations, 61 Fed. Reg. 60478 (1996) (to be codified at 34 C.F.R. pt. 682).

Federal Perkins Loan Program, Federal Family Education Loan Program, and William D. Ford Federal Direct Loan Program: Final regulations, 72 Fed. Reg. 55049 (2007a) (to be codified at 34 CFR Parts 674, 682 and 685).

Federal Perkins Loan Program, Federal Family Education Loan Program, and William D. Ford Federal Direct Loan Program: Final regulations, 72 Fed. Reg. 61960 (2007b) (to be codified at 34 C.F.R. pts. 674, 682 and 685).

Federal Perkins Loan Program, Federal Family Education Loan Program, and William D. Ford Federal Direct Loan Program: Notice of proposed rulemaking, 72 Fed. Reg. 32410 (2007c).

Federal Perkins Loan Program, Federal Family Education Loan Program, and William D. Ford Federal Direct Loan Program: Notice of proposed rulemaking, 73 Fed. Reg. 37694 (2008).

Federal Perkins Loan Program and Federal Family Education Loan Program: Final regulations, 64 Fed. Reg. 57528 (1999) (to be codified at 34 C.F.R. pts. 674 and 682).

Federal Perkins Loan Program and Federal Family Education Loan Program: Notice of proposed rulemaking, 63 Fed. Reg. 49798 (1998).

Federal Student Aid Programs: Final regulations, 67 Fed. Reg. 67048 (2002) (to be codified at 34 C.F.R. pts. 600, 668, 673, 674, 675, 682, 685, 690, and 694).

Federal Student Aid Programs: Interim final regulations, request for comments, 71 Fed. Reg. 45666 (2006) (to be codified at 34 C.F.R. pts. 600, 668, 673, 674, 675, 676, 682 and 685).

Fernández, S. A. (1994). Convergence in environmental policy? The resilience of national institutional designs in Spain and Germany. *Journal of Public Policy, 14*(1), 39–56.

Field, K. (2007, April 27). Negotiations over rules for 2 federal grant programs break down. *The Chronicle of Higher Education, 53*(34), A42. Retrieved from www.chronicle.com.

Field, K. (2009, April 20). Shireman is named deputy under secretary of education. *The Chronicle of Higher Education.* Retrieved from http://chronicle.com/article/Shireman-Is- Named-Deputy-Under/42772.

Field, K. (2014a, November 6). For-profit colleges sue again over federal gainful-employment rule. *The Chronicle of Higher Education.* Retrieved from http://chronicle.com/article/For-Profit-Colleges-Sue-Again/149871/.

Field, K. (2014b). Obama proposes incentives for student success. *The Chronicle of Higher Education.* Retrieved from http://chronicle.com/article/Obama-Proposes-Incentives-for/145121/.

Final guidance on maintaining, collecting, and reporting racial and ethnic data to the U.S. Department of Education: Final guidance, 72 Fed. Reg. 59266 (2007).

Flanagan, B., & Calandra, B. (2005). Podcasting in the classroom. *Learning & Leading with Technology, 33*(3), 20–23.

Freeman, J. L., & Stevens, J. P. (1987). A theoretical and conceptual reexamination of subsystem politics. *Public Policy & Administration, 2*(1), 9–24.

Furlong, S. R. (1998). Political influence on the bureaucracy: The bureaucracy speaks. *Journal of Public Administration Research & Theory, 8*(1), 39–65.

Furlong, S. R., & Kerwin, C. M. (2005). Interest group participation in rule making: A decade of change. *Journal of Public Administration Research and Theory, 15*(3), 353–370.

Gainful Employment Negotiated Rulemaking Committee. (2013, August 2). Retrieved from https://www2.ed.gov/policy/highered/reg/hearulemaking/2012/ge-negotiators2013.pdf.

Gaventa, J. (1980). *Power and powerlessness: Quiescence and rebellion in an Appalachian valley.* Urbana: University of Illinois Press.

Gersen, J. (2007). Legislative rules revisited. *University of Chicago Public Law & Legal Theory Working Paper* (No. 168). Retrieved from http://chicagounbound.uchicago.edu/cgi/viewcontent.cgi?article=1180&context=public_law_and_legal_theory.

Gilmour, J. B., & Lewis, D. E. (2006). Political appointees and the competence of federal program management. *American Politics Research, 34*(1), 22–50.

Gladieux, L. E., & Wolanin, T. R. (1976). *Congress and the colleges: The national politics of higher education.* Lexington, MA: Lexington Books.

Glaser, B. G., & Strauss, A. L. (1967). *The discovery of grounded theory: Strategies for qualitative research.* Chicago: Aldine.

Golden, M. M. (1998). Interest groups in the rule-making process: Who participates? Whose voices get heard? *Journal of Public Administration Research and Theory, 8*(2), 245–270.

Goodman, J. (1985). What students learn from early field experiences: A case study and critical analysis. *Journal of Teacher Education, 36*(6), 42–48.

Gorski, E. (2010, September 24). Govt. delays rule opposed by for-profit colleges. *Associated Press Online.* Retrieved from Lexis-Nexis Academic.

Grassley, C. (2015, June 11). *Grassley statement at judiciary hearing on examining the federal regulatory system.* Retrieved from Lexis-Nexis Academic.

Guthrie, J. W., & Springer, M. G. (2004). A *Nation at Risk* revisited: Did "wrong" reasoning result in "right" results? At what cost? *Peabody Journal of Education, 79*(1), 7–35.

Halstead, T. J. (2008). Presidential signing statements: Executive aggrandizement, judicial ambivalence and congressional vituperation. *Government Information Quarterly, 25,* 563–591.

Hamill, C. (1995). The phenomenon of stress as perceived by Project 2000 student nurses: A case study. *Journal of Advanced Nursing, 21*(3), 528–536.

Hannah, S. B. (1996). The Higher Education Act of 1992: Skills, constraints, and the politics of higher education. *The Journal of Higher Education, 67*(5), 498–527.

Harasim, L. (2000). Shift happens: Online education as a new paradigm in learning. *Internet & Higher Education, 3*(1–2), 41–61.

Harper, S. R., Patton, L. D., & Wooden, O. S. (2009). Access and equity for African American students in higher education: A critical race historical analysis of policy efforts. *Journal of Higher Education, 80*(4), 389–414.

Harter, P. J. (1982). Negotiating regulations: A cure for malaise. *Georgetown Law Journal, 71*(1), 1–118.

Hayden, F. G. (2002). Policymaking network of the iron-triangle subgovernment for licensing hazardous waste facilities. *CBA Faculty Publications,* paper 8. Retrieved from http://digitalcommons.unl.edu/cgi/viewcontent.cgi?article=1007&context=cbafacpub.

Heckathorn, D. D. (1997). Respondent-driven sampling: A new approach to the study of hidden populations. *Social Problems, 44*(2), 174–199.

Henderson, C. (1995). Undergraduate certificate programs of less than two years: 1991–92. *Research Briefs, 6*(1). Washington, DC: American Council on Education, Division of Policy Analysis & Research. Retrieved from ERIC database. (ED381202).

Higher Education Act, 20 U.S.C. §§ 1001 et seq. (2012).

Higher Education Opportunity Act of 2008, Pub. L. No. 110-315, 122 Stat. 3078 (2008).

Higher Education Task Force on Teacher Preparation. (2012, June). *Federal teacher preparation issues and concerns.* Retrieved from www.aau.edu/WorkArea/DownloadAsset .aspx?id=13454.

Hill, L. B. (1991). Who governs the American administrative state? A bureaucratic-centered image of governance. *Journal of Public Administration Research and Theory, 1*(3), 261–294.

Hillman, N. W., Tandberg, D. A., & Sponsler, B. A. (2015). Public policies for higher education: Strategies for framing a research agenda. *ASHE Higher Education Report, 41*(2), 1–98.

Horn, L., & Li, X. (2009, November). *Stats in brief: Changes in postsecondary awards below the Bachelor's degree: 1997 to 2007* (NCES 2010-167). Washington, DC: US Department of Education. Retrieved from http://nces.ed.gov/pubs2010/2010167.pdf.

House Education and the Workforce Committee. (2014, March 14). Members denounce new gainful employment regulation. Retrieved from http://edworkforce.house.gov /news/documentsingle.aspx?DocumentID=372950.

Howlett, M., Ramesh, M., & Perl, A. (2009). *Studying public policy: Policy cycles and policy subsystems* (3rd ed.). Don Mills, ON: Oxford University Press.

Huber, J. D., Shipan, C. R., & Pfahler, M. (2001). Legislatures and statutory control of bureaucracy. *American Journal of Political Science, 45*(2), 330–345.

Huntley, H. (2006, June 8). Program seeks debt relief for college grads. *St. Petersburg Times*, p. 2D. Retrieved from Lexis-Nexis Academic.

iLibrary—Dear colleague letters. (n.d.). Retrieved from https://ifap.ed.gov/ifap/byYear .jsp?type=dpcletters.

Ingram, H., Schneider, A. L., & deLeon, P. (2007). Social construction and policy design. In P. A. Sabatier (Ed.), *Theories of the policy process* (pp. 93–126). Boulder, CO: Westview Press.

Institutional eligibility under the Higher Education Act of 1965, as amended, and the secretary's recognition of accrediting agencies: Final rule, 74 Fed. Reg. 55414 (2009) (to be codified at 34 C.F.R. pts. 600 and 602).

Institutional eligibility under the Higher Education Act of 1965, as amended, Student Assistance General Provisions: Final regulations, 58 Fed. Reg. 13336 (1993) (to be codified at 34 C.F.R. pts. 600 and 668).

Jacobe, D. (2004, November 22). Bush's re-election: Good for the investment climate? *Gallup News Service*. Retrieved from www.gallup.com/poll/14110/Bushs-ReElection -Good-Investment-Climate.aspx.

Jaschik, S. (2015, January 2). Big union win. *Inside Higher Education*. Retrieved from https://www.insidehighered.com/news/2015/01/02/nlrb-ruling-shifts-legal-ground -faculty-unions-private-colleges.

Johnson, E. E. V. (1983). Agency "capture": The "revolving door" between regulated industries and their regulating agencies. *University of Richmond Law Review, 18*(1), 95–119.

Johnson, S. M. (1998). The Internet changes everything: Revolutionizing public participation and access to government information through the Internet. *Administrative Law Review, 50*(2), 277–337.

Jordi, B. (2015, October 2). Digitizing the *Federal Register* [Web log post]. Retrieved from https://www.federalregister.gov/blog/2015/10/digitizing-the-federal-register.

Kantrowitz, M. (2010, April 26). Elimination of the safe harbors for incentive compensation. *Student Aid Policy Analysis*. Retrieved from www.finaid.org/educators/20100426 incentivecompensation.pdf.

Kerwin, C. M., & Furlong, S. R. (2011). *Rulemaking: How government agencies write law and make policy* (4th ed.). Washington, DC: CQ Press.

Kingdon, J. W. (2003). *Agendas, alternatives, and public policies*. New York: Longman.

Laffont, J., & Tirole, J. (1991). The politics of government decision-making: A theory of regulatory capture. *The Quarterly Journal of Economics, 106*(4), 1089–1127.

Lederman, D. (2006, August 18). Gripes about grants. *Inside Higher Education*. Retrieved from https://www.insidehighered.com/news/2006/08/18/grants.

Lederman, D. (2007a, March 29). Explaining the accreditation debate. *Inside Higher Education*. Retrieved from www.insidehighered.com/news/2007/03/29/accredit.

Lederman, D. (2007b, May 29). Key GOP senator warns Spellings. *Inside Higher Education*. Retrieved from www.insidehighered.com/news/2007/05/29/alexander.

Lederman, D. (2010, March 24). Student loan bill scorecard. *Inside Higher Education*. Retrieved from www.insidehighered.com/news/2010/03/24/scorecard.

Library of Congress. (2012). *Chronological list of presidents, first ladies, and vice presidents of the United States*. Retrieved from www.loc.gov/rr/print/list/057_chron.html.

Lindblom, C. E., & Woodhouse, E. J. (1993). *The policy-making process* (3rd ed.). Upper Saddle River, NJ: Prentice Hall.

Lowi, T. J. (1970). Decision making vs. policy making: Toward an antidote for technocracy. *Public Administration Review, 30*(3), 314–325.

Lowi, T. J. (1972). Four systems of policy, politics, and choice. *Public Administration Review, 32*(4), 298–310.

Lowrey, A. (2012, March 21). 2 federal reserve nominees make it to a confirmation hearing. *The New York Times*, p. B3. Retrieved from Lexis-Nexis Academic.

Lowry, R. C. (2009). Reauthorization of the federal Higher Education Act and accountability for student learning: The dog that didn't bark. *Publius: The Journal of Federalism, 39*(3), 506–526.

Lubbers, J. S. (1998). *A guide to federal agency rulemaking* (3rd ed.). Chicago: American Bar Association.

Lukes, S. L. (2005). *Power: A radical view* (2nd ed.). New York: Palgrave Macmillan.

Makkai, T., & Braithwaite, J. (1992). In and out of the revolving door: Making sense of agency capture. *Journal of Public Policy, 12*(1), 61–78.

Malterud, K. (2001). Qualitative research: Standards, challenges, and guidelines. *The Lancet, 358*, 483–488.

Mantel, J. (2009). Procedural safeguards for agency guidance: A source of legitimacy for the administrative state. *Administrative Law Review, 61*(2), 343–406.

Marcus, J. (2012, July 13). For-profit colleges pumping campaign money to foes of regulation. *The Hechinger Report*. Retrieved from http://hechingerreport.org/content/for-profit-colleges-pumping-campaign-money-to-foes-of-regulation_8995/.

Marshall, M. N. (1996a). The key informant technique. *Family Practice, 13*(1), 92–97.

Marshall, M. N. (1996b). Sampling for qualitative research. *Family Practice, 13*(6), 522–525.

Matthews, L. K. (2012). Toward institutional autonomy or nationalization? A case study of the federal role in U.S. higher education accreditation. ProQuest Dissertations and Theses database. (UMI No. 3506040).

Maxwell, J. A. (2005). *Qualitative research design: An interactive approach* (2nd ed.). Thousand Oaks, CA: Sage.

McCubbins, M. D., Noll, R. G., & Weingast, B. R. (1987). Administrative procedures as instruments of political control. *Journal of Law, Economics, and Organization, 3*(2), 243–277.

McCubbins, M. D., Noll, R. G., & Weingast, B. R. (1989). Structure and process, politics and policy: Administrative arrangements and the political control of agencies. *Virginia Law Review, 75*(2), 431–482.

McCubbins, M. D., & Schwartz, T. (1984). Congressional oversight overlooked: Police patrols versus fire alarms. *American Journal of Political Science, 28*(1), 165–179.

Meier, K. J. (2008). The scientific study of public administration: A short essay on the state of the field. *International Review of Public Administration, 13*(1), 1–10.

Merriam, S. B. (1998). *Qualitative research and case study applications in education*. San Francisco: Jossey-Bass.

Mettler, S. (2014). *Degrees of inequality: How the politics of higher education sabotaged the American dream*. New York: Basic Books.

Miles, M. B., & Huberman, A. M. (1994). *Qualitative data analysis: An expanded sourcebook* (2nd ed.). Thousand Oaks, CA: Sage.

Mintrom, M., & Vergari, S. (1996). Advocacy coalitions, policy entrepreneurs, and policy change. *Policy Studies Journal, 24*(3), 420–434.

Moe, T. M. (2012). Delegation, control, and the study of public bureaucracy. *The Forum, 10*(2), Article 4. ISSN (Online) 1540–8884, DOI: 10.1515/1540–8884.1508.

Muñoz, C. (2014, October 30). What you need to know about new rules to protect students from poor-performing career college programs [Web log post]. Retrieved from https://www.whitehouse.gov/blog/2014/10/30/what-you-need-know-about-new-rules-protect-students-poor-performing-career-college-p.

National Association of Student Financial Aid Administrators. (2014, November 3). *NASFAA summary: Gainful employment final rules.* Retrieved from https://www.nasfaa.org/news-item/1087/NASFAA_Summary_Gainful_Employment_Final_Rules.

National Bureau of Economic Research, Inc. (n.d.). *Business cycle expansions and contractions.* Retrieved from www.nber.org/cycles.html#announcements.

National Center for Education Statistics. (n.d.). *About us.* Retrieved from https://nces.ed.gov/about/.

National Conference of State Legislatures. (2014). *NCSL standing committee on legislation special legislative summit education federal update.* Retrieved from www.ncsl.org/documents/summit/summit2014/onlineresources/educationcomm_summitupdate.pdf.

National Council of Higher Education Resources. (n.d.). *Organization directory.* Retrieved from http://c.ymcdn.com/sites/www.ncher.us/resource/resmgr/docs/ncher_organization_directory.pdf.

National Oceanic and Atmospheric Administration. (n.d.). *The National Sea Grant College Program.* Retrieved from http://seagrant.noaa.gov/WhoWeAre.aspx.

National Oceanic and Atmospheric Administration Office of Education. (n.d.). *Scholarships.* Retrieved from www.oesd.noaa.gov/scholarships/.

National Science Foundation. (n.d.). *About funding.* Retrieved from www.nsf.gov/funding/aboutfunding.jsp.

National Science Foundation. (2013, January 14). *National Science Foundation research terms and conditions, agency specific requirements.* Retrieved from www.nsf.gov/pubs/policydocs/rtc/agencyspecifics/nsf_113.pdf.

Natow, R. S. (2015). From Capitol Hill to Dupont Circle and beyond: The influence of policy actors in the federal higher education rulemaking process. *The Journal of Higher Education, 86*(3), 360–386.

Negotiated Rulemaking Act, 5 U.S.C. §§ 561 et seq. (2012).

Niles, M. C. (2002). On the hijacking of agencies (and airplanes): The Federal Aviation Administration, "agency capture," and airline security. *American University Journal of Gender, Social Policy, & the Law, 10*(2), 381–442.

1998 Amendments to the Higher Education Act of 1965, Pub. L. No. 105-244, 112 Stat. 1581 (1998).

Niskanen, W. A. (1971). *Bureaucracy and representative government.* Chicago: Aldine Atherton.

Nolter, C. (2012, July 5). For-profit colleges win in court, face new uncertainty. *The Deal Pipeline.* Retrieved from Lexis-Nexis Academic.

O'Connell, A. J. (2008). Political cycles of rulemaking: An empirical portrait of the modern administrative state. *Virginia Law Review, 94*, 889–986.

O'Connell, A. J. (2011). Agency rulemaking and political transitions. *Northwestern University Law Review, 105*(2), 471–534.

Office of Federal Student Aid. (n.d.a.). *Gainful employment information—Dear colleague letters and electronic announcements.* Retrieved from https://ifap.ed.gov/GainfulEmploymentInfo/GEDCLandEAV2.html.

Office of Federal Student Aid. (n.d.b.). *The US Department of Education offers low-interest loans to eligible students to help cover the cost of college or career school.* Retrieved from https://studentaid.ed.gov/sa/types/loans/subsidized-unsubsidized.

Office of Hearings & Appeals. (n.d.). *Organizations.* Retrieved from http://oha.ed.gov /organizations.html.

Office of Inspector General. (2015). *Home page.* Retrieved from www2.ed.gov/about/offices /list/oig/index.html.

Office of Management and Budget. (n.d.). *Office of Information and Regulatory Affairs.* Retrieved from https://www.whitehouse.gov/omb/oira.

Office of Postsecondary Education. (2009a, June 18). *Department of Education—Public hearing: Denver, CO.* Retrieved from www2.ed.gov/policy/highered/reg/hearulemaking /2009/presenters-denver.pdf.

Office of Postsecondary Education. (2009b, June 18). *Department of Education—Public hearing: Little Rock, AR.* Retrieved from www2.ed.gov/policy/highered/reg/hearule making/2009/presenters-little-rock.pdf.

Office of Postsecondary Education. (2009c, June 22). *Department of Education—Public hearing: Philadelphia, PA.* Retrieved from www2.ed.gov/policy/highered/reg/hearule making/2009/presenters-phila.pdf.

Office of Postsecondary Education. (2015a). *Fund for the Improvement of Postsecondary Education—welcome and overview of FIPSE programs and web resources.* Retrieved from www2.ed.gov/about/offices/list/ope/fipse/welcome.html.

Office of Postsecondary Education. (2015b). *Office of Postsecondary Education—home page.* Retrieved from www2.ed.gov/about/offices/list/ope/index.html.

Office of Postsecondary Education: Notice of intent to establish negotiated rulemaking committees under Title IV of the Higher Education Act of 1965, as amended: Notice of negotiated rulemaking, 72 Fed. Reg. 4221 (2007).

Office of Postsecondary Education: Notice of negotiated rulemaking for programs authorized under Title IV of the Higher Education Act of 1965, as amended: Notice of establishment of negotiated rulemaking committee, 71 Fed. Reg. 47756 (2006).

Office of Representative Glenn W. Thompson. (2010, September 29). *Thompson rallies with students for education rights.* Retrieved from http://thompson.house.gov/press -release/thompson-rallies-students-education-rights.

Office of Senator Bernie Sanders. (2010, September 10). *Senators call for "gainful employment" Dept. of Education rule.* Retrieved from www.sanders.senate.gov/newsroom /news/?id=4555fcd2-0c9d-4fd4-8774-68fda030eb20.

Office of Senator Lamar Alexander. (2007, May 25). *Statement of Senator Lamar Alexander—May 24, 2007—Accountability in Higher Education.* Retrieved from www .alexander.senate.gov/public/index.cfm/speechesfloorstatements?ID=a16ef618-bb53 -4373-af5d-34b6ee901219.

Office of the Federal Register. (2011, January). *A guide to the rulemaking process*. Retrieved from https://www.federalregister.gov/uploads/2011/01/the_rulemaking_process.pdf.

Paperwork Reduction Act, 44 U.S.C. §§ 3501 et seq. (2012).

Parsons, M. D. (1997). *Power and politics: Federal higher education policymaking in the 1990s*. Albany: State University of New York Press.

Pelesh, M. L. (1994). Regulations under the Higher Education Amendments of 1992: A case study in negotiated rulemaking. *Law & Contemporary Problems, 57*(4), 151–170.

Pell Grant Program: Final regulations, 57 Fed. Reg. 28568 (1992) (to be codified at 34 C.F.R. pt. 690).

Performance standards for retention of electronic records in the Student Financial Assistance Programs: Advance notice of proposed rulemaking, 66 Fed. Reg. 13034 (2001) (to be codified at 34 C.F.R. pt. 50).

Pew Charitable Trusts. (2015, June 11). *Federal and state funding of higher education: A changing landscape*. Retrieved from www.pewtrusts.org/en/research-and-analysis/issue-briefs/2015/06/federal-and-state-funding-of-higher-education.

Phelan, D. J. (2014). The clear and present funding crisis in community colleges. *New Directions for Community Colleges, 168*, 5–16.

Pitre, C. C., & Pitre, P. (2009). Increasing underrepresented high school students' college transitions and achievements: TRIO educational opportunity programs. *NASSP Bulletin, 93*(2), 96–110.

Pritzker, D. M., & Dalton, D. S. (1995, September). *Negotiated rulemaking sourcebook*. Washington, DC: Government Printing Office.

Program Integrity: Gainful Employment—Debt measures, final rule: Final regulations, 76 Fed. Reg. 34386 (2011) (to be codified at 34 C.F.R. pt. 668).

Program Integrity: Gainful Employment: Final regulations, 79 Fed. Reg. 64890 (2014) (to be codified at 34 C.F.R. pts. 600 and 668).

Program Integrity: Gainful Employment: Notice of proposed rulemaking, 75 Fed. Reg. 43616 (2010).

Program Integrity Issues: Final regulations, 75 Fed. Reg. 66832 (2010a) (to be codified at 34 C.F.R. pts. 600, 602, 603, 668, 682, 685, 686, 690, and 691).

Program Integrity Issues: Notice of proposed rulemaking, 75 Fed. Reg. 34806 (2010b).

Public Regional Hearing for Negotiated Rulemaking, U.S. Department of Education Office of Postsecondary Education. (2006a, November 2). Retrieved from www2.ed.gov/policy/highered/reg/hearulemaking/2007/transcript-fl.pdf.

Public Regional Hearing for Negotiated Rulemaking, U.S. Department of Education Office of Postsecondary Education. (2006b, November 8). Retrieved from www2.ed.gov/policy/highered/reg/hearulemaking/2007/transcript-dc.pdf.

Public Regional Hearing on Negotiated Rulemaking, U.S. Department of Education Office of Postsecondary Education. (2006, October 5). Retrieved from www2.ed.gov/policy/highered/reg/hearulemaking/2007/transcript-il.pdf.

Public Regional Hearing on Negotiated Rulemaking, U.S. Department of Education Office of Postsecondary Education. (2008a, September 19). Retrieved from www2.ed.gov/policy/highered/reg/hearulemaking/hea08/transcript-9-19-2008.pdf.

Public Regional Hearing on Negotiated Rulemaking, U.S. Department of Education Office of Postsecondary Education. (2008b, September 29). Retrieved from www2.ed.gov/policy/highered/reg/hearulemaking/hea08/transcript-9-29-08.pdf.

Public Regional Hearing on Negotiated Rulemaking, U.S. Department of Education Office of Postsecondary Education. (2008c, October 8). Retrieved from www2.ed.gov/policy /highered/reg/hearulemaking/hea08/transcript-10-08-08.pdf.

Public Regional Hearing on Negotiated Rulemaking, U.S. Department of Education Office of Postsecondary Education. (2009, June 22). Retrieved from www2.ed.gov/policy/highered /reg/hearulemaking/2009/transcript-phila.pdf.

Regulatory Flexibility Act, 5 U.S.C. §§ 601 et seq. (2012).

Richards, L., & Morse, J. M. (2007). *README FIRST for a user's guide to qualitative methods* (2nd ed.). Thousand Oaks, CA: Sage.

Rosenzweig, R. M. (2001). *The political university: Policy, politics, and presidential leadership in the American research university.* Baltimore: Johns Hopkins University Press.

Rourke, F. E. (1969). *Bureaucracy, politics, and public policy.* Boston, MA: Little, Brown.

Rourke, F. E. (1972). Editor's introduction. In F. E. Rourke (Ed.), *Bureaucratic power in national politics* (2nd ed., pp. ix–xi). Boston: Little, Brown.

Sabatier, P. A. (1986). Top-down and bottom-up approaches to implementation research: A critical analysis and suggested synthesis. *Journal of Public Policy, 6*(1), 21–48.

Sabatier, P. A. (1993). Policy change over a decade or more. In P. A. Sabatier & H. C. Jenkins-Smith (Eds.), *Policy change and learning: An advocacy coalition approach* (pp. 13–39). Boulder, CO: Westview Press.

Sabatier, P. A., & Jenkins-Smith, H. C. (Eds.). (1993). *Policy change and learning: An advocacy coalition approach.* Boulder, CO: Westview Press.

Sabatier, P. A., & Jenkins-Smith, H. C. (1999). The advocacy coalition framework: An assessment. In P. A. Sabatier (Ed.), *Theories of the policy process* (pp. 117–166). Boulder, CO: Westview Press.

Sabatier, P., & Weible, C. (2007). The advocacy coalition framework: Innovations and clarifications. In P. Sabatier (Ed.), *Theories of the policy process* (2nd ed., pp. 189–222). Boulder, CO: Westview Press.

Schlosberg, D., Zavestoski, S., & Shulman, S. W. (2007). Democracy and e-rulemaking: Web-based technologies, participation, and the potential for deliberation. *Journal of Information Technology & Politics, 4*(1), 37–55.

Schneider, A., & Ingram, H. (1993). Social construction of target populations: Implications for politics and policy. *The American Political Science Review, 87*(2), 334–347.

Scholz, R. W., & Tietje, O. (2002). *Embedded case study methods: Integrating quantitative and qualitative knowledge.* Thousand Oaks, CA: Sage.

Secretary of Education's Commission on the Future of Higher Education. (2006). *A test of leadership: Charting the future of U.S. higher education* (Contract No. ED-06-C0-0013). Retrieved from www2.ed.gov/about/bdscomm/list/hiedfuture/reports/final-report.pdf.

Selingo, J. (2006, May 26). Official of governors' group moves to Education Dept. *The Chronicle of Higher Education, 52*(38), A25.

Shapiro, S. (2007). The role of procedural controls in OSHA's ergonomics rulemaking. *Public Administration Review, 67*(4), 688–701.

Smith, K. B., & Larimer, C. W. (2013). *The public policy theory primer* (2nd ed.). Boulder, CO: Westview Press.

Solomon, D. F. (2011). Summary of administrative law judge responsibilities. *Journal of the National Association of Administrative Law Judiciary, 31*(2), 476–525.

Spiller, P. T., & Urbiztondo, S. (1994). Political appointees vs. career civil servants: A multiple principals theory of political bureaucracies. *European Journal of Political Economy, 10*(3), 465–497.

Stanley, J. W., & Weare, C. (2004). The effects of Internet use on political participation: Evidence from an agency online discussion forum. *Administration & Society, 36*(5), 503–527.

Stigler, G. J. (1971). The theory of economic regulation. *The Bell Journal of Economics and Management Science, 2*(1), 3–21.

Stone, D. (2002). *Policy paradox: The art of political decision making* (Rev. ed.). New York: W. W. Norton.

Stratford, M. (2014, October 3). Court victory for for-profits on recruiter bonus ban. *Inside Higher Education*. Retrieved from https://www.insidehighered.com/quicktakes /2014/10/03/court-victory-profits-recruiter-bonus-ban.

Stratford, M. (2015, November 30). Reversal on recruiter bonus pay. *Inside Higher Education*. Retrieved from https://www.insidehighered.com/news/2015/11/30/us-loosens -part-its-ban-college-recruiter-pay.

Stratford, M., & Fain, P. (2014, May 7). Backed into a corner. *Inside Higher Education*. Retrieved from https://www.insidehighered.com/news/2014/05/07/gainful-em ployment-fight-profits-make-familiar-arguments-against-different-landscape.

Strauss, A., & Corbin, J. (1998). *Basics of qualitative research: Techniques and procedures for developing grounded theory* (2nd ed.). Thousand Oaks, CA: Sage.

Student Assistance General Provisions, Federal Family Education Loan Programs, Federal Pell Grant Program: Interim final regulations with invitation for comment, 59 Fed. Reg. 22348 (1994) (to be codified at 34 C.F.R. pts. 668, 682, and 690).

Student Assistance General Provisions, Federal Pell Grant Program, Academic Competitiveness Grant Program, and National Science and Mathematics Access to Retain Talent Grant Program: Final regulations, 71 Fed. Reg. 64402 (2006) (to be codified at 34 C.F.R. pts. 668, 690, and 691).

Student Assistance General Provisions, Federal Perkins Loan Program, Federal Family Education Loan Program, and William D. Ford Federal Direct Loan Program: Notice of proposed rulemaking, 67 Fed. Reg. 51036 (2002).

Student Assistance General Provisions, Federal Perkins Loan Program, Federal Work-Study Program, Federal Supplemental Educational Opportunity Grant Program, Federal Family Education Loan Programs, William D. Ford Federal Direct Loan Program, and Federal Pell Grant Program: Final regulations, 61 Fed. Reg. 60578 (1996a) (to be codified at 34 CFR Parts 668, 674, 675, 676, 682, 685, and 690).

Student Assistance General Provisions, Federal Perkins Loan Program, Federal Work-Study Program, Federal Supplemental Educational Opportunity Grant Program, Federal Family Education Loan Programs, William D. Ford Federal Direct Loan Program, and Federal Pell Grant Program: Notice of proposed rulemaking, 61 Fed. Reg. 49874 (1996b).

Student Assistance General Provisions and Federal Pell Grant Program: Notice of proposed rulemaking, 59 Fed. Reg. 9526 (1994).

Student Assistance General Provisions: Final regulations, 60 Fed. Reg. 61760 (1995) (to be codified at 34 C.F.R. pt. 668).

Swail, W. S. (2000). Preparing America's disadvantaged for college: Programs that increase college opportunity. *New Directions for Institutional Research, 107*, 85–101.

Talent Search Program: Final regulations, 58 Fed. Reg. 59144 (1993) (to be codified at 34 C.F.R. pt. 643.

Teacher Quality Enhancement Grants Program: Final regulations, 64 Fed. Reg. 42837 (1999a) (to be codified at 34 C.F.R. pt. 611).

Teacher Quality Enhancement Grants Program: Notice of proposed rulemaking, 64 Fed. Reg. 27403 (1999b).

Team I—Program Integrity Issues. (2010, January 25). Retrieved from www2.ed.gov /policy/highered/reg/hearulemaking/2009/2009-2/team-one-negotiators.pdf.

Texas Guaranteed Student Loan Corporation. (2001, December 11). ED seeks nominations for Spring 2002 negotiated rulemaking. *Shoptalk Online, 134*, 1–2. Retrieved from http://tgslc.org/shoptalk/2001/st134/st134.pdf.

US Department of Education. (1998, September). *What should I know about ED grants?* Retrieved from www2.ed.gov/fund/grant/about/knowabtgrants/pt398.html#3-g.

US Department of Education. (2002). *Archived Information: 2002 negotiated rulemaking teams.* Retrieved from www2.ed.gov/policy/highered/reg/hearulemaking/2002/final negotiatorschart.pdf.

US Department of Education. (2006a, October 19). *Public Hearings for Negotiated Rulemaking—Presenters at the September 19, 2006 session.* Retrieved from www2.ed .gov/policy/highered/reg/hearulemaking/2007/presenters-uc.html.

US Department of Education. (2006b, October 27). *Public Hearings for Negotiated Rulemaking—Presenters at the October 5, 2006 session.* Retrieved from www2.ed.gov /policy/highered/reg/hearulemaking/2007/presenters-lu.html.

US Department of Education. (2006c, November 21). *Public Hearings for Negotiated Rulemaking—Presenters at the November 2, 2006 session.* Retrieved from www2.ed.gov /policy/highered/reg/hearulemaking/2007/presenters-fl.html.

US Department of Education. (2006d). *Title IV Negotiated Rulemaking Team—Loans Committee.* Retrieved from www2.ed.gov/policy/highered/reg/hearulemaking/2007 /loans-summary-1.pdf.

US Department of Education. (2007a). *Meeting Summary—U.S. Department of Education—Negotiated Rulemaking Accreditation Committee.* Retrieved from www2 .ed.gov/policy/highered/reg/hearulemaking/2007/accred-session-1-sum.pdf.

US Department of Education. (2007b, January 5). *Public Hearings for Negotiated Rulemaking—Presenters at the November 8, 2006 session.* Retrieved from www2.ed.gov /policy/highered/reg/hearulemaking/2007/presenters-dc.html.

US Department of Education. (2007c). *Title IV Negotiated Rulemaking Team—ACG / National SMART Grants Team.* Retrieved from www2.ed.gov/policy/highered/reg /hearulemaking/2007/acg-session-1-sum.pdf.

US Department of Education. (2007d). *2006–07 Negotiated Rulemaking for Higher Education—Accreditation Team.* Retrieved from www2.ed.gov/policy/highered/reg /hearulemaking/2007/accred.html.

US Department of Education. (2008). *Student Loans Negotiated Rulemaking Team: Meeting Summary.* Retrieved from www2.ed.gov/policy/highered/reg/hearulemaking/2008 /loans-session-1-summary.pdf.

US Department of Education. (2010, November 30). *Negotiated Rulemaking for Higher Education 2009–10*. Retrieved from www2.ed.gov/policy/highered/reg/hearulemaking /2009/negreg-summerfall.html.

US Department of Education. (2013a, September 26). *Education Department awards $20.1 million in grants to strengthen 39 higher education institutions*. Retrieved from www.ed .gov/news/press-releases/education-department-awards-201-million-grants -strengthen-39-higher-education-institutions.

US Department of Education. (2013b, May 21). *Negotiated rulemaking public hearing— May 21, 2013—Washington, DC*. Retrieved from https://www2.ed.gov/policy/highered /reg/hearulemaking/2012/may21presenters-dc.pdf.

US Department of Education. (2013c, May 23). *Negotiated rulemaking public hearing— May 23, 2013—Minneapolis, MN*. Retrieved from https://www2.ed.gov/policy/highered /reg/hearulemaking/2012/may23presenters-mn.pdf.

US Department of Education. (2013d, May 30). *Negotiated rulemaking public hearing— May 30, 2013—San Francisco, CA*. Retrieved from https://www2.ed.gov/policy/highered /reg/hearulemaking/2012/may30presenters-ca.pdf.

US Department of Education. (2013e, June 4). *Negotiated rulemaking public hearing— June 4, 2013—Atlanta, GA*. Retrieved from https://www2.ed.gov/policy/highered/reg /hearulemaking/2012/june4presenters-ga.pdf.

US Department of Education. (2014a). *Academic Competitiveness Grants and National Science and Mathematics Access to Retain Talent (SMART) Grants*. Retrieved from www2 .ed.gov/programs/smart/index.html.

US Department of Education. (2014b). *U.S. Department of Education releases list of higher education institutions with open Title IX sexual violence investigations*. Retrieved from www.ed.gov/news/press-releases/us-department-education-releases-list-higher -education-institutions-open-title-ix-sexual-violence-investigations.

US Department of Education. (2015a). *Accreditation in the United States: National recognition of accreditors by the U.S. Secretary of Education*. Retrieved from www2.ed.gov /admins/finaid/accred/accreditation_pg3.html#Recognition.

US Department of Education. (2015b). *Federal TRIO programs—home page*. Retrieved from www2.ed.gov/about/offices/list/ope/trio/index.html.

US Department of Education. (2016, February 8). *Student Aid Enforcement Unit formed to protect students, borrowers, taxpayers*. Retrieved from www.ed.gov/news/press-releases /student-aid-enforcement-unit-formed-protect-students-borrowers-taxpayers.

US Department of Justice. (n.d.). *Educational opportunities section*. Retrieved from www .justice.gov/crt/educational-opportunities-section.

US Department of Labor. (2011). *Trade Adjustment Assistance Community College and Career Training Grant Program—program summary*. Retrieved from www.doleta.gov /taaccct/.

US General Accounting Office. (2000). *Federal rulemaking: Agencies' use of information technology to facilitate public participation* (Publication No. GAO/GGD-00-135R). Washington, DC: Government Printing Office.

US General Accounting Office. (2003, September). *Rulemaking: OMB's role in reviews of agencies' draft rules and the transparency of those reviews* (GAO-03-929). Retrieved from www.gao.gov/new.items/d03929.pdf.

US Government Accountability Office. (n.d.). *Government Accountability Office (GAO) Watchdog report.* Retrieved from www.gao.gov/podcast/watchdog.html.

US Government Accountability Office. (2009, June). *Department of Education: Student Assistance General Provisions, Teacher Education Assistance for College and Higher Education (TEACH) Grant Program, Federal Pell Grant Program, Academic Competitiveness Grant Program and National Science and Mathematics Access to Retain Talent Grant Program* (Publication No. GAO-09-756R). Washington, DC: Government Printing Office. Retrieved from www.gao.gov/decisions/majrule/d09756r.pdf.

US House of Representatives. (n.d.). *Party divisions of the House of Representatives.* Retrieved from http://history.house.gov/Institution/Party-Divisions/Party-Divisions.

US House of Representatives. (1992). *Higher Education Amendments of 1992: Conference Report. H.R. Rep. 102–630.* Washington, DC: Government Printing Office.

US Office of Government Ethics. (2007, October). *Understanding the revolving door: How ethics rules apply to your job seeking and post-government employment activities.* Retrieved from https://ethics.od.nih.gov/topics/RevolvingDoor.htm.

US Senate. (n.d.). *Party division in the Senate, 1979–present.* Retrieved from www.senate.gov/pagelayout/history/one_item_and_teasers/partydiv.htm.

Wagner, W., Barnes, K., & Peters, L. (2011). Rulemaking in the shade: An empirical study of EPA's air toxic emission standards. *Administrative Law Review, 63*(1), 99–158.

Waterman, R. W., & Meier, K. J. (1998). Principal-agent models: An expansion? *Journal of Public Administration Research & Theory, 8*(2), 173–202.

Weible, C. M. (2007). An advocacy coalition framework approach to stakeholder analysis: Understanding the political context of California marine protected area policy. *Journal of Public Administration Research & Theory, 17*(1), 95–117.

West, W. F., & Raso, C. (2013). Who shapes the rulemaking agenda? Implications for bureaucratic responsiveness and bureaucratic control. *Journal of Public Administration Research & Theory, 23*, 495–519.

Wheeler, D. L. (2006, July). Empowering publics: Information technology and democratization in the Arab World—lessons from Internet cafés and beyond. *Oxford Internet Institute, Research Report No. 11.* Retrieved from http://ssrn.com/abstract=1308527.

White House. (n.d.). *The cabinet.* Retrieved from https://www.whitehouse.gov/administration/cabinet.

White House Office of the Press Secretary. (2015, September 12). *Fact sheet: Empowering students to choose the college that is right for them.* Retrieved from https://www.whitehouse.gov/the-press-office/2015/09/12/fact-sheet-empowering-students-choose-college-right-them.

Wilson, J. Q. (1989). *Bureaucracy: What government agencies do and why they do it.* New York: Basic Books.

Wood, B. D., & Waterman, R. W. (1991). The dynamics of political control of the bureaucracy. *The American Political Science Review, 85*(3), 801–828.

Yackee, S. W. (2003). An agent, but an agent of whom? Organized interests and the U.S. bureaucracy. ProQuest Dissertations and Theses database. (UMI No. 3086656).

Yackee, S. W. (2006). Sweet-talking the fourth branch: The influence of interest group comments on federal agency rulemaking. *Journal of Public Administration Research & Theory, 16*(1), 103–124.

Yin, R. K. (2003). *Case study research: Design and methods* (3rd ed.). Thousand Oaks, CA: Sage.

Zahariadis, N. (2007). The multiple streams perspective: Structure, limitations, prospects. In P. A. Sabatier (Ed.), *Theories of the policy process* (pp. 65–92). Boulder, CO: Westview Press.

Zemsky, R. M. (2007). The rise and fall of the Spellings Commission. *The Chronicle of Higher Education, 53*(21), B6–B9.

Zemsky, R. (2013). *Checklist for change: Making American higher education a sustainable enterprise.* New Brunswick, NJ: Rutgers University Press.

Note: Page numbers in *italic* indicate figures and tables.

CPSIA information can be obtained
at www.ICGtesting.com
Printed in the USA
LVHW101317300523
748324LV00002B/4

9 781421 421469